Legacy

Legacy

*Pastoral Praxis
in 2 Timothy*

T. Patrick Jensen

FOREWORD BY
Virgil P. Travis Jr.

WIPF & STOCK · Eugene, Oregon

LEGACY
Pastoral Praxis in 2 Timothy

Copyright © 2024 T. Patrick Jensen. All rights reserved. Except for brief quotations in critical publications or reviews, no part of this book may be reproduced in any manner without prior written permission from the publisher. Write: Permissions, Wipf and Stock Publishers, 199 W. 8th Ave., Suite 3, Eugene, OR 97401.

Wipf & Stock
An Imprint of Wipf and Stock Publishers
199 W. 8th Ave., Suite 3
Eugene, OR 97401

www.wipfandstock.com

PAPERBACK ISBN: 978-1-6667-8865-5
HARDCOVER ISBN: 978-1-6667-8866-2
EBOOK ISBN: 978-1-6667-8867-9

VERSION NUMBER 01/04/24

Scripture quotations are from New Revised Standard Version Updated Edition (NRSVUE), copyright © 1989 National Council of the Churches of Christ in the United States of America. Used by permission. All rights reserved worldwide. Citations of poetry are considered free domain.

Permissions were obtained for publication of both the foreword and pastoral interview. Tables from Pew Research are appropriately cited. Names in all pastoral anecdotes in the book have been altered to prevent libel of any sort.

For Jesus, to whom my heart is devoted.

For Aubrey, who never stopped believing.

For my beloved children who illustrate the wonders of the kingdom.

Contents

List of Figures | ix
Foreword by Virgil P. Travis Jr. | xi
Acknowledgments | xv
Introduction | xvii

Chapter 1: Legacy of Apostolic Fatherhood | 1

Chapter 2: Legacy of Kindling | 19

Chapter 3: Legacy of Suffering | 32

Chapter 4: Legacy of Sound Doctrine | 43

Chapter 5: Legacy of Endurance | 55

Chapter 6: Legacy of Honor | 82

Chapter 7: Legacy in Perilous Times | 109

Chapter 8: Legacy of Deliverance & Departure | 128

Chapter 9: Legacy of Irrelevance | 152

Chapter 10: Legacy of Apologetic Evangelism | 176

Chapter 11: Legacy of Invitation | 200

Afterword | 219
Appendix A: Pastoral Transition Screen | 221

Appendix B: Liturgy of Acceptance | 223
Appendix C: Legacy Interview | 231
Bibliography | 237
Scripture Index | 241

List of Figures

Figure 1: Integrity vs. Despair | xxii

Figure 2: Signs of the Apostolic Office | 18

Table 1: Weeping Emotions and Transformation of Self | 25

Figure 3: Sound Doctrine | 54

Table 2: Types of Christian Suffering | 80

Figure 4: Harbingers of a Hardened Heart | 104

Figure 5: Signs to Depart a Church | 147

Table 3: Biggest Declines Seen Among Mainline Protestants | 190

Table 4: Composition of the Religious "Nones" | 191

Figure 6: Size of the Unaffiliated Population: Long Term Trends | 192

Appendix A: Pastoral Transition Screen | 221

Foreword

MAGNIFICENT PIECE OF WORK! Dr. T. Patrick Jensen is an accomplished author and has served in the ministry for over twenty-two years and for over twelve years as a psychiatrist. He is a very gifted pastor and unique in that God has equipped him with the great ability to integrate theology and mental health ministry. His experiences serving as a pastor and his professional insight as a Christian psychiatrist give him firsthand knowledge on how to help those in pastoral transition to deal with the subjects of ecclesiology, theology, and emotional and spiritual issues. This is why *Legacy* is a must read for those aspiring to work in the ministry of our Father in heaven and the one, holy, apostolic church. This work is an awesome sequel to his first book, *The Coming Winter*. A must-read for anyone who has or is experiencing rejection, hurt, and pain from a church-related experience. The Emmaus Center and School for Ministry of Knoxville trains pastoral counselors and these two works are requirements for those aspiring to a call into any type of ministry in our church or community.

This book is truly written in the context of his own pastoral transition and a sincere longing to reflect systematically and theologically on where and how God works in us through these pastoral transitions. Dr. Jensen takes the mask off and helps the reader focus through the biblical lens of Paul's guidance to Timothy on matters of ecclesiology. His chosen audience is all those who have ever experienced a time of ministry transition and struggle with the grief of the emotional and spiritual angst of unmasking their own hurt and pain.

The main thesis of his work presents to his readers a vulnerability that many fathers, mothers, priests, and pastors would not dare to disclose in the church, to their friends, to their spouses or families. As a pastor, Dr. Jensen shares this work out of the personal pain he felt transitioning from his first pastoral charge. He states that "being in a state of confusion during this time," he was seeking God to understand himself through using the book of 2 Timothy as a lens to guide him through his present need to further serve God through this time of transition. He used the ancient sources of inspirational truths of the early church fathers to guide him back into the focus of his present ministry of clinical theology and psychiatry.

He hits right at the heart of the spiritual, emotional, and stressful transitional experiences that every father, mother, priest, and pastor will face when confronted with church and relational conflict. In fact, he takes us immediately to the Scriptures, to plant our feet directly into the narrative of Paul's guidance to Timothy. Paul uses the term "son" (1 Tim 1:2) to help the reader see Paul's admiration for Timothy. The apostle in 2 Timothy doesn't shy away from focusing on his personal relationship with Timothy. When we look at 2 Timothy 1:8, Paul is exhorting his audience to "Remember Christ by remembering me and my gospel." Paul with intentionality is passing his torch to Timothy. Timothy accepts his new role of leadership.

Dr. Jensen so delicately underscores the unsettling tie between Paul and Christ. When we read the many examples and illustrations in the book, we are to see and grasp the depth and implications of our own humanity and the depths of our grief in our own transitions in life. These same relational struggles are the same today in the twenty-first-century pastorate.

In my combined forty-plus years of pastoral ministry as an army chaplain, licensed pastoral counselor, missionary, rector of a very active parish, and dean of a school, I have seen, listened to, and watched the anguish tales of ministers, priests, rabbis, and missionaries relate their experiences about entanglements with members of their congregations, parishes, and synagogues. I have seen conflicts within major denominations, conflicts within many religious hierarchies, that spiraled into pastors' homes, relatives, and communities. I have witnessed, counseled, and sat with numerous colleagues and others whose pain, struggles, and emotional plights have caused them to further fail. And others use the principles in this book to move ahead of the struggle to find a merciful God leading them into the next chapter of their life and ministry.

Ministry, as you will read in *Legacy*, is generational. God did not send His Son just to die on a cross. God sent His Son into the world to save the least, the lost, and the poor, to pass down His legacy to His disciples. St. Paul, when he accepted Christ, was given a mission, a calling, a *sentness* instilled in his total being. Paul embraced Timothy as Christ embraced Paul. St. Timothy became Paul's disciple, his companion, his coworker, in preaching. Timothy was with St. Paul in his winter of last days in Corinth. St. Paul's persecution was given to Timothy. Bishop Timothy carried out the ministry until his final winter. Paul tried to halt a procession in honor of Diana by preaching the gospel. They dragged him through the streets and stoned him to death. Timothy then took on his legacy of ministry.

In closing, the scarlet thread of this jewel of a book is that we all have a legacy. So many of us have gotten where we are by standing on someone else's shoulders. The question begs in each of us: to whom and in which way will you leave your legacy?

Rev. Dr. Virgil P. Travis Jr.
Emmaus Abbey Church
Center for Christian Counseling

Acknowledgments

Without the constant support of my wife and children, this work would not have been possible. Without the early-morning whispers of the Lord to bring healing, comfort, and insight, this work as well would not have been possible. O, how the Scriptures breathe new messages for any circumstance. O, what a responsible legacy I must leave to my children and to my brothers and sisters in the faith. I pray that we all may hear what the Spirit is saying to the bride!

I also want to thank those pastors and friends who graciously entered a discourse with me as I explored the tenets of this book. I would like to thank priest and pastor Virgil P. Travis Jr., who taught me to see life through the lens of liturgy, to worship God in the natural rhythms of life. I want to thank those who took great pains to assist in the editing, including all the team at Wipf and Stock, to ensure a more coherent read. They have labored well and procured a more precise manuscript. I want to thank my Lord, who gives us an answer for the hope that we have in Christ Jesus!

Introduction

Paul's Appeal to Loyalty

PAUL, IMPRISONED IN ROME, writes his second letter to Timothy. In irony, the captive writes to the free on the nature of freedom. Paul is nearing the end of his life and seeks to leave a legacy with Timothy, a legacy of pastoral praxis. Paul is entrusting the gospel and his associated work to the tender care of Timothy. The assignment is Ephesus. Ephesus must be won to Christ, and the opposition must be defeated.

Paul is bound, which, again with wonderous irony, is a victory for the gospel. For "the word of God is not chained (2 Tim 2:9)." The second letter to Timothy has as an impetus an exhortation for Timothy to endure as he would face his own winter fraught with persecution, turmoil, and fierce opposition. Paul is charging Timothy as a "good soldier of Christ Jesus" to continue in the warfare ahead (2 Tim 2:3).

Paul's situation also influences the content of his second letter. For Paul has already experienced a preliminary hearing (4:16–18) and is awaiting a final hearing. He certainly anticipates a verdict of execution (4:6–8). Paul knows that the situation in Ephesus has deteriorated and is reaching a critical crossroad where intervention is necessary. Some have abandoned him (1:15; 4:10), some have gone away to other missions (4:10, 12), and Hymenaeus remains at work to undermine the gospel despite having been excommunicated (2:17–18).

Thus, what we have here is a highly personal letter appealing to Timothy that he would stay the course. The ultimate appeal is for Timothy to remain loyal to Christ and his testimony. And yet, there is a penultimate appeal as well; Paul asks for Timothy's loyalty to him (1:13). It is this second appeal that offers a contrast between the first and second letter to Timothy. The loyalty is predicated on the strength of the relationship. Paul's imprisonment occasions a more visceral and affectionate tone that offers all pastors, whether senior or transitional, to launch out and find a Timothy. Indeed, it is captivity that creates an even greater potential for this kind of transaction. In the kingdom, the paradox abounds, the bonds of love are strengthened by the woes of imprisonment. So, theological inquiries remain. What if imprisonment acts as a catalyst for mentoring? What if it is captivity and even pending death that awakens the soul to legacy? Pastors who were once in the field and find themselves hemmed in by circumstances beyond their control have been divinely appointed the space to mentor a Timothy God has sent them.

The Integrity-Despair Crisis

Erik Erikson's writing on stages of development may be relevant to our discussion of Paul's second letter to Timothy. Erikson is keen on observing various "crises" over one's lifetime. These crises assist in the matriculation to and through the next stage of development. As such, Erikson posits a *crisis-dialectic* paradigm of emotional and psychic growth that requires a crisis that catapults one to the next stage of maturation or development. Paul, in writing his second letter to Timothy, would be in his last stage of Erikson's development, which he has coined "integrity vs. despair."

Erikson describes this stage by first recognizing that integrity has as its central context a wisdom that he defines as a "kind of informed and detached concern with life itself in the face of death itself."[1] That is, life is informed by a dialectic. One one hand, we all matriculate through the various stages of development, but we also face an end or telos of that very life. The tension of both concern and detachment is the dialectic of the crisis. But this is not the only dialectic inherent in this stage. Where wisdom provides the dialectic of concern and detachment, disdain creates a monolithic antipathy to wisdom in the form of

---

1. Erikson, *Life Cycle Completed*, 61.

"a reaction to feeling (and seeing others) in an increasing state of being finished, confused, helpless."[2]

Thus, the pathos of wisdom is concern and detachment, breaking from one pattern and embracing the next. Disdain is anti-pathos, which is a state of remaining in past stages that were never faithfully resolved. This results in a gestalt of anxiety about the hopelessness of the self and the others to whom the self is connected.

Two Critical Virtues

Erickson continues his dialectical crisis theorem with the claim that the end of life is a return to the beginning of life. In this way, maturation embraces the likeness of a child. He provides two virtues that are critical at the end of life when navigating integrity vs. despair. First, hope is necessary, for it is the "most basic quality of 'I-ness,' without which life could not begin or meaningfully end."[3]

Second, Erikson suggests that the last possible form of hope is faith. Faith is the second critical virtue and a teleological extension of hope. Hope is confidence in the life to come. Hope that the next generation will go on and that we will all have a home that can be confidently anticipated. The work, assignment, and faith are all teleologically complete and kept. Paul signifies this when he states that he has kept the faith and fought a good fight (see 2 Tim 4:7).

Erikson asserts that it is a return to childhood that enables one to ascertain the matriculation of hope into faith, or a hope that is the confidence of a child who believes his Father can do anything! Thus, he claims that hopefulness is one of the most childlike of all human qualities. Indeed, Jesus calls us to return to childhood when he likewise states,

> He called a child, whom he put among them, and said, "Truly I tell you, unless you change and become like children, you will never enter the kingdom of heaven. Whoever becomes humble like this child is the greatest in the kingdom of heaven. (Matt 18:2–4)

For Jesus, the return to childhood is a similitude of humility. It is the acknowledgement of powerlessness in the face of situations beyond our control. It is the subjugation of the self to God Himself. It is the yielding up of the spirit at death. It is the loosening of the grip and a

---

2. Erikson, *Life Cycle Completed*, 61.
3. Erikson, *Life Cycle Completed*, 62.

condescension to the truth that we are mere mortal. It is the embrace that our life is a mist, appearing in the morning and fading in the evening (see Jas 4:14). It is joy in today and hope for tomorrow. It is delight in play and peace about our work. It is belief for the impossible and a non-anxious abiding in His presence. We return to childhood as we need physical assistance in our old age; we cannot be as independent as we once were. We condescend to ascend. The kingdom is waiting for children. But can we allow ourselves to become one in the process of our aging? Erikson would assert that in order to navigate this last phase and find integrity, we must return to becoming a child through the means of the final consummation of hope—that being faith.

Agape as *Finalis Virtus*

I would add to Erikson's observation the need for *agape* as the *finalis virtus* in ending life with integrity. If hope is translated into faith, then *agape* is the means of this transformation. Paul himself states elsewhere that among the three cardinal virtues that remain, love is the greatest (see 1 Cor 13:13). Therefore, I would imagine that integrity is very much tied to the practice of faith, hope, and love at the end of life that mediates a return to childhood, which is a process of condescension into humility that precipitates and anticipates the ascension to heaven in peace and joy.

If, indeed, a return to childhood is the arguable epicenter of the final crisis-dialectic, one can then aspire to maintain also that a return to family is a primary destination of this journey. Indeed, Erikson maintains that many of the elderly seek psychotherapy precisely because they are dislocated from family. They have lost a relational influence, having been unable to secure intimacy and sense of generativity that comes with childhood.[4]

Perhaps this is why Paul is insistent that Timothy "come before winter" (2 Tim 4:21). Perhaps this would be the last communion with his *son* before his death. Even as he writes a letter of impartation, he also seeks an encounter to finalize the impartation. In 1 Timothy the winter is coming; in 2 Timothy the winter has passed, and Paul stands on the precipice of spring. But Timothy needs Paul to face his own winters in life. First Timothy is the throes of battle; 2 Timothy is the deliverance from "every evil deed" (2 Tim 4:18).

---

4. Erikson, *Life Cycle Completed*, 63.

Integrality

Erikson would go on to offer a more nuanced definition of integrity in coining the term "integrality." That is, integrity can be envisaged as the integration of *soma, psyche,* and *ethos* in a way that I would argue potentiates an epistemology of *shalom*. Erikson argues that navigating each dialectical crisis creates relational lines that connect the three human constitutions. In a way, Erikson is arguing for an anthropology of *soma, psyche,* and *ethos* that can correspond with Paul's use of the words "flesh," "will/soul," and "spirit." The disunity or disintegration of these human constituents results in a kind of despair at the end of life. The integration or integrality of such constituents enables a unity that is a herald of integrity. However, I would assert a more theological framework that includes the concept of shalom as a sign of integrity.

To support this claim, Apolos Landa, in revisioning a shalom framework of health and healing, offers this contrastive definition of shalom when he asserts,

> True shalom, then, is not the absence of conflict or the cessation of hostility, but a state achieved by bringing equilibrium to what is unbalanced, justice where there is inequity, integrity where there is unrighteousness, wholeness where there is disintegration, and healing and health where there is sickness and disease.[5]

Shalom deconstructs the dualistic and gnostic conception of anthropology as a chasm between body and soul and seeks rather to integrate the organism in such a way that wholeness can be achieved. Shalom is therefore an anthropology of integration, wholeness, peace, and justice. It is inter- and intrapersonal wholeness.

As shalom is integrity of the human in relationship to self and others, it is the existential pinnacle at the end of the life. Therefore, a theological framework for the end of life may be a return to the beginning of shalom, which is the integration of self with self, God, and others in pure trust. This journey is navigated through the means of faith, hope, and love, with love being the *virtus finalis* of shalom. Shalom is the ego integrality with God and others that underscores justice, peace, well-being, and harmony. See figure 1 below for a composite illustration of this integrity-vs.-despair crisis-dialectic.

---

5. Landa, "Shalom and Eirene," 58.

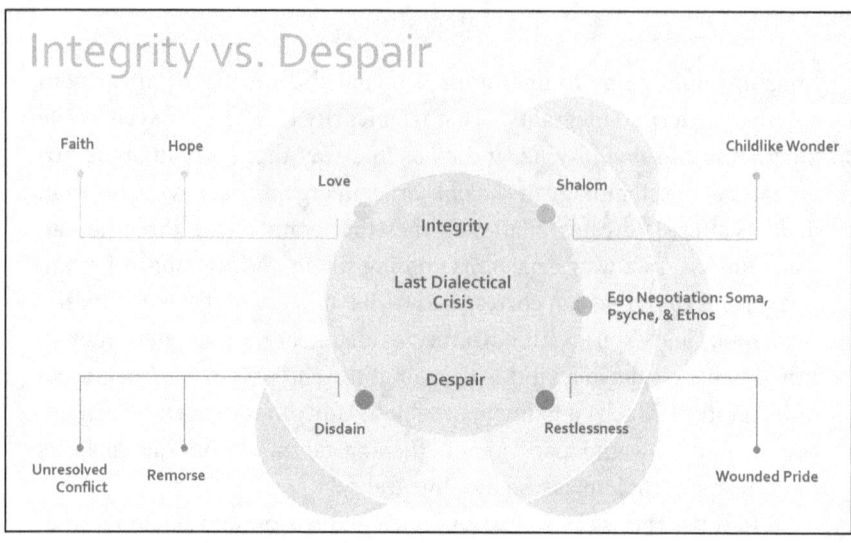

Figure 1: Integrity vs. Despair. Virtues contributing to integrity include the cardinal virtues of faith, hope, and love, with love (*agape*) being the *finalis virtus*. Dispositional traits contributing to integrity include childlike wonder, or going back to the beginning, and shalom, a type of integrality of peace. In contrast, despair is the consummation of antipathy, which includes unresolved conflict, persistent remorse, and disdain or animosity toward the self. Dispositional traits contributing to despair include wounded pride and restlessness, a state of discontentment with the life that was lived. The ego or the self negotiates between integrity and despair, which includes an intrapersonal conversation that includes the whole person, *soma* (body), *psyche* (soul), and *ethos* (spirit).

This is Paul's account in the second letter to Timothy. It is his time of shalom, his departure, and his impartation of faith, hope, and love to Timothy. Therefore, we will explore the pastoral reflections on deliverance from this life to another. We will pay special attention in the pages ahead to a theological framework and *praxis* of mentoring and impartation. Namely, I hope to provide a framework for pastoral legacy. In the process, we might also unexpectedly discover a framework of legacy from spiritual father/mother to spiritual son/daughter. Thus begins our journey to discover what legacy means for us as pastors and for us as Christians.

Chapter 1

Legacy of Apostolic Fatherhood

> Paul, an apostle of Christ Jesus by the will of God, for the sake of the promise of life that is in Christ Jesus, To Timothy, my beloved child: Grace, mercy, and peace from God the Father and Christ Jesus our Lord. (2 Tim 1:1–2)

The Election of the Apostle

WE BEGIN WITH AN introduction of defense. Paul defends his apostolic credentials by divine injunctions. That is, it is the explicit will of God that Paul be an apostle and this will is rooted in the promise of life, and the author of this life is Christ Himself. In other words, Christ commissioned Paul, and as Christ is divine, it was God's will that Paul be an apostle. As Christ is the author of life, the apostle's credentials live on. So, we learn that impartation and legacy often includes such acts that defend one's call. The beginning of the commission sets the tone for Timothy. In this light, he can defend his commission as well.

The apostle is an interesting office within an ecclesiastical and evangelistic framework. Spiros Zodhiates has defined "apostle" in the form of an adjective. That is, he describes one as being sent forth. It has the connotation of an ambassador sent into a foreign land to represent the king.[1] And perhaps Paul, more than any, utilizes this definition when he writes that "we are ambassadors for Christ, since God is making his appeal through us; we entreat you on behalf of Christ: be reconciled to God" (2 Cor 5:20),

---

1. Zodhiates, *Key Word Study Bible*, 1693.

or when he writes in his own captivity that he is "an ambassador in chains. Pray that I may declare it boldly, as I must speak" (Eph 6:20). This then raises the implication that an apostle is not only sent but sent with a certain audacity to undo the golden calves of the age.

The word "apostle" is rarely used in classical Greek, and yet our Lord, perhaps with significant intention, verbalizes this construction when announcing the commission of the twelve apostles. The Gospel of Luke is keen to describe an all-night prayer meeting by which perhaps Christ received from His own Father the names of the twelve apostles, who were chosen "from" the disciples (see Luke 6:12–16). The implication here is that there were more than twelve disciples but there would not be more than twelve apostles. For the first time, we see herein a clear distinction between disciple (follower) and apostle (sent one). The apostle is clearly a disciple as the gospel informs us that the apostle designation is one that is in addition to the disciple designation. However, the inverse is not true. Not all the disciples that day were given the designation of apostle. So, is it then a possibility that not all followers will be sent, or at least in the form of an apostolic commission?

Second, is the apostolic designation subjected to an element of arbitrary selection through the casting of lots (see Acts 2:26)? After choosing two, lots were cast that indicated that Matthias would be numbered among the apostles. And if this is the case, does one necessarily require a direct commission from Jesus either in person or through a vision to be assigned the office of apostle? Were the apostles limited to the Twelve plus Paul? It seems, in imitating Christ, any selection of an apostle necessitates a prolonged period of prayer. Jesus prayed all night prior to choosing His twelve apostles. Do we pray before we choose? Do we seek the Lord until names are named? How does the church choose its leaders? How do we choose certain designations? How can we get back to prayer being the primary substrate of any apostolic charge? How can we reform our souls to ensure a steady appeal to God to unveil the apostles, to disclose our leaders, to reconstruct our ecclesiastic defenses?

Jesus seems to allude to the *sentness* of apostolic commission when he prays for the twelve apostles with the following: "As you sent me into the world, so I have sent them into the world" (John 17:18). So, apostolic commission is a direct extension and iteration of Christ's work upon the earth. Christ leaves a legacy to the twelve apostles; Paul leaves a legacy to Timothy. The question remains whether Paul is imparting an apostolic legacy to Timothy. He has already sent Timothy to Ephesus and recalls him one last time, but for what purpose?

Paul numbers himself with the apostles and seems to imply that his credentials correlate with his Damascus Road encounter. For in writing to the Corinthian church, he is insistent that "Last of all, as to one untimely born, he appeared also to me. For I am the least of the apostles..." (1 Cor 15:8–9). Thus, this also raises the question as to whether seeing Christ, or rather seeing and being seen by Christ, is an authenticator of some sort. That is, is this required for being an apostle? Must one receive a direct commission in the form of a theophany?

Paul opens most of his letters with his apostolic charge as a form of authority received from Christ to legitimize the letter. We would typically end our letters with our signature and credentials to authenticate their content, but Paul chooses rather to open his letter with his signature and provides certain nuances that clarify his understanding or perhaps revelation concerning his apostolic call.

In Romans 1:1, the apostle is "set apart for the gospel," and one who is a servant (likely with a *doulos* connotation of slave) of Christ. In 1 Corinthians 1:1, the apostle is "called," and the calling is initiated by the "will of God." Thus, Paul's theology of apostolic call is inherently clear; it is a divine commission, call, and appointment. But this still leaves the question as to whether this call is individualistic, that is, a personal call; or is there a type or form of communal affirmation? That is, does the community witness to some degree this divine appointment? The call was witnessed by those who traveled with Paul and affirmed by Ananias, who also had a vision that Paul would be divinely called to the Gentiles (see Acts 9:15–16). The "will of God" is an important substrate of apostolic calling as it is again reiterated in 2 Corinthians 1:1.

Paul would specify that an apostle is not a corporeal designation. That is, men cannot render the designation as some other title that we create to fill certain job descriptions within the ecclesiastical community. Paul states "not of men," likely as a polemic against the self-proclaimed teachers at the church of Galatia that he is preparing to confront. His apostolic designation appears to also carry with it the authority to confront the heresy in Galatia, as he spares no words in stating how perplexed he is that the churches in Galatia would be removed from the gospel and would become bewitched (see Gal 3:1).

The will of God is also the premise of his apostleship in Ephesians 1:1. Timothy is with him when he addresses the Philippian church and so "servants" are used rather than the invocation of his apostolic call (see Phil 1:1). Paul asserts the "will of God" yet again in rendering the apostolic designation when writing to the church at Colossae (see Col 1:1). In most of the introductions to Paul's epistles, Timothy is mentioned, yet another indication of the bonds between them. Timothy was there as Paul constructed many of these letters, and all the while he was receiving a legacy and a spiritual deposit with each one (see 2 Cor 1:1; Phil 1:1; Col 1:1; 1 Thess 1:1; 2 Thess 1:1).

Finally, we come to Paul's use of the term "apostle" in the Pastoral Epistles. In his first letter to Timothy, Paul states that his apostolic designation was by the command of Christ (1 Tim 1:1). We have noted above the issue of a promise of life in correlation with the apostolic designation (2 Tim 1:1). And finally, when writing to Titus, Paul employs a curious description of his call, stating that it is according to the faith of God's elect (Titus 1:1). Indeed, Paul expresses three statements that both confirm and describe his commission as an apostle. First, it is according to the faith of God's elect. Second, it is in the context of acknowledging truth. Third, it is in the hope of eternal life, which is subsequently manifested through Paul's preaching (see Titus 1:1–3).

The "elect," or the ἐκλεκτός (ek-lek-tos), are the ones spoken out of or chosen with a specific intention in mind. There is a special relationship between the One calling and the one hearing. ἐκλεκτός is a choice or selection among many and again brings up the twelve apostles narrative once more as they were chosen among many (see Luke 6).[2] Paul was chosen to be an apostle among many. So, is the apostolic designation imbedded in the doctrine of election? Our purpose here provides no room for expositing this doctrine, but one must note the curious correlation here. Paul advances the notion of his *chosenness* to be sent and brings emphasis to his being chosen by subsuming the apostolic designation within God's freedom to elect offices. God is free to choose some and not others, but this ought not to denigrate the ubiquitous nature of salvation. However, this does inherently create a certain charismatic impartation from God to certain individuals within God's redemptive metanarrative (see Matt 22:14).

By beginning with God's choice or ἐκλεκτός, Paul not only defends his commission but also affirms the authority that comes from his election so that his letter carries the weight of divine injunction. Paul

---

2. Zodhiates, *Word Study Bible*, 1712.

models a kind of determination to defend his appointment perhaps so that Timothy would not fear in doing the same. Paul does not confer the apostolic designation to Timothy as this is done by Christ, but he does repeatedly encourage him to exercise his pastoral authority regardless of his age (1 Tim 4:12).

Jurgen Becker writes on the designations given to Paul and comments that Paul's understanding of his commission is a watershed moment that recapitulates creation (see 2 Cor 4:6).[3] Just as light was created to penetrate the darkness, a completely new way of seeing has penetrated Paul's soul. Everything has been transformed! And this transformation has as an etiological center, the Damascus Road encounter. That is, vision of Christ precedes apostolic mission to the gentiles. Mission must be predicated on vision. That vision must be of Christ and His direct commission for it to be apostolic. The fact that Paul's apostleship is validated by a post-resurrection theophany of Christ may leave the door open for future apostolic commissions as Christ is free to manifest Himself in a vision to any He may set apart.

In Matthew's gospel, the twelve apostles are called to Jesus but then given a special commission that may also be apostolic in nature. They are given "authority over unclean spirits, to cast them out, and to cure every disease and every sickness" (Matt 10:1). In this sense, the apostle is also charismatic and authoritative. He is given power for the task of an itinerant missionary or preaching endeavor.

The apostle was sent to a specific people group. Where Paul was an apostle to the Gentiles, the Twelve were apostles to Israel. Jesus was particular in His commission of the apostles that they were not to enter the "road leading to gentiles," but rather go to the "lost sheep of the house of Israel" (Matt 10:5–6). The apostles were to preach with the authority given to them by Christ. The content of the preaching was a simple but profound message to be reiterated in every town they would enter: "The kingdom of heaven has come near'" (Matt 10:7).

Signs of the Apostle

The apostles were given a commission in the imperative, "Cure the sick; raise the dead; cleanse those with a skin disease; cast out demons" (Matt 10:8). In a sense, we find the summary of the apostolic commission

---

3. Becker, *Paul, Apostle to the Gentiles*, 77.

accompanied by kingdom signs. Indeed, one could argue that these signs indicate and validate an apostolic call. A contemporary anecdote of the noteworthy sign of resurrection is articulated in Reinhard Bonnke's account of a miracle during a gospel crusade. While preaching an evangelical service, the body of a dead man was brought into the church in an adjoined room and laid out on a table. The father of the corpse provided the gathering more clarity as to the condition of his deceased son when he gave the following remarks: "I am his father. It is true that he is now breathing. But he is still as stiff as iron. He has been dead since Friday and has been in a mortuary."[4]

Further prayer and worship ensued in that room as pastoral staff members believed for the miracle of resurrection. One of the pastoral staff members "laid hands on his chest and announced that heat was returning to the torso."[5] The prayers continued all day, with the deceased's wife standing in faith that her husband would be returned to her. And then, all at once, he "sneezed and sat up on the table."[6]

The resurrected man, named Daniel, was escorted to cooler rooms for his full recovery and he asked for water. He kept asking for an enigmatic file as the fog of confusion was lifting from his slumber. He was escorted to the church sanctuary, where a man with his crippled wife entered, amazed to see this man raised from the dead. She immediately threw down her crutches and began running throughout the sanctuary in joyful fervor and praise. The husband who witnessed this miracle immediately erupted with repentance, saying, "I am a sinner. I repent. God, please forgive me of my sins."[7]

A miracle begat a miracle. The miracle of resurrection created the potential for a miracle of healing and a miracle of repentance. It is as if the kingdom signs were proliferating as witnesses came and hearts were exposed. The apostolic commission was manifest in that the kingdom of heaven was most certainly at hand. It was a *break-in* of God's kingdom into our own.

---

4. Bonnke, *Raised from the Dead*, 116.
5. Bonnke, *Raised from the Dead*, 117.
6. Bonnke, *Raised from the Dead*, 118.
7. Bonnke, *Raised from the Dead*, 120.

Apostleship and Theophany

Thus, was Reinhard Bonnke then an apostle to Africa? Looking more intently into his biography, we find that Bonnke experienced a call to Africa as a child.

> Not long after this conversation I attended a life-changing Sunday service. On this particular day, a husband and wife missionary team has been invited to speak. I do not remember much about them because as they were speaking the Spirit of God spoke to me in my heart. It was as if He said very clearly, "Reinhard, one day you will preach My gospel in Africa.[8]

Now, we must earnestly inquire as to whether Bonnke experienced a theophany as a sign of apostleship. There may be an implicit theophany when Bonnke describes a dream or vision that became the encounter that would forever change his trajectory and ministry.

> I had a dream that changed everything. I saw a map of Africa. Not South Africa, not Lesotho, not Johannesburg, but the entire continent. The map began to be splashed and covered with blood. I became alarmed. I thought surely this meant some kind of apocalyptic violence was coming—perhaps a Communist revolution. But the Spirit whispered to me that this was the blood of Jesus that I saw. The terrible violence that spilled His blood happened 2,000 years ago on a cross. Then I heard the words, *Africa shall be saved*.[9]

Bonnke's recurrent dream of a blood-stained Africa washed in the blood of Jesus was a Spirit-revealed commission that was Christocentric in its content, given the sign of redemption and the symbolic appeal to all of Africa. The clarion call "Africa shall be saved" became the recurrent vision statement of Bonnke's ministry as the claim was a cacophony among the crusades. What started with a healing miracle in his first crusade of one hundred people evolved into a million-soul campaign at subsequent crusades throughout all of Africa. The dream was being realized. Although we do not hear directly from Christ in Bonnke's dream, we do hear from the Holy Spirit, who connects the commission to the blood of Christ. We also do not obtain a nuanced clarity for who is speaking the words "Africa shall be saved." Is this Christ Himself?

---

8. Bonnke, *Living a Life of Fire*, 77.
9. Bonnke, *Living a Life of Fire*, 235.

Even without the full nuance provided from Bonnke concerning his vision, we still get the sense that his commission originated in the mind of Christ, for the dream was specific to a certain people group and an image that revealed the redemptive work of Christ.

Apostleship as Passing the Mantle

Furthermore, we have a legacy from Bonnke to Kolenda, one generation to the next, in Bonnke's farewell crusade in Africa. He states that the Lord revealed to him that the "anointed must be appointed." He prays that the "torch" would be passed to Daniel Kolenda. He prays that the old would give birth to the new.[10] He, like the apostle Paul before, lays hands on Kolenda and prays for the signs of the kingdom to accompany his ministry and for the harvest of multiple souls to be the fruit. We will see later how Paul calls Timothy to stir up the gift that was imparted by the laying on of Paul's hands (see 2 Tim 1:6). Here we find the final act of the apostle in securing an apostolic legacy by imparting a *gift* to the next generation. It is not that Bonnke commissions Kolenda to be an apostle, as this is a commission solely belonging to Christ.[11] However, it is that Bonnke, like Paul, exhorts Kolenda to the task of leadership, evangelism, and preaching in the power of the Holy Spirit. This is the legacy aspect of apostolic ministry.

Christ being the sole sender of the apostle would imply a special office rather than a successive office. That is, there may not be successive apostles to a certain people or work. Rather, God provides the apostolic office at the time and people of His own choosing. Thus, I would like to propose a sixth Christocentric attribute to the full gospel paradigm of Christ as Savior, Christ as Sanctifier, Christ as Healer, Christ as Holy Spirit Baptizer, and Christ as Soon-and-Coming King. The fivefold gospel so central to early Pentecostalism focuses on the work done in the individual without emphasis on the work done through the individual. To this we add Christ as Apostolic Sender. That is, He commissions

---

10. See Bonnke commission Kolenda during his final crusade at the following link: Bonnke. "Evang Reinhard Bonnke Transferred," https://www.youtube.com/watch?v=NK0Y80YM560.

11. See Becker, *Paul, Apostle to the Gentiles*, 80, where he describes the apostolic call as an office that "does not come out of the church and also has no succession in the church, because that would do away with the immediate link between the person and God or Christ as sender."

apostles and sends them to particular people groups with kingdom signs, with resurrection of the dead being a special apostolic sign. This sixth attribute of Christ adds to the paradigmatic model, a missional component that speaks to vocation but also to the fact that Christ alone provides this office to the church (see Gal 1:1).

I am not calling the church to designate or create this office. I am not calling the church to begin appointing or ordaining apostles. Quite the contrary; I am apprehensive whenever the apostolic designation is used with so much liberality that many self-proclaim this office over their ministry without the kingdom affirmation. Rather, I am calling the church to recognize the office of apostle as one that Christ fills with appointments in the fullness of times with the characteristics we have already explored. Paul is "the symbolic figure of the worldwide Gentile mission," whereas Bonnke became the symbolic figure of the African mission.[12]

Suffering as Apostolic Sign

Next, we have not yet explored yet another dimension to the apostolic commission, suffering. The signs of the resurrection, the kingdom, and glory are subsequent to the fellowship of suffering (see Phil 3:10). Paul will provide a litany of sufferings in his second letter to the church at Corinth as credentials of his apostolic labors.

> Are they ministers of Christ? I am talking like a madman—I am a better one: with far greater labors, far more imprisonments, with countless floggings, and often near death. Five times I have received from the Jews the forty lashes minus one. Three times I was beaten with rods. Once I received a stoning. Three times I was shipwrecked; for a night and a day I was adrift at sea; on frequent journeys, in danger from rivers, danger from bandits, danger from my own people, danger from gentiles, danger in the city, danger in the wilderness, danger at sea, danger from false brothers and sisters; in toil and hardship, through many a sleepless night, hungry and thirsty, often without food, cold and naked. And, besides other things, I am under daily pressure because of my anxiety for all the churches. Who is weak, and I am not weak? Who is made to stumble, and I am not indignant? (2 Cor 11:23–29)

12. Becker, *Paul, Apostle to the Gentiles*, 80–81.

Therefore, weakness and suffering are also the credentials of apostolic ministry. Paul would rather boast in his weaknesses than in the glory, and yet there was also glory when Paul preached. However, the apostle joins the sufferings of Christ, boasting in the "thorn" as a medium of God's glory. The apostle suffers in the caring for many churches and to the people he has been called to commit the gospel. He suffers from his own family and from those without, with both physical and emotional perils. There is no aspect of the human constitution where the suffering does not touch. But the suffering must be. It is a sign of the apostolic call, and I would argue the seed for resurrection power. John Chrysostom also brings a sense of the apostolic necessity for suffering when he states that "He [Christ] hath not made us Apostles only that we might encounter dangers, but that we might even suffer and die."[13] So, when one seeks the apostolic office, one ought to weigh what will follow this office: suffering to a great extent and God's glory to a greater extent.

Father-Son Dyad as Apostolic Call

There is another designation, perhaps not as divine as Paul's commission but an appointment nonetheless worth noting. It is the appointment of a "dearly beloved son." Timothy is the recipient of this Pauline designation, a unique human designation. Paul employs the term ἀγαπητός τέκνον (ag-ap-ay-tos' tek'-non) as one who endears Timothy unto himself. It is most often translated as "beloved child."[14]

There are two instances in the ministry of Christ where this phrase is also articulated, and it is within the Father-Son relationship. We find ἀγαπητός τέκνον uttered at the baptism of Christ, where the Father proclaims this over His Son, adding that He is "well pleased" with Him (Matt 3:17). Second, God declares ἀγαπητός τέκνον at the Mount of Transfiguration when Moses and Elijah appear to Jesus for what appears to be a counsel of some sort. To ἀγαπητός τέκνον the Father adds "hear Him" (Luke 9:35). Thus, I would like to argue that ἀγαπητός τέκνον is a divine address to illustrate the declaration of a father over a son. As the Father employs the beloved title at the baptism and transfiguration of Christ, Paul adopts this same address over his son in the faith, Timothy. Jesus has commissioned Paul as an apostle and Paul has commissioned

---

13. John Chrysostom, *Homilies of John Chrysostom*, 166.
14. Rogers Jr. and Rogers III, *New Linguistic and Exegetical Key*, 500.

Timothy as a son. And for the rest of this letter, we see the acts of a father, indeed, an apostolic father imparting to his son. The appointment is divine as it recapitulates the fatherly affection first displayed over the eternal Son. Nothing is mentioned of Timothy's father, though much is said of his mother and grandmother. Perhaps this is the reason for Paul's proclivity to act as a father to Timothy. In any regard, it is perhaps yet another sign of apostolic calling to have sons in the faith! And not just any sons, but ἀγαπητός τέκνον, the "dearly beloved son."

Indeed, in introducing his first letter to Timothy, Paul adds the clarity that Timothy is his "son in the faith" (1 Tim 1:2). Thus, I wonder what it was like for Timothy to read these words as an introduction to the commission he was to receive. Perhaps there was a sense of affection and endearment that would renew his fervency for the kingdom and his role as the one who would be instrumental in advancing the Pauline legacy. Perhaps he felt like he belonged to a family, one with divine purpose, and one with a divine apparatus that had brought two people together not just for a task, but for a relationship.

Now we must draw an etymological distinction between the Heavenly Father's declaration over the Son and Paul's declaration over Timothy. We have already explored the similarities, but there is also a distinction. The Son is described as the υἱός rather than the τέκνον. Thus, the υἱός of God denotes a certain relational character that goes beyond mere begetting although it includes this. He is not simply a child of the Father; He is the unique Son of God! In contrast, Timothy is described as a τέκνον to Paul. The difference involves a certain kind of unique peculiarity that is not replicated. One cannot exactly replicate the relationship between the Father and the Son, but can emulate it in the mirroring formulation of a father-child relationship in the faith. Paul and Timothy are an image of apostolic ministry where the apostle is divinely appointed and the child is the one affectionately chosen to carry out the legacy of the gospel.

Dwight's Father Conflict

The ἀγαπητός τέκνον relationship is given further complicated nuance in the biography and conflicted work of Timothy Dwight, a revolutionary caught between the loyalist legacy of his father (the Dwight side of the family) and the awakening legacy of his grandfather (the Edwards side of the family). Peter Kafer captures the emerging contradictions in the life of Timothy Dwight when he draws attributes from Dwight's biographers with the following statement.

> Part revolutionary, he was part reactionary.; part neoclassic, he was incipiently Romantic; agrarian idyllist, he was a mercantile Capitalist. He was even a Calvinist who tended toward Arminianism. For though Timothy Dwight to many different, and sometimes contradictory, aspects of late eighteenth century America, . . . he followed a flawless logic, that of his own inner experience.[15]

Timothy, aptly named for our purposes, oscillated with an internal dilemma in his attempts to identify his father. Torn between the prospects of his influential father with loyalist sentiments to the British government and the revolutionary ideas of his grandfather Jonathan Edwards, he resided in a dialectic of law and theology, ultimately finding some sort of expression of this conflict through the medium of poetry. The Dwights were prominent figures in Hampshire County, with a legacy of law, land, and laud. Indeed, Dwight's grandfather of the same name, Col. Timothy Dwight, was arguably the most influential man in the region.[16]

In contrast, Dwight's mother was the fourth daughter of Jonathan Edwards, who was one of the fathers of the First Great Awakening, but whose scrupulous piety compelled him to refrain from other forms of income when he lost his parish in Northampton with "nothing visible to depend upon for my future usefulness, or the subsistence of my numerous family."[17]

Thus, his daughters were encouraged to marry, and Mary Edwards was wedded into the Dwight family at age sixteen. Timothy Dwight was born to a family with two distinct legacies, and thus a gestalt that would posit an internal tumultuous conflict that Dwight would work through amid revolutionary America. Indeed, the ἀγαπητός τέκνον relationship appeared more prominent, implicitly if not explicitly, between Dwight and his grandfather as Dwight considered Edwards a "moral Newton and the second Paul."[18] And though these accolades were not overtly ascribed to his father, Dwight was torn between the pursuit of theology (the Edwards legacy) and law (the Dwight legacy). In the end, Dwight leaned into his

---

15. Kafer, "Making of Timothy Dwight," 189.
16. Kafer, "Making of Timothy Dwight," 190.
17. Kafer, "Making of Timothy Dwight," 190.
18. Kafer, "Making of Timothy Dwight," 191.

Edwards legacy, but with a distinction that was his very own. He rather enjoyed the medium of poetry. But in his pursuit of this legacy, he would adopt the ascetic and rigorous practice of study that recapitulated his grandfather's tenure at Yale, which would likewise precipitate both a physical and emotional undoing to the extent that Dwight required a fourteen-month period of convalescence to recover. Ironically, Dwight locates his conversion experience just before his emotional breakdown.[19]

Dwight's fate as an Edwards would become sealed when the foment for revolution heightened to the extent that sides were taken and conflict ensued. Dwight would become a revolutionary at Yale even as his father suffered back home as a Tory and British sympathizer. Indeed, Timothy Dwight remained at Yale when his father Major Dwight was ousted from his political posts and forced to flee to the more pro-British colony of West Florida with only some of his family. The Dwight estate was plundered, and the family terrorized as one of Timothy's brothers was incarcerated, having developed a severe case of PTSD. He was considered insane, never to recover. Major Dwight would die in Florida as Timothy Dwight was ascending in influence as an Edwardian revolutionary. He attempted and failed to be chosen as Yale's president in his early twenties, but would continue to support the war effort, enrolling as a chaplain in the militia.[20]

It is in this context that Timothy Dwight chooses his path and begins his seminal work, *The Conquest of Canaan*. It was meant to be the epic poem of America. Dwight sought, in this manner, to be the Milton of a new nation, taking the biblical narrative of Joshua conquering the promised land within the contemporary and existential ideology of America's rise into glory during the Revolution and putting this into verse. Many have argued that Dwight also includes his own psychology and inner conflict as he creates characters that parallel his own relationship with his father and wife. What was meant to be the epic poem of America would not garner attention or recognition as such. Again, Dwight is unable to accomplish the idealization of purpose that characterized his own appraisal of his work. Nonetheless, there is a lesson in Dwight's monolith, for in Book 7 there is a dream lamenting the death of a father, which posits the universal human experience of the ἀγαπητός τέκνον. That is, in the lament and subsequent luminary dream

19. Kafer, "Making of Timothy Dwight," 192–93.
20. Kafer, "Making of Timothy Dwight," 195.

of Irad (one of Dwight's characters and arguably most like himself), we find a vision of a ghastly figure, Irad's father.

Let us explore this dream as one with a web of complicated human nuance in describing ἀγαπητός τέκνον in a way that explicates a more complicated relating nuance between father and son. In exploring Dwight's conflict, we may see it within ourselves.

Irad's vision of his father is one of seeming silence for several stanzas as Irad is alone with his thoughts and thus verbalizes in monologue fashion his lament, with a notable reference to being absent.

> And art thou fled forever? this thine end,
> Thou best of parents, and thou surest friend?
> And could'st thou fall, a prey to murdering war?
> What cruel demon drove my feet so far?
> Was no kind angel hovering o'er the throng?
> Where look'd the Power, thy virtue serv'd so long?[21]

Irad attributes his absence from his father as a potential demonic excursion that achieved an absence that was quite lamentable. For in Irad's absence, his father and "surest friend" fell by the sword. And then the divine appeal is issued forward as an existential question that likely crosses the tongue of all who have lost his or her love. On whom did divine Power of heaven, for whom Irad's father served and by implication gave his life, look when in the throes of battle he died? The lament is a question of why. Why did God not protect the vicissitude and vitality of his father, for whom his father virtuously and with great fidelity gave of his best years? And for Dwight, perhaps he finds his own lament in this verse, as he was absent when his father died. And more so, Dwight encouraged the movement that would be the demise of his father. Could it be that there is a form of regret imbedded in verse? It is quite possible as Dwight continues his visionary excursus,

> Thy soul so pure—thy life so firmly just—
> Scarce Heaven's own law could more demand from dust.
> Why, O thou righteous Mind? but cease my tongue,
> Nor blame the dread decree, that cannot wrong.
> Mine the sole fault—and mine the single blame—[22]

---

21. Dwight, *Conquest of Canaan*, 159.
22. Dwight, *Conquest of Canaan*, 160.

Irad places the sole blame for his father's death on himself. Even as he appeals to God for the elusive answer to the why of grief, the why of loss, and the why of theodicy, he is also quick to temper his tongue to look inward. Irad goes on to specify why he assumes the responsibility for the demise of his father.

> Wild with the magic of that phantom, fame.
> Didst thou for this the guilty shield bestow,
> To leave thee naked to the fatal blow?
> Didst thou for this the sword accurs'd impart,
> That should have plung'd beneath the murderer's heart?[23]

The confession is made, and the intent is exposed. Irad's seeking of fame is what he perceives was the fatal blow to his father. And perhaps, just perhaps, he longs to be the one to have died vicariously on his father's behalf. Perhaps Dwight exposes his own lament. For as he was rising in the ranks of recognition at Yale, his father was suffering at home—persecuted, imprisoned, and then exiled. Therefore, perhaps Irad's and Dwight's vision is one to warn the young ambitious and prodigious pursuit be tempered by love and relational pathos. Fame is no comparison to love.

Finally, we have the description of a father's nurture of a son who needed direction and consolation with the following stanza.

> Far other love, far other faithful cares
> Nurs'd my young limbs, and watch'd my rising years;
> My early steps, from pleasure's slippery road,
> Lur'd with soft smiles, and led them up to GOD;
> Thy own bright actions prompting to pursue,
> To virtue charm'd me, and to glory drew;
> With Joshua's self my wishes forc'd to vie.
> Boast of mankind, and chosen of the Sky.[24]

Irad and Dwight reflect on what appears to be a clinical metaphor of the father-son dyad. A father can strengthen his son's limbs, perhaps an unwitting reference to Moses aiding his son in the faith. Moses strengthened Joshua with hands extended that caused Israel to prevail in battle (see Exod 17:11). And even as the father lifts his hands and, by extension, his son's fighting arm, he himself requires the assistance of others in the same

---

23. Dwight, *Conquest of Canaan*, 160.
24. Dwight, *Conquest of Canaan*, 160.

way. The father is a guide to avoid the slopes of pleasure and overcome the obstacles of hedonism that can so easily lure youthful pride away. And in the end, Irad is cradled within a kind of virtue that is also glorious, and one with a providential context. For Irad, who was fashioned of his father to fulfill a destiny by alignment with Joshua, also views this same destiny as the sword to deal the blow of his father's death. What a dilemma! What conflict bestowed upon the mind that one must both agonize the grief of a lost father while pursuing the glory of victory, as if life preserved and victory in battle are mutually exclusive.

In the end, Irad is elected or chosen to fight at Ai, despite the bitter defeat and loss of his own father. It is not soon after his vision of his father that Joshua calls everyone to arms, for it is to Ai they must once again go to lock shields and exchange blows. Irad is hardly allowed to grieve until he is shouting a visceral and resounding war cry. Dwight does not provide space for the ghost of Irad's father to speak those words of wisdom he so earnestly craved as a son.

What if Dwight would have had Irad's father speak? We find the grave silent and Irad's imagination wild with speculation. Perhaps Irad's father was as silent even as he was ghastly because Dwight's father suffered in silent exile, estranged from family, and cut off from further influence upon his son. What son does not long to hear from his own father or father in the faith, "Job well done"? But what if a son turns to traverse an antagonistic path, as did Dwight from the path of his father? What words are thus reverberated in his imagination? What does a father say? Perhaps if Dwight had explored the vision, created a poetic dialogue between father and son, perhaps punctuating the universal human longing to make his or her father proud, maybe the universal application of human appeal would have been felt. We read the verse and yearn for more words to cut through the tension of grief.

The tides of war may be coming with Ai, but pale in comparison to the war that occurs throughout every generation—what do we do with loss? What do we do with theodicy? How do we relate, respect, but also individuate from our fathers? Where are the fathers today? Have they all been slain on the altar of mistrust? Are there no spiritual fathers because there are no trustworthy sons whereby a father can throw the mantle? Are there no fathers because the ones who would become fathers are themselves fatherless? Is fatherlessness the unspoken epidemic upon humanity that has become a breeding ground for gender confusion? Perhaps we have created a cultural construct where fathers distrust sons and sons resent fathers. We have lost the ἀγαπητός τέκνον, father-son dyad, which is all too important to leave undone. What if Paul is calling spiritual fathers to account through the Holy Spirit by modeling a legacy instilling father-son apostolic paradigm for the church to once again capture? I would argue that the church must once again both reclaim the recognition of apostles by individuals commissioned by Christ Himself and reify the father-son dyad through spoken word and legacy for the next generation.

A Contemporary Application

Like Dwight, I was born into a family with a maternal legacy of ministry. My grandfather was a minister in the Foursquare Church. Unlike Dwight, both my mother and father groomed me for a vocation in medicine. Financial security was a virtue for our family as we were anything but secure. Filing for bankruptcy was a watershed moment for our family; we could no longer pay our mortgage. Thus, when I announced my intention to pursue ministry, like Dwight's father, my father was puzzled and saw it as a waste of my undergraduate degree and investment in medicine. The genesis of my calling to preach was also my genesis of a journey for a spiritual father. I hoped to have found it when I pastored my first church and sought meetings and counsel from the previous pastor of the church. The previous pastor had incidentally been my very own pastor for four years. However, with each meeting, I became more and more discouraged as I felt the shame of not personally evangelizing or growing the church as expected. I needed help with a staff member seeking to undermine authority and overall counsel with how to lead the church and staff. Within the first year, sexual impropriety was uncovered within the church, and I sought counsel on how to navigate this sensitive debacle as well. In short, I needed help, a father, a sense of consolation and encouragement, a sense that God would be with me in the mess. However, what I received was lamentation over the church's seeming lack of evangelism and witness.

Thus, I would journey the pastoral road without a father in the faith, without a Paul, and without the defense that Paul would provide for Timothy through the medium of a letter and admonition to Ephesus. Paul defended Timothy and upbraided the influential vying for authority. Alas, this would not be my story. And as such, I buckled under the pressure of contempt, as there became a confluence of antipathy and false accusations that arose to have me ousted. Thus, I wonder if my story is not entirely unique to a generation of pastors who are emerging without a Paul to defend and mentor them in the faith. This paucity of the father-son dyad may be one explanation as to why ministers exit the field, with loneliness as the harbinger as they fought the beasts of Ephesus in a silo. It seems to me that the church is in desperate need to revive the father-son, mother-daughter dyad for an effective legacy to be transferred to subsequent generations. I have wondered on many occasions whether the outcome of that first pastoral experience would have been different if there had been a defense or an apostolic polemic toward those with influence within the church. But more than this, I wonder what Timothy remains out there waiting for a Paul to invite him in to dine, to laugh, to cry, and to contemplate the kingdom work together. I am at an age where I must now turn to Timothys in the faith whether or not I will ever have a Paul for discourse.

In summary, we have discussed several signs to the apostolic legacy. We have exposited a few attributes, including theophany, population, miracles, suffering, and fatherhood. Please see figure 2 below.

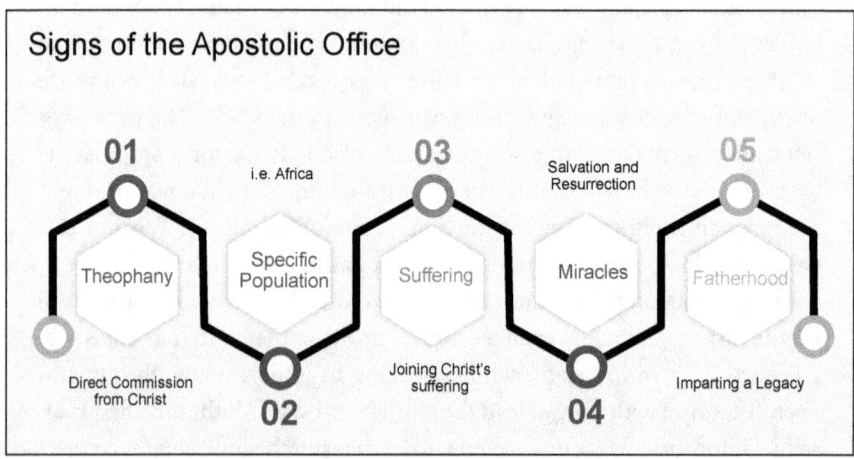

Figure 2: Signs of the Apostolic Office

However, it is the last of these signs, the legacy of fatherhood, that I have longed to underscore. Legacy is the result of a father-son dyad. It is also the fruit of apostolic commission. It is a dyad to be reclaimed by the church. It is apostolic to identify children in the faith and cast a mantle upon them. As for me, I look to my own children and children in the faith. How am I interfacing with them in a way where this dyad dynamic is effectively alive and well? The next generation very well depends on such filial dynamics. Perhaps my lesson is not how I can have a father in the faith, but how I can be a father in the faith.

Chapter 2

Legacy of Kindling

> For this reason I remind you to rekindle the gift of God that is within you through the laying on of my hands . . . (2 Tim 1:6)

PAUL PROVIDES THREE IMPERATIVES to Timothy throughout the rest of chapter 1, explicated by a context of relationship, history, and present vocation. The three imperatives begin with Paul's charge that Timothy "rekindle" the gift of God deposited to him by the laying on of Paul's hands (2 Tim 1:6). The second charge is that he be not ashamed of the testimony and of Paul, who represents this gospel testimony (2 Tim 1:8). A correlated charge follows in that he must courageously face the afflictions of the gospel that come with declaring this testimony over and against a hostile culture. Third, he is to adhere with sincere fidelity to the sound words entrusted to him by Paul. Timothy is to do this with divine enablement of the Holy Spirit (2 Tim 1:14–15).

I would like to explore these three imperatives of Paul as legacy imperatives. That is, this is the charge given to the next generation of pastors, preachers, and teachers. Any movement or church institution may benefit from intentionally charging its students with the same legacy as they are launched into mission. Each imperative also has an imbedded context and formulation by which the charge is realized. The imperative of rekindling the gift is realized in the context of intercession, tears, and the laying on of hands (see 2 Tim 1:3, 4, 6). The second imperative, being unashamed of suffering, is rooted in the context of soteriology and elective calling (see 2 Tim 1:9). The third and final imperative of fidelity to sound doctrine is contingent upon divine enablement by the Holy Spirit through the virtues of faith and love (see 2 Tim 1:13–14).

I would like to explore the context of this first imperative by investigating what comes before. Paul appeals to generations of those who have served God and ultimately passed on to Paul a legacy of a pure conscience (see 2 Tim 1:3). This pure conscience Paul now seeks to pass on to his son in the faith, Timothy. But rather than a conspicuous mantle, Paul seeks a more invisible one to be placed upon Timothy. This is, therefore, the work of intercession. Paul never ceases to remember Timothy in prayer, both night and day. Thus, the rekindling of the gift is as much an imperative for Timothy as it is for Paul. He is praying fervently that Timothy be enabled to rekindle the charisma, the evidence of grace, the infused power of the Holy Spirit for the manifestation of God's kingdom through him. Thus, it can be observed that in terms of legacy, there is as much that is not seen as is seen. The unseen legacy is one that enjoys the dew of intercession and one that responds to a prayer burden for sons and daughters in the faith.

Moreover, Paul is mindful as he prays that Timothy has had episodes of weeping. Curiously, we may ask the question, of what or over whom does Timothy weep? Was Timothy present when Paul met with the Ephesian elders to announce his final departure (see Acts 20)? Did Timothy weep with the other elders and does Paul now conjure up those tears as a father affectionately recalls the loving pleas of a son? Does Paul now see a prophetic burden being passed to Timothy, one that he no less carried for at least three years, wherein he "did not cease night or day to warn everyone with tears" (Acts 20:31)? That is, does Timothy inherit the pastoral medium of tearful intercession and tearful preaching? And is this what Paul references when he states that Timothy's tears ironically induce a sense of joy? Or does Paul allude to joy because of an anticipated visit with Timothy as he calls him to his side before winter (see 2 Tim 4:21)? Maybe there is an ironic juxtaposition of weeping and joy that is necessary in the impartation of legacy but also in the vicissitude of pastoring. That is, perhaps pastoring brings with it the most ironic and intense of emotional displays for the transformation of self and identity.

Rekindling as Weeping

Jack Barbalet explores the social and personal substrates of weeping, beginning with a thesis that may bring a nuanced understanding to human weeping,

> [T]he physical process of weeping plays a signal role in harmonizing or reintegrating a person's self-concept after events that have disrupted a prior self-image and self-feelings.[1]

Is weeping thus an instrumental medium by which identity is transformed? Does it integrate the pain of disruption with the birth of a new chapter? That is, a self-concept is fundamentally altered by disruptions or insults upon that concept, and perhaps weeping assists to reify or recreate a new self-concept after such a disruption.

Barbalet will further accentuate the concept of self-reifying identity by drilling down to the source of weeping that acts as a catalyst for transformation:

> It is therefore loss of a self-meaningful condition or opportunity or, to put it more generally, a negative change in the condition of self, which tears express.[2]

Loss is the catalyst of transformation. So that loss, re-envisioned here, can be a phenomenon with great potential. We expect one thing but arrive at another. The loss of the expectation, the opportunity, the idealized utopia of our imaginations, and the insertion of something or someone wholly different, creates the context for weeping. We come to understand ourselves in a convulsive way, which at first undermines our perceived self-image so that space is created for this very image to be reconstructed in a way that integrates the loss as perhaps something to be gained. One must mourn the loss of an identity, for it is certainly a meaningful loss as if a death has indeed occurred. One must express tears at the grave of oneself, for one often feels helpless to revive the old self. And yet, I would argue that it is tears that hold the kingdom key to a form of resurrection.

Jesus wept twice during his earthly ministry; at least twice in terms of what is recorded. He wept at the grave of Lazarus, which was pre-emptive in creating a context of resurrection (see John 11:35). The second was over Jerusalem, who had rejected their Messiah and who in

---

1. Barbalet, "Weeping and Transformations of Self," 126.
2. Barbalet, "Weeping and Transformations of Self," 128.

a short time would see destruction from Roman wrath (see Matt 23:37–39). In both instances, tears became the seedbed for resurrection. For Lazarus the resurrection was immediate; for Jerusalem the resurrection will come in the eschaton (see Rev 21). Thus, I would argue that tears, more than a mere expression of loss, hold theological significance in that the weeping that is in response to loss is the foundation that permeates the beginning of a resurrection. And perhaps this resurrection is of a different self, a lively self that integrates loss with gain. In this sense, it is a dialectical phenomenon and can be embraced as a form of transformation and work of the Holy Spirit. Indeed, in the context of an enemy's pursuit and slander, David evokes a phrase that brings comfort to all those who mourn. He states that it is God who keeps a record of sorrows, as if this human experience has kingdom potential. Moreover, if it were not enough for sorrows to be recorded, tears are preserved in the economy of heaven (see Ps 56:8). And this kind of heavenly preservation of tears is once again affirmed when the weeping prayers of the saints draw up to heaven as a form of incense before the Lord with eschatological ramifications (see Rev 5:8). Thus, where tears may be invoked by meaningful loss, the fruit of weeping can be existential gain!

Perhaps this is why Paul is filled with joy in the context of Timothy's tears. Perhaps his joy is more than just the happiness of an anticipated visit with Timothy, but a sense of joy that Timothy is being transformed into the bold leader Paul has prayed that he would become in the context of a brooding heresy filling the Ephesian church. Perhaps Paul notes Timothy's tears as fulfillment of Paul's earnest desire that Timothy inherit the legacy he is leaving. Perhaps Timothy is experiencing the prophetic burden of the gospel manifested by tears of transformation with the loss of timidity and the birth of audacity. Tears then become a sign of a gift being rekindled!

And of course, immense joy can also produce tears, but as Katz has asserted, this joy is a more poignant reminder of what is lost:

> What is discharged in weeping, according to Katz, is an image of self that is not tolerable, and . . . weeping offers positive rewards in the form of relief that may be found in dissolving and washing away a spoiled self-image.[3]

---

3. Katz, *How Emotions Work*, 186; and in Barbalet, "Weeping and Transformations of Self," 130.

Do tears really wash away an unpalatable self-image? Does joy really remind us of loss, at least the kind of joy that erupts in weeping? Was Timothy being changed from one image to the next? Or was it simpler than this? Was it the tears of separation between a father and son? Maybe it was as simple as that, and perhaps this *simple* transaction transforms. And perhaps weeping from separation is itself an existential medium that changes one's perspective of self.

Forward momentum easily evokes weeping, for it can also serve to remind us of a nearing death. Katz adds, "It is not just philosophers or poets who agonize over the realization that every great step forward in life is a step closer to death."[4]

Is Timothy weeping over the pending death of Paul? Certainly, suffering was revealed to Paul and that this would happen in Rome, and here Paul is in a Roman jail and anticipates his own death. Does Timothy anticipate this loss with weeping as the commiserate sign? And yet, without this loss, Timothy may not feel the compelling pathos to complete his mission. Timothy must find his way, albeit with a letter from Paul. What if tears move us forward in a way to something great but this also entails the death or leaving behind of something or someone else?

And in contrast, tears also indicate a certain raptness or joy that is sometimes only explicable through tears. I think Barbalet is right to add to some of the psychoanalytic thinkers that joy is not only a mechanism that reminds us of loss, but also a medium by which the self is "augmented," or transformed. In this way, raptness can be defined as

> a change in the material self through connection to a larger whole, as resulting from the augmentation of self through contact with a self-enhancing experience in aesthetic, religious or intimate personal experiences.[5]

Indeed, conversion is perhaps the most emotional experience one may have. In conversion, one both sorrows over one's sins in mourning while at the same time celebrating the newfound freedom in Christ with a kind of joy that culminates in tears. Conversion becomes the manifestation of a dialectic of both mourning and ecstasy, both associated with tears resulting from two contrasting emotions, both enacting transformation of the self.

---

4. Katz, *How Emotions Work*, 191.
5. Barbalet, "Weeping and Transformations of Self," 132.

Katz and Koestler have both written on the ego transformation enacted by tears and Barbalet has constructed a table contrasting the positive and negative transformations of the self as etiologically based in the source producing the tears. That is, as raptness produces a positive transformation of self, mourning may engender a negative transformation of self.[6] However, what if rather than envisioning either a negative or positive transformation, we remove these appraisals and rather look at the concept of weeping as phenomenological and transformative without confining the etiology of the tears to what may be intuitive appraisals of transformation? For example, why could not mourning be a positive transformation of the self? Why could relief not also be a negative transformation of the self?

Thus, in dialogue with some of these psychoanalytic thinkers, I would like to offer a theological polemic. This theological polemic is summarized in table 1 below. Certainly, we can describe the type of weeping with an openness that either negative or positive transformations can be occurring to the self, contingent upon contextual causes. Moreover, some tears of transformation can be both joyful and sorrowful, such as is the case with a conversion experience. Moreover, in terms of theological praxis, weeping tears that are joyful in nature appears to culminate in a kingdom virtue of shalom, which is peace and well-being. Shalom can also be characterized by right relationships with God and neighbor. Moreover, sorrowful weeping tears, I would argue, move the self to a culminating kingdom virtue of compassion, which is the ability to suffer with others.

These two kingdom virtues manifested by the same phenomenon of weeping tears can also be mediums by which the self becomes fully integrated. That is, the cognitive, emotive, spiritual, somatic, and willful selves come into a communicative whole. Indeed, shalom is a state of both intra- and interpersonal wholeness. Compassion is a state of self-confidence to risk the consequences of suffering with another. Jesus models shalom and compassion both in His earthly ministry and also in his passion upon the cross. He enters the suffering with the two thieves upon the cross and vicariously suffers for all who deserve to die.

---

6. See Barbalet, "Weeping and Transformations of Self," 122–23.

Table 1: Weeping Emotions and Transformation of Self

Concept of Self	Tears of Joyful Transformation	Tears of Sorrowful Transformation	Tears of Disintegrated Transformation
Somatic Self	Euphoria/Awe/Wonder	Hopeful Mourning	Destructive Mourning (depression and anxiety)
Social Self	Restoration/Reconciliation	Self-Pity (reaching for comfort)	Shame (loss of community)
Spiritual Self	Deliverance (freedom and forgiveness)	Conversion (conviction and guilt)	Rejection (refusing divine comfort)
Emotive Self	Joy (restoration of hope)	Anger/Wrath (seeking justice/vindication)	Despair (loss of hope)
Cognitive/Willful Self	Justice/Vindication/Victory	Sympathy/Empathy	Suicidal/Homicidal Ideations (actual or fantasy)
Dis-, Integrated Self	*Shalom*	*Compassion*	*Death*

Often, one might say in the context of sorrowful transformation, "This is not who I am," even as they weep. The emotional state of such an individual may be so discrepant from his or her former concept of self that the only way to communicate this is through tears of mourning. It is the loss of one's self and the birth of another. Every sorrow, however, has the potential to birth a greater state of compassion as one comes to empathize with the suffering of another with greater veracity.[7]

According to Helmuth Plessner, it is the surrender of self to the full gamut of the emotional experience and the manifestation of the tears that instigates the transformation of self. One must submit to the loss of control by releasing the self-concept for the new to come into

---

7. See also Barbalet, "Weeping and Transformations of Self," 136, where he notes the following: "experience of raptness, or relief, or shame, and so on, is possibly as intense and discrepant emotion that is not necessarily assimilated into self-processes: 'What I'm experiencing is not me. This is not who I am'. Any failure of assimilation of changes of self leads to a discharge of emotional energy that frequently takes the form of tears."

fruition.[8] And from an existential perspective, weeping can very much feel as if one has lost control of one's bodily eruptions. But perhaps this is the transformational aspect of weeping, to invoke a state of surrender or loss of control so that the prior self or concept of self is lost and a new one emerges. Thus, could it be that Timothy's tears, albeit tears of pending loss concerning his mentor, but also loss of his self-concept in relation to Paul, are transformational? His social self is changing, Timothy is becoming a new self; not just an ambassador of Paul, but the appointed pastor of the church at Ephesus.

But perhaps this is the transformational aspect of weeping, to invoke a state of surrender or loss of control so that the prior self or concept of self is lost and a new one emerges. Thus, could it be that Rachel's tears are leading Israel somewhere, to an integration of a new national identity? The other question that I find myself asking is: can one weep beyond the integration phenomenon to the extent that it becomes complicated and harmful? That is, can one suffer from destructive bereavement that leads to depression, anxiety, despair, and even perhaps suicidal ideations? Perhaps this is why the Lord instructs Rachel to refrain from weeping (see Jer 31:16). The work of her weeping is complete; to further mourn would not add to the work but rather complicate the national reformation God is performing as a response to her weeping. What if all of Israel continued to weep with sorrow even as God restored them to their land from captivity? What if they were unable to weep out of raptness? Would they then reject the integration of the shalom of God in their restoration? The other theological question remains: is there a way to cease from weeping in the context of one refusing comfort, unless there is a divine injunction? This divine injunction, transformation, and conversion, if you will, appears to be necessary for one to be consoled and to consider an altogether different emotional state.

And if there is an integration or reintegration of the self because of tears, the converse may also be true. That is, perhaps there is a fragmentation of the self from the kind of tears that erupt from despair, self-loathing, rejection of consolation, and even the contemplation of death. Tears birthed from a loss of hope, loss of community, loss of self,

---

8. See Plessner, *Laughing and Crying*, 116–17, 126, 137, where Barbalet cites his work with the following statement: "a crucial aspect of this process almost uniquely understood by Plessner is that weeping involves an act of self-surrender to the force of the relevant emotion, a yielding or inner capitulation and, to that degree, a loss of self-control."

seek annihilation as the pain becomes too much to endure. Judas comes to mind, who loses community, becomes "one destined to be lost," and unable to convert from the sinful act of betrayal (see John 17:12). Satan enters Judas and cultivates the kind of complicated bereavement that is tormenting, and a rigid therapeutic arises in his imagination—death (see John 13:27 and Matt 27:1–10).

Another, more physiological approach to tears can also take on theological undertones if, as McNaughton has observed, we consider the notion that tears are activated by the parasympathetic nervous system. Where the sympathetic nervous system prepares an individual to fight, flight, or freeze, the parasympathetic system reorients the body to a state of recovery. In the sympathetic state, there is only the reflex to act in offense or defense, but it is in the parasympathetic state that we assume the more vulnerable self once danger has passed. Tears, therefore, may signify a kind of recovery from the devastation or threat to the self or self-concept. Tears can be surmised as both physiologically and emotionally reflective, assisting the individual in the assimilation of the new self.[9]

Finally, I would like to offer a personal anecdote as an illustration. I had just returned from Ecuador on a mission trip and was boarding the down escalator to baggage claim, anticipating there a reunion with my family, who was eagerly awaiting my return. We had just adopted our daughter within the year, and she was still adjusting to the new dynamic that is the Jensen family. Although I had anticipated smiles and hugs upon my return, I had not expected what happened as I turned the corner after stepping off the escalator. My adopted daughter jumped up into my arms, cupped my face in her hands, and began to scream with utter excitement. There were no words, just repeated screams of joy. She seemed both surprised and overjoyed that I would have returned and that her new-fledged family was indeed intact.

As she drew me close to her, I found tears of joy erupting from my eyes. I could not hold back the tears that, I now wonder, were washing away my self-concept that I was to control what number of and by

---

9. See McNaughtan, *Biology and Emotion*, 148, where he states the following: "th[e] view of the function of tears, as a means of returning the body to normal after emotional disturbance, fits with the fact that tears are controlled by the parasympathetic rather than the sympathetic nervous system. It also accounts for the observation of tears of joy as well as tears of sadness—any arousing of emotion whatever its affective sign could require a chemical mopping up operation. The pattern of occurrence of tears is also consistent with this theory— tears occur during recovery from emotion rather than at the peak of arousal."

what means I was to bring children into my home. There was a change convulsing on the inside that was creating a new sense of self. I was a dad, and not just a dad to those who came through the womb of my wife, but to those birthed in the hearts of our dreams. I am paternal in nature; I am to take care of a family; I am to weep with joy at the love of my children on display in the sincerest of ways. Perhaps this was a sign of greater shalom at work in my life.

Touch as Kindling

The imperative of rekindling the gift is first deposited by the laying on of Paul's hands. It is as if physical touch remains a part of imparting legacy. Now, it is entirely possible that the gift Paul refers to is the spiritual gift of faith, as he has noted this gift in Timothy's grandmother and mother. It is as if spiritual genetics are implied, where faith is familial in nature. Although, this is the closest intimation we have as to the identity of the gift, there is no explicit exposition, and it behooves us to therefore consider that the identity of the gift is not as important here for Paul as the utilization and display of the gift.

A spiritual father is therefore one who continually encourages the gift in his sons and daughters. And more, a spiritual father communicates this encouragement through touch. Paul uses the Greek χάρισμα (*khar'-is-mah*), which is the same referential term used in 1 Corinthians 12:1–11, where Paul provides a litany of spiritual gifts, manifestations of grace, and deposits of the Spirit. The χάρισμα imparted to Timothy appears to have occurred during his ordination to the ministry,

> Do not neglect the gift that is in you, which was given to you through prophecy with the laying on of hands by the council of elders. (1 Tim 4:14)

Thus, though not an absolute protocol, we do have a pattern of legacy through the medium of ordination where gifts can potentially be imparted through prophecy and the laying on of hands. In this instance, it is possible that the touch was a sign of prophetic fulfillment. First, Timothy was given a prophecy concerning a certain gift; and second, the elders laid their hands on him, suggestive of a prayerful act for this prophecy to be realized. In both instances, Timothy was encouraged that the gift is not to be neglected and rather is to be kindled into activity. This is yet another indication that both the local pastor (presiding elder) and the body of elders or presbytery is involved in the ordination of ministers, with the specific task of praying over the ordained for the impartation of a spiritual gift or gifts.[10] This is intimated in Paul's warning to Timothy that he be cautious in whom he appoints as an elder at the church of Ephesus. That is, he is to lay hands on no one in a sudden fashion, but rather let time prove an individual faithful and sincere in the faith (see 1 Tim 5:22).

We have explored the context of Paul's imperative here as one of constant intercession, tears, and now touch. But how and in what way does this ἀναζωπυρέω (*an-ad-zo-poor-eh'-o*), or the rekindling of the gift, occur within Timothy? The early Pentecostals would define the kindling in a concrete manner that paints a picture of kindling that occurs when starting a fire. Many would use the phrase "fan into a flame" to describe the charge Paul gives Timothy in his second letter. While some may see Paul's imperative as a rekindling of or recalling of salvation through baptism, early Pentecostals envisioned this as a reification of Spirit baptism or stirring of zeal and fervency through acts of encounter and devotion.[11]

Kindling as Spirit Baptism

In the Church of God Evangel's early periodicals, we find an anonymous author correlating Paul's imperative of ἀναζωπυρέω to Jesus' admonition to the church of Laodicea concerning their lukewarm state (see Rev 3:15–16). The hermeneutic is certainly common among early Pentecostals as zeal and fervency is understood with metaphors of fire or Spirit baptism. An examination of this early periodical may assist in a nuanced understanding of ἀναζωπυρέω from the perspective of a burgeoning revival movement and may aid in our understanding of Paul's imperative to Timothy.

First, the author implores that ἀναζωπυρέω be understood by proximity when he says,

> We never reach this state while advancing but always when losing, hence, it is positive proof that we are getting further from God, for nothing gets lukewarm when kept close to the fire.[12]

---

10. One should note that as early as the letters of Ignatius, the πρεσβυτέριον, or body of elders, was seen as an office that was subordinate to the overseer or *episkopos*. See Tsuji, "2 Timothy 1:6," 68.

11. See Tsuji's article "2 Timothy 1:6" for a polemic on rekindling the gift as a recall of salvation and the laying on of hands as a reference to the rite of water baptism.

12. "Lukewarmness or Fervent in the Spirit."

The author will illustrate his point with a reference to Barnum's circus, which had declined at the time. Indeed, the author indicates that Barnum stuffed his circus animals and traveled as an exhibition rather than a circus. Likewise, the author contends "we stuff our dead graces and starved resolutions, and our professions and forms and then try to pass the dead show off as something living and real..."[13] And thus, the form is without fervency, the pretense is without power, the feigned is without faith, the hubris is without heat, the gift is without glory, and one is encumbered by stagnation. Therefore, the call to Timothy is the call for us all: stir up, rekindle, and fan into flame by drawing near to the Flame. Proximity and presence is the context of enduring consumption.

Second, the author contends that ἀναζωπυρέω is enacted by hot, fervent, and enduring prayer. He asserts that prayer is the "breath of the soul," and brings to bear yet another metaphor of anemic prayers, stating that they "become like a disabled balloon that ascends a little ways, then it is tossed and driven by the wind, and falls back without reaching the higher altitude."[14] Prayer is therefore yet another medium of ἀναζωπυρέω whereby one persists in kindling the gift. Prayer is conducive to proximity, drawing one yet nearer to God, and is greater than the "wireless telegraph" in that one communicates not overseas but through planetary systems.[15] Just as ἀναζωπυρέω is enacted through proximity, proximity is imbedded in the context of prayer.

The author continues his polemic on ἀναζωπυρέω by correlating it also to preaching and purity. That is, the one ἀναζωπυρέω is the one who craves to hear the Word preached, seeking conviction rather than offense or naivete. The one ἀναζωπυρέω is the one caught up with purity of soul and character rather than the justification of sin. The one ἀναζωπυρέω is, yes, one baptized in water, but one who also has gone to be baptized in fire and the Holy Spirit. The author calls for a "fresh baptism of old time power and holy zeal."[16] The ἀναζωπυρέω is also the one who propagates the gospel, as the author invokes the fruit of Spirit baptism in reference to visions and dreams. He asserts that the prayerful "could see brown-skinned Chinese with their faces turned toward them with their feeble

---

13. "Lukewarmness or Fervent in the Spirit."

14. "Lukewarmness or Fervent in the Spirit."

15. "Lukewarmness or Fervent in the Spirit." The author marvels at the modern invention of the wireless telegraph as a contrasting example to prayer, which ought to invoke greater marvel as such communication reaches a higher plain directly to God Himself.

16. "Lukewarmness or Fervent in the Spirit."

hands raised, begging for the bread of life."[17] One cannot help but also note the author's contention that ἀναζωπυρέω is walking in freedom over form, loosing meetings over holding meetings, repentance over reputation,[18] consecration over criticism, dynamism over static liturgy, and refilling over punctiliar baptism. Indeed, he makes reference to 2 Timothy 1:6 through the metaphor of a steam engine, which requires added "refire" for an eschatological purpose. That is, refiring the line is a refilling of the engine with the fuel to make steam in order to reach our destination, the "city of gold."[19] Thus, a Pentecostal perspective of ἀναζωπυρέω would entail all of what we have noted above, the need for ongoing refiring of the line of our souls for the purpose of enduring to the end, where our citizenship is realized in the city of our belonging.

The author concludes this notion of ἀναζωπυρέω with the following prayerful plea:

> Oh that God would give us such a mighty baptism of holy fire until the things of this world would sink into insignificance and that His great cause would have first place in our lives and that we would be so filled with life, fire and power that we would sweep over this world, like a mighty fiery cyclone and convince the world that we have been with Jesus.[20]

The thrust of rekindling is thus tightly aligned with refilling and fanning the flame of Spirit baptism for early Pentecostal thought. We find that this is accomplished with proximity, presence, purity, preaching, and propagation. Perhaps this is the same zeal that consumed Christ, which facilitated a purging of the temple of the consumeristic commodification of that which can never be sold or bought (see Matt 21:12–23). The legacy of the imperative to rekindle the gift has thus been explored as one that is facilitated by prayer, weeping, and touch. Now we will investigate the second imperative to Timothy in Paul's introductory remarks, where one is to leave a legacy of suffering.

---

17. "Lukewarmness or Fervent in the Spirit."

18. "Lukewarmness or Fervent in the Spirit," where the author admonishes pastors and leaders who restrict the form of services for "fear something will happen that will hurt their reputation and drive people away, when possible they haven't got enough reputation to fuss over or guard." He goes on also to describe repentance as a "sweat box of genuine repentance," implying the kind of visceral sorrow that accompanies repentance.

19. "Lukewarmness or Fervent in the Spirit."

20. "Lukewarmness or Fervent in the Spirit."

Chapter 3

Legacy of Suffering

> Do not be ashamed, then, of the testimony about our Lord or of me his prisoner, but join with me in suffering for the gospel, in the power of God ... (2 Tim 1:8)

THE SECOND IMPERATIVE IS for Timothy to be unashamed of the gospel, and in doing so to accept the afflictions that come with audacity. Being unashamed therefore appears to be necessarily tied to afflictions that follow boldness. Paul knows this experientially and prepares Timothy for the same. We must recall that Timothy faithfully inherits this imperative as he is also imprisoned for the testimony of Jesus Christ (see Heb 13:23).

By correlating audacity with afflictions, Paul underscores a theological maxim—afflication is necessary for discipleship. That is, the more one is afflicted, the greater the audacity. The greater the imprisonment, the greater the freedom. The more resistance, slander, stripes, and oppression, the more emboldened is the prophetic speech, love, truth, and fidelity to our Lord. In an ironic sense, therefore, afflictions form one for audacity. Paul desires to leave a legacy for Timothy to not only endure but to partake in afflictions.

Suffering and Proximity

The Greek construction συγκακοπαθέω (*soong-kak-op-ath-eh'-o*) is found only here in the New Testament and is a compound phrase joining *sun* and *kakopatheo*. The prepositional phrase *sun* is literally rendered "together" and, as a preposition sometimes meaning "with," implies a more proximal connection with the subject than if the preposition *meta* (also meaning "with") were used. The preposition is employed in Romans 6:8, where Paul emphasizes the intimate connection with Christ's death when he says, "But if we died with Christ, we believe that we will also live with him" (Rom 6:8). Thus, *sun* also takes on the meaning of "in like manner." The preposition is also used in intimating possession as in 1 Corinthians 15:10, where the grace of God is "with" Paul, enabling him to labor in the kingdom. The preposition also entails a "together with" concept that invokes communal cooperation as in 1 Corinthians 5:4, where Paul states, "When you are assembled and my spirit is present with the power of our Lord Jesus." In summary, the preposition *sun* implies a companionship, a consorting, a togetherness, a unity, a completeness, a wholeness, and may be better understood with the English "altogether."[1]

The preposition itself implies that afflictions are not meant to be experienced in isolation. One is never alone if one is in Christ who suffers. The suffering is always in solidarity with Christ, who has preveniently suffered before us and to whom we join when we partake of afflictions. Indeed, suffering when in Christ is related to *paschal*, which is suffering intended toward purpose. The suffering in Paul's use of συγκακοπαθέω is specific to suffering from evil motives, acts, or intentions. Paul uses *kakos* to indicate that the afflictions are at the hands of evil mercenaries who intend harm.[2] The word is used in 2 Timothy 1:8, but also in 2:9, where Paul specifies the irony of chains when he says, "for which I suffer hardship, even to the point of being chained like a criminal. But the word of God is not chained." Indeed, evil cannot accomplish what it intends, to muzzle the gospel, but rather disseminates it more widely.

Moreover, Paul's sufferings are appointed, as the afflictions in and through the body of Christ must be made full. And within God's election, there is an appointment unto suffering for certain servants so that the eschatological impetus for the body of Christ can be made glorious once more. Glory can be the result of affliction (see Col 1:24). Why some suffer and others do not is in the providence of God. But we should all know this: that providential suffering is not without purpose. There is no vanity where godly affliction remains. Pastors, the charge is a refrain

---

1. Zodhiates, *Key Word Study Bible*, 1758.
2. Zodhiates, *Key Word Study Bible*, 1726.

of a song meant to encourage you onward to endure the hardship of the pastoral task. It is a song sung over you, a song of deliverance, beckoning that you not faint, nor grow weary. If you find yourself as a castaway, know that a fruitful season is yet ahead.

Now, let us explore the context for the formational transaction of affliction unto audacity as power, soteriology, and election. It is to this dynamic that we turn to better understand the divine enablement of affliction and the fruit, which is audacity. We find God's power is at the center of endurance, for without it one could hardly endure suffering, destruction, and persecution. The innate drive to be accepted, to belong, and to be loved is a universal human longing that when threatened requires divine enablement to endure such isolation in the wilderness. The scapegoat phenomenon requires divine community.

Second, soteriology is the context of abiding through afflictions. And more specifically, there seems to be an election aspect of affliction. I dare not become encumbered in the election debate concerning the *via saludis* but rather would like to argue a polemic that in soteriological election, God has appointed some to suffer as a part of their salvation. Indeed, their growth in *fear and trembling* depends upon the afflictions God has appointed for them to endure. The calling unto salvation is first a *holy* calling. This holy election is given emphasis in Ephesians 1:4–5, where the adoption bears the fruit of being accepted. This is one of the paradoxes of the kingdom. To be rejected by your own is to be accepted into the company of heaven. And so, why does it feel so solitary, so isolating, so alone? Perhaps God is fashioning one for divine communion through the affliction of corporeal rejection.

Suffering and Election

Clarity emerges when one looks intently into the term Paul uses to refer to soteriological election, πρόθεσις (*proth'-es-is*), which can be rendered "purpose" in 2 Timothy 1:9. The term has come to be translated with phrases such as "setting forth," "setting up," or "exposition." The term connotes purpose, design, and resolve.[3]

It is a curious term used by Paul, as it invokes the imagery of the shewbread, which was "exposed" in the temple for the consumption of the priests. In this way, an exhibition is most closely aligned with this concept.

---

3. Zodhiates, *Key Word Study Bible*, 1752.

The shewbread was to be a display within the temple, open to full view. The bread was designed for display, not to be hidden in a pantry closet or kitchen, but within the consecrated space for God's holiness.

The calling prefigures the creation of the cosmos. The calling is toward many; the choosing is for the few (Matt 22:14). The calling is motivated and engendered by God's good pleasure, and not by anything we could contrive or offer (see 2 Tim 1:9; Rom 8:28; Eph 1:8–9). The purposes of God are therefore theologically bound to the called of God. The called are to accomplish God's purposes and the calling itself is an extension of God's purpose. In a more specific manner, the calling to exhibition, display, and exposure to others is a means of incurring affliction, which paradoxically manifests God's glory.

Thus, if we are to understand πρόθεσις, we must turn to the rite of the shewbread as the Septuagint conveys. Indeed, πρόθεσις, is the term utilized as the sole reference to the shewbread, a foreshadow of God's redemptive work. When referring to the shewbread, the phrase "setting before" is most fitting, as in Matthew 12:4, which says David "ate the bread of the Presence, which it was not lawful for him or his companions to eat, but only for the priests" (Matt 12:4). The shewbread was appointed for consumption to the weary, oppressed, and persecuted.

What is curious in the Septuagint's use of πρόθεσις is that the term makes no reference to time, but rather to position, intimating that election has more to do with position than time. One's location in the kingdom's economy and whether one suffers affliction appears to be an appointed task with glorious outcomes.

The shewbread was to be set "on the table before me continually," according to the command of God (Exod 25:30). The location was in proximity to the presence of God and to be seen and viewed by God. The shewbread was to be anointed with frankincense and a portion of this frankincense was to be burned upon the altar as a memorial of the bread itself. Moreover, Aaron and his sons were to eat the shewbread in the holy place (see Lev 24:5–9).

It then becomes clear that the shewbread was to typify Christ, who is the bread that comes from heaven, and of which if we do not eat, we have no part with Christ (see John 6:51). It is also clear why frankincense was offered at the birth of Christ to foreshadow His role as priest to intercede and vicariously provide atonement for all of humanity, a perfume unto the Father (see Exod 30:34).

The second meaning of πρόθεσις is how we traditionally think of election as a predetermination, purpose, intent, or design of God to call people in general unto salvation (see Rom 8:28). This meaning also entails the gathering together of all things in Christ (see Eph 1:9–11). It is the determination to make gentiles fellow heirs with the Jews as the same body (see Eph 3:6, 11). Finally, it is the choosing of one nation rather than another to enjoy certain privileges and blessings (see Rom 9:11).[4]

Suffering as Consumption for the Poor

In terms of Paul's use of πρόθεσις in 2 Timothy 1:9, I would like to explore the first rendering concerning the shewbread. For it appears to closely align with his exhortation to Timothy not to be ashamed of the gospel, but to freely suffer affliction. If indeed the bread was made to be consumed, the purpose of some in the kingdom is also to suffer affliction in the pattern typified by the shewbread, most fully consummated in the person of Christ. In this way, πρόθεσις or election becomes a certain election for some to be afflicted with the intended outcome of glory, namely, the glory of God's name and purpose in redeeming the world.

We begin with an allusion to David's consumption of the shewbread (see 1 Sam 21:1–9). David is a fugitive in his own land, running from the murderous threats of Saul. He is joined by a few men who have aligned themselves with his plight and thus are following his leadership. He chances upon Nob, where there is an enclave of priests and a holy tabernacle. David inquires of food for himself and his men, and herein Ahimelech, the priest, is faced with a certain dilemma. The dilemma concerns the law of consecrating the shewbread. The shewbread was to be consumed only by the priests who lived in the sanctuary,

> They shall be for Aaron and his descendants, who shall eat them in a holy place, for they are most holy portions for him from the offerings by fire to the Lord, a perpetual due. (Lev 24:9)

And yet, we find that the shewbread illustrates for us a higher law and appointment or election than that of the Levitical ordinance. It is the law of love—that is, love of God and neighbor over ritual and liturgy.

---

4. Zodhiates, *Key Word Study Bible*, 1752.

> All who eat it shall be subject to punishment, because they have profaned what is holy to the Lord, and any such person shall be cut off from the people. (Lev 19:8)

So even here we find a higher law whereby lower legal injunctions must be surrendered. We have this more explicitly stated by Jesus in his Matthean polemic on the Ten Commandments, where he pronounces the two greatest commandments. All other commandments are to be subsumed under these commandments and ought to fulfill these commandments.

> He said to him, "'You shall love the Lord your God with all your heart and with all your soul and with all your mind.' This is the greatest and first commandment. And a second is like it: 'You shall love your neighbor as yourself.' On these two commandments hang all the Law and the Prophets." (Matt 22:37–40)

We find, therefore, that the typology of the shewbread is for the consumption of not only the priest, but also the one oppressed and persecuted. This illustrates what I would argue is the polemic of election—appointment to be consumed and afflicted. However, the affliction is for the nourishment of the persecuted, marginalized, and oppressed.

Jesus refers to this story when confronted by the Pharisees for picking grain on the Sabbath (see Matt 12:3–4). Again, Jesus is referencing greater and lesser laws by utilizing Himself as an example. He will argue that He is greater than the temple and thus Levitical jurisprudence must surrender to His authority. In this instance, it is a jurisprudence of mercy and a kind of mercy that triumphs over judgment (see Jas 2:13). The Sabbath must submit to the One who rules the Sabbath. That is, Christ will argue a polemic that utterly dismays the Pharisees, for the Sabbath had become engrained in Jewish culture as a law *prima facie* overruling other laws. Jesus reinserts the purpose of Sabbath as subordinate to the One who created Sabbath, namely, Himself. He also repositions ritual as subordinate to mercy. That is, the sacrificial system is meant to remind the people of God's mercy, not to exercise condemnation, which is already inherent in the trespasses committed by all. Jesus is greater than the temple and, as an analogy, mercy is greater than judgment.

I say all of this to indicate that the shewbread is a parable of this kingdom principle. For the shewbread is elected to be on display but also to be consumed. The shewbread is to be afflicted and was created for this purpose. In like manner, the elect are to be on display before the presence of the Lord and are to be consumed by acts of mercy for the oppressed. One can be free to envision election as consumption and consumption as consummation.

Roland DeVaux writes of ancient Israel and specifies the temple and its furniture as a prophetic sign of the elect. He writes of the shewbread as *lehem happanim*, which is the "bread of the face of God" or the "bread of the Presence." Incense was placed along each row, consisting of six loaves for a total of twelve as a representation of the twelve tribes of Israel. The incense would burn every Sabbath as the priests would consume the shewbread, again a beautiful typology for the Eucharist.[5] Indeed, the prophet Ezekiel is intentional to specify the very table where the bread lies as an "altar" when he is given the vision of the temple (see Ezek 41:22). This indicates that the shewbread itself is indeed consecrated as a sacrificial component in temple life. The conjoining of incense with consumption indicates an ironic beauty. The bread, although destroyed, is done so within the context of an aroma that permeates the entire holy place.[6] Paul would allude to this metaphor when writing,

> For we are the aroma of Christ to God among those who are being saved and among those who are perishing: to the one group a fragrance from death to death, to the other a fragrance from life to life. Who is qualified for these things? For we are not peddlers of God's word like so many, but as persons of sincerity, as persons sent from God, we are speaking in Christ before God. (2 Cor 2:15–17)

The incense also illustrates election in that there is one fragrance but two distinct and contrasting receptions of this fragrance. The bread that alludes to Christ also alludes to those who follow Christ. For just as Christ is a permeating and sweet aroma unto the Father with eternal life as this fragrance, we share in this fragrance. However, this fragrance is perceived by the *unelect* or unbelieving as one that smells of a corpse. The unelect cannot fathom consumption as an indicator of eternal life.

Furthermore, we can extrapolate analogous claims between Jesus and David in relation to the shewbread, but also to Sabbath practice in general (see 1 Sam 21:1–9 and Mark 2:23–28). For example, William

---

5. See DeVaux, *Ancient Israel*, 422, where he specifies that the burning of incense was an *azkarah*, or an offering burnt on the altar of perfumes.

6. See DeVaux, *Ancient Israel*, 432, where he refers to the incense ritual in Israelite temple life as *qtoreth sammim*, which is "offering of aromatics," and alludes to Exodus 32:34–38.

Herzog is keen to observe that both Jesus and David are "real but unacknowledged kings on a campaign." As such, the entire pericopes of David and Jesus coalesce to indicate alignment with the fugitive and the marginalized. Both are under the oppression of royal authority. Any perceived threat to the institution is stamped out. For both David and Jesus, their authority (David's anointing via Samuel and Jesus' anointing at His baptism) gives them permission to "commandeer" what is needed as an act of mercy.[7] Both pericopes involve food and both therefore have an underlying excursus on consumption.

Herzog continues to glean from Jesus identifying with David by drilling down to David's situational zeitgeist as fugitive or "coyote figure." That is, Jesus does not necessarily associate with David as king, but as a fugitive who "lives by his wits while others are seeking to destroy him." This is an important observation in terms of procuring an idea of election. When we speak of elect and then utilize the term πρόθεσις as a reference to shewbread, we are thus confronted with Jesus' reference to the shewbread in the context of marginalization. Jesus is overturning theological foundations built in error. The royal consciousness of the day had turned Sabbath from freedom to slavery. By fulfilling His elect role as fugitive, Jesus is like David, the rogue king, who exemplifies mercy through embodiment of the "face of God" to be consumed.

Indeed, Walter Brueggemann also accentuates the juxtaposition of the royal institution of the temple tradition with the tribal association of Jesus as reforming and standing in contrast to the temple tradition when he defines a tribe as

> a unit of society standing apart from and over against the regimentation and legitimation of the state. I do not mean simply rustic, ethnic prestate communities, but units of the marginal who are cast into the marginal role by social necessity, and social coercion, who do not have access to the wealth and power of the state and who tend to be irreverent to the civilities of the state.[8]

Sabbath and its systems of worship were never intended for oppression but for mercy. The shewbread was consumed because in the sacrifice of its contents, it fed the hungry. Similarly, the disciples are hungry and chance upon provision on the Sabbath through God's mercy and are fed. The royal institution, however, is offended by this act as it predicates and

---

7. Herzog II, *Jesus, Justice, and the Reign of God*, 187.
8. Brueggman, *David's Truth in Israel's Imagination and Memory*, 10–11.

thrives on judgment, ritual, power, and prestige. Jesus not only aligns with the marginalized but becomes the oppressed. In doing so, he asserts the reformation voice that the oppressed can exercise by challenging various assumptions of ritualistic practice.

Jesus is brokering a new covenant "of God's forgiveness of sin and call to merciful living."[9] Now to intensify Jesus' polemic in opposition to the pharisaical charge of violation, Herzog draws attention to the citation of Hosea 6:6 in the Matthean account of this pericope (see Matt 12:7). This citation will necessarily create a conundrum of sorts, pitting mercy and sacrifice as opposing one another. This disrupts the traditional notion that sacrifice is a certain manifestation of mercy. Herzog asks the question that likely disturbed the minds of the Pharisees: "How can sacrifice be construed as merciless?"[10] Herzog answers the question by an appeal to synecdoche. That is, "sacrifice" is a term to intimate the entire temple paradigm and practice, which had become oppressive and exploitative. Command had become demand, mercy had been transformed to coercive material support for the temple, rest had become work, mercy had been supplanted by judgment, and sacrifice was no longer from affection but from oppressive obligation. Rather than giving and supporting life, the Sabbath was threatening the survival of the tribes and, in particular, the poor of the tribes.

Jesus turns the charge of the Pharisees back on them. The violation of the Sabbath is not incurred by Jesus' disciples, but rather the system of oppression propped up by the Pharisees themselves, which glorifies a system of sacrifice and squeezes out the mercy intended by the sacrifice itself. Jesus will reorient them to the true nature of the Sabbath (i.e., including the purpose of the shewbread) by redefining Sabbath in Mark 2:27–28. They had "forgotten that the Sabbath was God's provision for restoring human life and renewing human community."[11] Task-driven piety is the mainstay of temple life, which in a sense *profanes* the Sabbath, indicating the Pharisees with the same charge they had uttered.

Now Herzog is not yet finished with Jesus' subversive claims, for Herzog will note the "Son of Man" reference in Mark 2:28 as an intentional remark claiming that it is the human aspect of Jesus that stakes authority over the Sabbath. That is, the human agents of God, which includes the oppressed, are those who creatively observe the Sabbath

---

9. Herzog II, *Jesus, Justice, and the Reign of God*, 189.
10. Herzog II, *Jesus, Justice, and the Reign of God*, 189.
11. Herzog II, *Jesus, Justice, and the Reign of God*, 189.

in a way that cultivates human flourishing. Anyone who is under and promoting God's covenant of mercy and love can broker a movement of Sabbath observation. It is not exclusive to the spiritual elite or a religious caste system. "Peasants and Pharisees are on the same footing and can claim the same prerogatives."[12]

Contemporary Application

It has been over a year since the fateful day in October when brokenness entered in to fracture a dream that had been building for at least a decade. The sting of slander entered Pastor Cory's soul from his own brothers and sisters. Misunderstandings had transformed into allegations and accusations that tore asunder a concept of safety, togetherness, and future. He now looks back with a heart that is now mending, although not altogether whole. He wonders if he, like so many who choose the work of ministry, appreciates the display for God's presence. Or, he contemplates whether he can speak for God while becoming the shewbread once the Sabbath arrives. But the bread on display is to be consumed. The elect is elected to join Christ in His sufferings. If Christ's body is broken for the consumption of the whole world, how much more are Christian servants to be broken for the consumption of our neighbor?

The church board sought his removal as a means of restoring the former glory of the church. A return to glory was the intent, but perhaps true glory, true display in the face of God, is our own surrender to the election of consumption. Pastor Cory would stand with a message prepared looking out on a congregation with some who had contempt in their hearts.

Pastor Cory had made attempts to align with the oppressed and poor. He had begun a medical and counseling clinic for the mentally ill and those who suffer from substance use. He had moved the church to plant a sister church in a neighboring town with differing socioeconomic demographics, namely, a community with greater poverty and marginalization. However, these two missions became controversial and "too expensive." Pastor Cory can still hear the echo of the words of one board member who said, "We must keep our money here, at our church, and for our expenses." He recalls another board member lamenting that she was uncomfortable with the clientele that the clinic brought to the church.

---

12. Herzog II, *Jesus, Justice, and the Reign of God*, 190.

Negotiations eventually collapsed and Pastor Cory, broken and battered, relented to dissolve the clinic, under pressure to resign. When conversations heated up about the church plant, Pastor Cory resigned, no longer able to withstand the constant blame for the church's financial woes.

Unfortunately, Pastor Cory's story is not unique in the contemporary church. Today's church is more concerned with comfort than compassion, trends than total surrender, statistics than suffering, and fame than faithfulness. We are not teaching the next generation to prepare for suffering, to prepare to be on display for the express purpose to be consumed, to be a fervent advocate for the oppressed and poor. We are preparing the next generation for fame, celebrity status, stage presence, entertainment, and luxuries.

However, what is needed as the day of the Lord approaches is a pastor who is willing to suffer as a legacy for the next generation. I think of Bonhoeffer, Sister Theresa, Lottie Moon, and countless others who have served as the shewbread of the Lord. May we not forget their legacy, the legacy of Christ's sufferings, and in so doing recapitulate such a kingdom pathos to the next generation. Are we preparing the next generation for persecution and suffering and more to count it all joy? What better legacy can one leave but to lay one's life down for another? Pastor Cory had given himself to be on display as the shewbread. And as the shewbread, he was elected to be consumed. He had been torn asunder by his own, and yet who knows if this was for a great display of God's glory yet to come. Time will yet reveal as Pastor Cory awaits his next assignment.

Chapter 4

Legacy of Sound Doctrine

> Hold to the standard of sound teaching that you have heard from me, in the faith and love that are in Christ Jesus. Guard the good deposit entrusted to you, with the help of the Holy Spirit living in us. (2 Tim 1:13–14)

WE COME TO THE third and final imperative of the first chapter of Timothy, which is one alluding to the posterity of the gospel. It is the legacy of Paul's message that he entrusts to Timothy to preserve with all faith and love. Paul realizes that many have abandoned him and his message: "All who are in Asia have turned away from me" (2 Tim 1:15). An entire block of the early church not only questioned Paul's message but wholesale rejected it. This may have been in the context of the Neronian persecution, where one would risk death unless one recanted the faith.

I can only imagine the pain that Paul is experiencing as he is likely on death row, writing to Timothy to preserve the legacy of his message even as he realizes that an entire people group has rejected him. It is here where Paul thinks of the future and realizes that the message can only be preserved by the work of the Holy Spirit. It is the Spirit that will perpetuate the gospel in the context of persecution and provide great courage to the servants of God to consider not the value of this corporeal life but to speak of the life to come.

Paul will turn again to the legacy of sound doctrine when he encourages Timothy toward the end of the epistle,

> But as for you, continue in what you have learned and firmly believed, knowing from whom you learned it and how from childhood you have known sacred writings that are able to instruct you for salvation through faith in Christ Jesus. (2 Tim 3:14–15)

Paul appeals to this godly heritage that was no doubt instilled by his mother and grandmother. This is the sound doctrine Paul refers to, one imbedded in the christological lens of the whole of Scripture. Paul validates the sound doctrine of Lois and Eunice, stating that it is the same doctrine that he has also proclaimed.

Indeed, when writing to Titus concerning the qualifications of an elder, this ability to hold to sound doctrine is included in the litany of qualities:

> . . . holding tightly to the trustworthy word of the teaching, so that he may be able both to exhort with sound instruction and to refute those who contradict it. (Titus 1:9)

We find in this instruction the polemic of sound doctrine. Holding fast to sound doctrine functions to both exhort and convict those who offer contradiction. The question is not whether one will contradict sound doctrine, but when. Paul realizes this and is making his final injunction to preserve the legacy of sound doctrine through a next generation of preachers, namely, Timothy and Titus. Sound doctrine encourages and judges. It is to be spoken and fallout is to be expected. One need not be surprised if "all of Asia" leaves one who adheres to sound doctrine, as many may be offended by Christ.

In many ways, Pastor Louis blamed himself, or rather his perceived ineptitude as a leader, for the church's continual decline. Repentance had been a hallmark message throughout his pastoral tenure and there was little response to these messages. For reasons that became clearer later, the Lord continued to place a burden of repentance on him for the church he was pastoring. But rather than the revival he hoped to realize, he witnessed a continual decline. Rather than expecting rejection, he was bereft with himself. He could not identify with Paul's insight that abandonment, rejection, and refusal are part of ministry. There will always be a Phygellus and Hermogenes to lead some or an entire block of people away from the message of sound doctrine. He sought to preach the whole Bible rightly divided and was accused of *nonrelevance*. For some in the congregation, relevance became defined as exclusive New Testament preaching. That which was the Lord's work was attributed to the devil.

But more painful, and what became untenable for him and his wife, is that his very salvation was questioned. A church board member made the allegation with none coming to his defense. It is so as a pastor; the loneliness is palpable and those who persecute and reject you will think they are doing a service unto the Lord. However, regardless of these occurrences, albeit painful as they may be, our task is to continue the legacy of sound doctrine. Christ has entrusted it to Paul, Paul has entrusted it to Timothy and Titus, and they have entrusted to the next generation and so on. We must endure the rejection and hold to sound doctrine regardless of church growth or decline.

Now we find that Paul will define what is contrary to sound doctrine in his first epistle to Timothy. It is likely not a comprehensive list, but one that provides a notion of what sound doctrine is not.

> . . . this means understanding that the law is laid down not for the righteous but for the lawless and disobedient, for the godless and sinful, for the unholy and profane, for those who kill their father or mother, for murderers, the sexually immoral, men who engage in illicit sex, slave traders, liars, perjurers, and whatever else is contrary to the sound teaching . . . (1 Tim 1:9–10)

I am curious as to why Paul explicates these specific acts of wickedness to elucidate the contrary notion of sound doctrine. Perhaps these were the acts that Timothy was facing at the church in Ephesus. Perhaps Paul had been personally injured by these acts being perpetrated against him. Paul is referring to law and the godly use of the law, which is further explained in *The Coming Winter*.

Our purpose here is to underscore what sound doctrine is not. It is not defined by those who are consistently insubordinate to appointed and godly authority. It is not profaning God and injuring the reputation of His servants. It is not murdering fathers and mothers so that there remains a silo of orphans to contend for themselves. It is not practicing adultery, or any other form of lascivious sexuality. It is not sexual exploitation, human trafficking, lying, or perjury. Human trafficking has become a pandemic and is, by very nature, what is contrary to sound doctrine. Those who lie or engage in perjury to avoid church discipline and preserve a certain status also remain contrary to sound doctrine. Such was the case of a certain church member who lied to all the staff and the church leadership for the purpose of having Pastor Louis removed. There was no acknowledgment of perjury. Pastors must not be afraid to identify Phygellus and Hermogenes and warn the next generation to preserve sound doctrine.

Paul continues to provide pastoral guidance in what sound doctrine is and what it is not toward the end of his first epistle to Timothy.

> Whoever teaches otherwise and does not agree with the sound words of our Lord Jesus Christ and the teaching that is in accordance with godliness is conceited, understanding nothing, and has a morbid craving for controversy and for disputes about words. From these come envy, dissension, slander, base suspicions ... (1 Tim 6:3–4)

We find that sound doctrine is an intimation of wholesome words, which Paul explicates as the very words of Jesus Christ, so that even the judgment pronouncements Jesus makes of the Pharisees and Sadducees are wholesome words. When He calls them snakes and unveils the true nature of their hearts, this is wholesome, for it is truth, and is meant for freedom. Christians are to replicate the words of Jesus Christ by making His vocabulary our own. Those who are unable to do so still deal with a proud heart, relishing dispute, debate, and conflict. There are some who thrive from envy and as such will engender strife and conflict with a sardonic smile. They are operatives to revile the servants of God and create an environment of suspicion. If one suspects evil intentions, then perhaps these will fall away and slander the servants of God as well. Indeed, it is quite clear that this is not sound doctrine. How often does one's political ambition lead one down the slippery slope of rejecting sound doctrine?

Sound Doctrine and Dogmatics

Paul is entrusting Timothy with something quite precious, the doctrine and gospel of the Lord Jesus Christ. Timothy has been chosen by Paul, alongside Titus, to preserve, propagate, and protect the gospel. It is the legacy of Paul and the main purpose for writing this second letter.

Karl Barth has defined church dogmatics as

> ... the science in which the church, in accordance with the state of its knowledge at different times, takes account of the content of its proclamation critically, that is, by the standard of the Holy Scripture and under the guidance of its confessions.[1]

---

1. Barth, *Church Dogmatics in Outline*, 9.

In defining dogmatics in this fashion, Barth alludes to doctrine as a science, or rather an "attempt," albeit frail, to expound Scripture in the form of facts that bring revelatory awareness to the hearer in the form of doctrine. Moreover, the object of doctrine is clear in Barth's mind—it is the church. Indeed, he states the impossibility of divorcing doctrine from the church. Indeed, "dogmatics will always be able to fulfill its task only in accordance with the state of the Church at different times."[2]

This is a profound statement, for it requires a *conditio sine qua non*[3] of doctrine—that condition being the life and work of the church. The church, therefore, is an indispensable condition to doctrine. We cannot simply write about sound doctrine; we must live it! We cannot simply place volumes of literature under the rubric of textual and literary criticism; we must flesh out these directives in community. The church—with all its flaws, its faithfulness and infidelity, its humility and pride, its paradoxes of power, abuses, glories, and error; as redeemed and yet earthly, organic and yet with a divine imprint—must be the object of doctrine. Perhaps this is why Paul entrusts sound doctrine to Timothy; for the purpose of organizing and living among the community at Ephesus. And yet, it was Paul's doctrine that caused many to fall away from him in Asia—or was it? Perhaps it was the doctrine that unveiled the true from false, the wheat from the tares, the genuine from the disingenuous, Phygellus from Onesiphorus.

Doctrine that is pure, sound, and *scientific* thus requires a beginning and standard from which to draw conclusions that result in proclamation. Proclamation is the function of the church and must continue in a *hic et nunc*[4] manner that draws on the Torah, Prophets, Wisdom, and New Testament. Barth goes on to explicate that dogmatics is not an extrapolation of human "thoughts, or my heart, but the evidence of the apostles and prophets, as the evidence of God's self-evidence. Should a dogmatic lose sight of this standard, it would be

---

2. Barth, *Church Dogmatics in Outline*, 11.

3. Translated as "indispensable condition," as in Barth, *Church Dogmatics in Outline*, 10.

4. See Barth, *Church Dogmatics in Outline*, 12, where he states that dogmatics is a science of history and present. The history informs the present and moves into proclamation within the context of the church. *Hic et nunc* is a here and now informed by historicism. This is a corollary with another kingdom principle that alludes also to doctrine. This synonym is the already–not yet phenomenon, where the kingdom is here and now but not fully realized in the confession, work, sacraments, and manifestations within the community of faith.

an irrelevant dogmatic."[5] The science is one that draws from the wells of God's self-disclosure over the course of the human epoch and history, which extends into the way we proclaim this disclosure. It is not an exact science, for it is a human initiative, but with divine unction, proclamation is at its best. Doctrine is not doctrine unless it takes the testimony of God through the Scriptures seriously.

Barth will turn to the Apostles' Creed as a reference to tackling the science of doctrine or dogmatics and will begin with "I believe." He writes that belief is trust and is the start of doctrine—that is, in whom and in what do we believe? Barth offers the following when defining faith and its necessary commingling with doctrine:

> Christian faith is the gift of the meeting in which men become free to hear the word of grace which God has spoken in Jesus Christ in such a way that, in spite of all that contradicts it, they may once for all, exclusively and entirely, hold to His promise and guidance.[6]

Doctrine is meant to be heard; it is meant to engender and energize faith. It is meant to hold to promise and to accept divine guidance. Doctrine requires faith inasmuch as words are transformed from mere formalities to ways of living. And doctrine is meant to be believed; we should note the distinct and yet valid paradigmatic ways of believing. As Augustine first contended, there is *fides qua creditur* and *fides quae creditur*. Murphy offers a definition of each phrase when she says that belief is both an "act that believes (*fides qua creditur)* and faith [is] a content to be believed (*fides quae credtiur).*"[7] What a difference one letter can make!

Doctrine is thus birthed out of both objective and subjective experiences of faith. The apostles and prophets encountered the Word of God. That is, they heard the voice of God either as a gift from above or through theophany. This act was believed and proclaimed. These acts were also written down as content to be believed by subsequent generations whether in encounter or simple faith. Encounter and content appear to be ever engaging in a perichoretic dance over one's lifetime as one responds to doctrinal statements prayerfully and one continually encounters God as an act.

---

5. Barth, *Church Dogmatics in Outline*, 13.
6. Barth, *Church Dogmatics in Outline*, 15.
7. Murphy, *Illuminating Faith*, 13.

This faith becomes increasingly personal when one conceptualizes the *qua* of faith in the Augustinian fashion of human faces.

> The eyes of faith are my eyes and my seeing, they are deeply seated within me, as my personal matter . . . Our face expresses our faith, at least in the sense that our faith, just as our face, must be ultimately personal.[8]

Perhaps this is the kind of faith that becomes fully realized in Paul's concept of identity consummation when he states that we are fully known when coming face to face with Christ (see 1 Cor 13:12). Face-to-face encounter is a kind of faith by which we believe (*fides qua creditur*), which emboldens the faith in what we believe (*fides quae creditur*).

Doctrine's subject is God, its object is the church, and its engagement is encounter. We should have always known that doctrine would be advanced by relationships. It must be so; it is contingent upon God's self-disclosure in relational terms and heralds to ontology—we are made in the image of God, one intently personal and relational. Faith is not mere proposition; it is also encounter. Faith and doctrine are yet another work of divine enablement where the Holy Spirit is working in the human heart. Augustine uses the term *facies*, or human countenance, to conjure up the personal nature of faith when referring to *qua*. And yet, he is also getting at something of a conformation that occurs with encounter. For the face is not static, but finds its contours, expressions, and illuminations changing. The human face is ever changing into the face of Christ in likeness vis-à-vis encounter (*fides qua*) and assimilation of faith (*fides quae*). As Augustine puts it, "For when too, we see two men exceedingly alike, we wonder, and say that both have one countenance."[9]

We must ask the question, therefore, does doctrine, however published, move one to encounter? Does it compel one to preach and teach? Does it cause one to meditate upon the precepts of God's Word? Does it move one to prayer? Does it advance conformation of human character and countenance? Paul is intent on doctrine being sound, for perhaps it is this medium that he knows encourages one to remain faithful to Christ! Timothy is to hold to sound doctrine for in it lies the potential to his own conformation—being in the likeness of Christ! Paul's letter to Timothy is obviously personal, perhaps because Paul is intimating a faith and doctrine that is personal. And yet, the letter is also quite

8. Murphy, *Illuminating Faith*, 13–14.
9. Augustine, "On the Holy Trinity," 346.

ecclesiological so that the personal faith of Timothy (*fides qua*) could be translated into the ecclesiastical practice and discipline (*fides quae*) that would be required of him to set the church in order.

It is noteworthy to assess Barth's elevation of the objective (*quae*) aspect of the Apostles' Creed. He identifies the opening statement "I believe" in juxtaposition with what follows, which are the credal statements of the confession. In doing so, he creates a type of dichotomy that I would hope to somewhat dismantle. He asserts that the Apostles' Creed speaks at its best the "deepest and completest about what happens to us men, about what we may be, do and experience."[10]

However, was the *what* of Paul's belief only informed by his mere understanding of the Torah, Prophets, and burgeoning witness of Christ? Or was Paul's belief utterly transformed with a theophany and subjective experience of the Lord Jesus Christ, who commissioned him to the gentiles? I would argue that it is the latter of Paul's experience that radically transformed the trajectory of Paul's life and faith. His encounter with Christ also becomes canon for the witness of subsequent generations. Indeed, we sometimes liken our own conversion to a Damascus Road experience where our entire lives are halted by the direct word and appearance of our Lord to upend our carnal ambitions, even our false security that we are doing God a favor when we are unknowingly persecuting Him.

Barth goes as far to assert that if attempts are made to preserve subjective faith, then we run the risk of losing our faith. He alludes to the gospel where Jesus asserts that one who attempts to preserve one's life will surely lose this life (see Matt 16:25; Mark 8:35; Luke 9:24; John 12:25). He summarizes this allusion by stating that "whoso means to rescue and preserve the subjective element shall lose it; but whoso gives it up for the sake of the objective, shall save it."[11]

And yet, does this historically and personally resonate as the universal possibility? Again, if we refer to Paul, and in a particular sense his writings to Timothy, Paul refers to the gospel as "my gospel" (2 Tim 2:8; Rom 2:16). Paul is not timid to identify with the gospel completely and existentially in such a way that the testimony of Christ becomes his testimony. To reject Paul's message in this sense is to reject Christ as well. Perhaps the intensity of Paul's identification is to consolidate his subjective faith in such a way where the objective faith is also preserved. Rather than creating separate categories of faith, we should also identify

---

10. Barth, *Church Dogmatics in Outline*, 16.
11. Barth, *Church Dogmatics in Outline*, 16.

with the gospel in such a way where it becomes our own. If we own the gospel, then we proclaim it as something precious and affective. If we own the gospel, the objective aspect of our faith is tied into the burning passion of our love. We move from intellectual ascent to transforming affections. We take principles and baptize them with a fiery love. Thus we must, with Paul, not only identify with the gospel or with doctrine, but also own the gospel and doctrine. We can assimilate an ownership such as this with an interdependence of both *qua* and *quae* faith, both objective and subjective faith. Indeed, many a Christian has written to make sense of what he or she is experiencing in the Lord and from interacting with the precepts of Scripture. Indeed, I am writing in this moment to understand my albeit painful experience as a pastor leaning into the Holy Spirit to shed light upon this experience through divine revelation in and through the pastoral epistles of Paul.

Paul is leaving a legacy, but not just a doctrine of objectivity, but also a gift that is imparted to Timothy, which is highly personal to Timothy. Timothy may not have the same subjective Damascus Road experience that was given to Paul, but he does have a gift imparted by the laying on of hands by Paul himself (see 2 Tim 1:6–7). Timothy has a subjective experience of a gift that was also noticeable in his mother and grandmother. Paul conjures up such an experience to encourage Timothy in both the subjective and objective task of ministry. Timothy is to affectively rekindle his gift (*quae*) even as he actively defends the faith (*qua*). Therefore, I would modify Barth in that doctrine is at its best when it becomes a faithful integration of both subjective and objective aspects of our faith within a rubric where one confirms and affirms the other. It seems to me that this is the good dance of orthodoxy with orthopathy. When at its best, this becomes a perichoretic dance of love.

Indeed, Barth has already defined faith as a meeting, and this meeting is with the Lord Jesus Christ through His Word.[12] Indeed, this meeting can also be highly personal while at the same time ubiquitous. That is, Christ meets at any time, any place, and any condition to reveal His grace, His love, His intent, and His purpose for any one individual throughout the epochs of time. This grace deserves witness, testimony, and a language for us to communicate the glories of God among us. For example, how many

---

12. See Barth, *Church Dogmatics in Outline*, 17, where he asserts that meeting is a gift and that this gift is freedom. "Freedom is God's great gift, the gift of meeting with Him." Thus, one can extrapolate from this that God takes the initiative in formulating such a meeting and we receive this meeting as a gracious and freeing divine initiative that also engenders our freedom. Freedom is vis-à-vis divine meeting. Freedom is in the hearing of God's Word as hearing is the beginning of faith (see Rom 10:17).

of us have described our own Damascus Road experience because Christ first met with Paul in this way, but we have also, in a sense, made it our own as well? Subjective faith is preserved as confession in this way, as experiences of faith in the Lord are translated through the ages. In this regard, I have an affinity for Barth's description of faith as both trust and meeting, for this description affirms encounter, relationship, and trust. Faith as trust knows that God alone is trustworthy, at least in the way that is eternally consistent. Human trust is frail and often broken.

Sound Doctrine and Trust

Pastor Marcus unintentionally broke trust with certain staff members when he proposed a budget that included the painful reality that the church could no longer maintain the current number of staff. So, the staff members affected could no longer trust Pastor Marcus as an advocate and thus worked with board members to reverse this proposal and see that he be removed as pastor. Perhaps this was an effort on their part to restore trust in the church institution as a whole. Trust was broken when certain staff members consorted with board members to press Pastor Marcus to resign without speaking to him personally to clarify the financial proposal.

Pastor Marcus still feels the conundrum, for the board was unwilling to entertain the selling of the building to relieve the financial burden of a pending deficit. The building and certain staff members had become a sort of sacred cow that could not be changed. And yet, every year for the past eight to ten years, ministry budgets were cut to preserve the building and staff. As ministry budgets dwindled to about 10–15 percent of the budget, Pastor Marcus proposed a reduction in staff size. The staff size was one for a church of one thousand members, largely unchanged since the church had declined to four hundred members. Pastor Marcus was attempting to restructure the staff in a way in which a four-hundred-member congregation could support them. Nonetheless, one can understand the breach of trust this likely created. This broken trust disseminated to the board and many members of the board were persuaded to ask for Pastor Marcus to resign. Barth is clear that one human encounter after another is a "human path from one disloyalty to another, and it is the same with the way of the gods of this world."[13]

And more importantly, Barth wrestles with a cultural god and philosophy that has only grown in what has become the golden age

---

13. Barth, *Church Dogmatics in Outline*, 19.

of humanism and individualism. We live in a world that worships humanity potential. Our culture, through the industry of entertainment, the arts, and education, underscores the philosophy that everyone ought to be true to him- or herself. But even the *self* will betray the *self* given enough time and space. The trust we place in whatever identity or act of industry we can muster will eventually lead to our own betrayal. We cannot trust our frailty; we cannot trust our insecurity; we cannot trust our works to produce anything but hay and stubble without divine injunction (see 1 Cor 3:12). The whole world is proclaiming a humanistic message that one ought to be true to oneself. The church, however, can proclaim a countercultural message that human institutions are not trustworthy apart from the God of all trust. We can only wholly, entirely, utterly, and with great abandon place our full trust in the Lord, who knows, creates, and sustains all things.[14]

Trust is a good and wholesome way of thinking of faith. This trust is always preserved because God can be trusted indefinitely. He brokers a trust through the gospel and this kind of love can always be trusted because love is the beginning of trust. Trust is not trust unless love is the foundation. Love is the very seed of trust, which becomes the largest of shrubs to provide refuge for the living (see Matt 13:32). God can be trusted for God is love. Faith is a trust with abandon, recklessly and yet prudently giving all one is to be loved of God!

Pastor Marcus sometimes wonders if he would have brokered greater trust if he had submitted a wholly different budget, one that required the church to raise money for ministry while preserving the salaries of staff members. Or was this bound to happen at some point as crisis is the revealer of true motives in the human heart? Pastor Marcus often wonders what legacy he might leave. And of course, any pastor longs to leave a legacy where sound doctrine is epitomized and proliferated. He can only hope that this is a type of legacy that persists even after his departure.

In conclusion, Paul is clear, one legacy of utmost importance is sound doctrine wedded to trust that faithfully proclaims the testimony of Jesus Christ. This sound doctrine is an integration of both *qua* (objective) and *quae* (subjective) encounters with God vis-à-vis Word, prayer, worship, and community that result in the faithful proclamation of God's speech. See figure 3 below.

14. See Barth, *Church Dogmatics in Outline*, 19, where he states that "we ourselves will never be true to ourselves." Human potential and the word of human authority both have the potential to be gods to be worshipped, and Barth is clear that these gods can "never keep what they promise. So with them, there is never real peace and clarity."

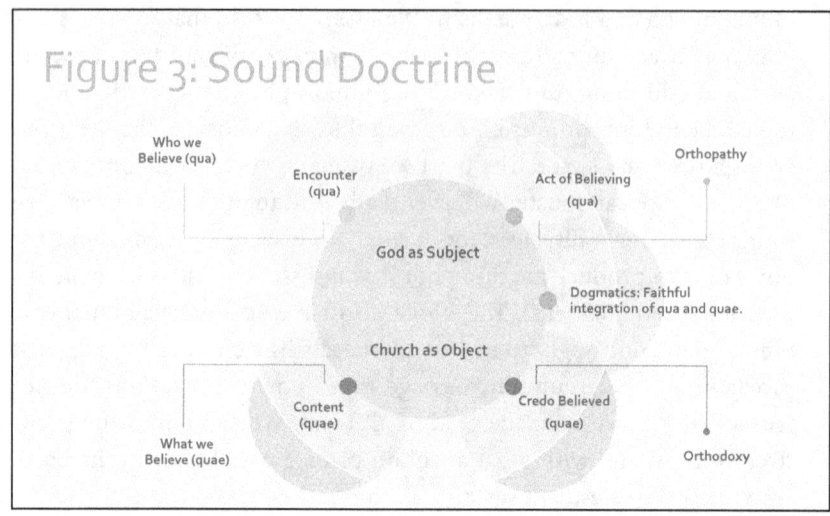

Figure 3: Sound Doctrine. Doctrine is the faithful integration of *qua* and *quae* faith, with God as subject and the church as object for the proclamation of divine speech.

This transaction is bidirectional with God as subject and church as object. The modern pastor is caught in the dilemma of a church that has become so corporate that he acts as a CEO who hires and fires staff. But then he is also judged as a CEO, coming under fire if attendance begins to dwindle, and thus he may be asked to resign himself from a board that typically runs the church organization as an institution with a service or product to be consumed. The loyalty of the modern church is to the institution's success and glory, typically achieved by larger attendance, budgets, and a proliferation of programs. In contrast, Paul says nothing of the sort, but underscores the need for a pastor to leave a legacy of sound doctrine, which will likely cause many to actually leave the church. Nonetheless, a pastor can be consoled if he leaves a legacy of encounter and credo—meetings with God and proclamation of sound doctrine. For Pastor Marcus, as he must cope with the pain of his own departure, I like to believe that God has prepared an Onesiphorus who will refresh him with genuine love and friendship (see 2 Tim 1:16).

Chapter 5

Legacy of Endurance

Share in suffering like a good soldier of Christ Jesus. (2 Tim 2:3)

Paul will mention endurance twice in the opening verses of 2 Timothy 2. He will first encourage Timothy to share in suffering as a good soldier in Christ and will subsequently refer to his own endurance of affliction as purposeful endurance that is mysteriously correlated with assisting the elect to endure. These two references are given nuanced explications, ending with an early church credal statement (see 2 Tim 2:11–13). The legacy Paul leaves to Timothy is one of endurance and perseverance, proliferating the gospel. Thus, it behooves us to learn the value of endurance and suffering as this is a paradoxical fashion in which God works to further advance our own salvation while also procuring the salvation of others.

Paul asks that Timothy endure hardship; that is, he is to συγκακοπαθέω (*soong-kak-op-ath-eh'-o*), which intimates both community and unity. Timothy is to suffer together as if he were suffering with another as a display of unity and oneness. The suffering is not altogether an act of solitude, but a joining with Paul, and more than this, a joining with Christ, until the hardship or suffering is consummated, and the fruit becomes life. Moreover, we should note that included in the Greek word is *kakos*, which we cannot deny is a reference to evil, so that the suffering or endurance is not an amoral suffering. That is, this type of hardship comes from a sinister purpose. This kind of suffering is an affliction meant to incur harm to the individual person or reputation. Evil is lurking to withdraw one's confession of Christ through the medium of hardship or suffering. This was the intent of Satan with Job and continues to be the intent of Satan with countless believers.

We have heard this refrain before from Paul. He brings clarity to the mystery of suffering when he urges that Timothy be a partaker of afflictions *of the gospel* (see 2 Tim 1:8). The prefix *sun* again brings the experience into a type of fellowship so that the gospel necessarily will create a potential of suffering. Why? Because evil is always determined to thwart the gospel's advancement. What is lovely, however, is that the suffering is with all the prophets, the apostles, and with Christ Himself. It is not a lonely suffering, because in it one is tied hand to hand with those who have gone before, who urgently appeal, "Endure, good soldier of Christ!" Paul will echo this refrain again in a series of final charges to Timothy when he calls him to "endure suffering, do the work of an evangelist, carry out your ministry fully" (2 Tim 4:5). And Timothy may recall something familiar to Paul's echo of endurance from his first letter, when Paul urged that Timothy should wage good warfare (see 1 Tim 1:18).

Paul is keen also on explaining the methodology of endurance, which is a legacy for all pastors who are enduring in and with the gospel. It is the power of God that sustains all feeble hands to keep to the plow and advance one step at a time. Paul continues his military metaphor by expositing the life of a successful soldier. The kind of soldier that endures is one that is, first, not concerned with investments in the affairs of this life. These kinds of investments work like a millstone hung about one's neck to create a kind of slothfulness where one becomes paralyzed. There is but one Commander, one General, one King. The soldier who finds himself enduring will be seeking to wholly please Christ, our General, who issues missions and who sends the Holy Spirit as both comfort and guide. So, the first strategy to endurance is obvious, but always needs reiteration: do not become entangled in the affairs of this life. We can recall this very same warning in Jesus' Parable on the Seed and the Sower. The one who becomes occupied with the winds of the age and who is deceived by wealth will have the seed of God's word choked from his or her soul (see Matt 13:22). Therefore, we endure by having affections attuned to our first Love, by loyalty to our Savior, by attending to the commands of our General, and by seeking to advance the mission of Christ. I suppose a question we could all ask ourselves is: Which mission are we advancing? From where do we receive our commands, and from whom do we leap into action?

Second, Paul will change the metaphor from a military one to an athletic one. He refers to an athlete who seeks the crown through some competitive event. The mastery that the athlete seeks is the one over his or her event. The crown is not received except that it is earned through lawful means. That is, an athlete cannot cheat his or her way to mastery. If he or she does, in the end the crown is tainted, unearned, and his or achievements nullified. This is the case in our modern games if an athlete enhances his or her agility through exogenous hormones, or if one is to learn the signs of his or her adversary and exploit them to win a game. All of society frowns upon such action and the crown, if not withdrawn, is marred in perpetuity. The Houston Astros had their victory called into question in 2017. Their World Series success was cast into doubt when it was discovered that they may have been stealing signs from the catcher to the pitcher of the opposing team. The Yankees lost their sixth and final game against the Astros by a home run hit by Astro Jose Altuve, but watch the scene as Altuve signals to his team to not remove his jersey as he rounds third base to home. Indeed, he rushes to the dugout to change shirts before celebrating the victory with the team.[1] It was discovered that Altuve may have had a device under his shirt that indicated when he might receive a favorable pitch.

Or think of Lance Armstrong, a champion American cyclist who won an unprecedented seven grueling Tour de France races only to be stripped of the medals once it was discovered that he had been using performance-enhancing drugs.[2] We think of athletes who have mastered their sport, but only through lawful training, hard work, and endurance. Such is the case with the Christian and with the pastor. There are no back-room deals or consorting to ruin the reputation of another to get ahead or to preserve a title. The good soldier of Christ is forever following Christ, emulating His character in every way possible.

Paul will also use this athletic metaphor when writing to the Corinthian church (see 1 Cor 9:25–27). He writes that temperance is required for mastery. A temperate tongue, behavior, relationship, and life is one having worked diligently to follow Christ. This kind of temperance is the fruit of discipleship. Paul will go on to specify the need to coerce or beat his

---

1. See the following video from the sixth game of the American League Championship in 2017, "Jose Altuve Sends Astros to World Series," https://www.youtube.com/watch?v=XC34yua88z0.

2. See the following site for a biography that accounts the story of Lance Armstrong, "Lance Armstrong Biography," https://www.biography.com/athlete/lance-armstrong.

body into subjection for temperance. He himself wishes not to be disqualified for a lapse of the tongue or a lapse in judgment. He cannot preach to others while he himself is being cast away from the faith. Oh God, let us learn again the power of temperance; let us strive to subject our carnal nature to Your righteousness! Let temperance become the fruit of our lives on display as a means of enduring Christian warfare!

Finally, Paul references a farmer and his crop, and the fact that the farmer is to enjoy the fruit of his harvest as an *a priori* act during sowing. This implies that the farmer is also the first to labor for the harvest and thus is the first to enjoy the harvest. Paul, again writing to the Corinthian church, provides additional clarity when he writes,

> Or does he not speak entirely for our sake? It was indeed written for our sake, for whoever plows should plow in hope and whoever threshes should thresh in hope of a share in the crop. (1 Cor 9:10)

Paul certainly writes about this hope concerning ministerial compensation as he will later add to this statement with, "In the same way, the Lord commanded that those who proclaim the gospel should get their living by the gospel" (9:14).

But we should also note that a pastor or minister is also a purveyor of hope in general; not just hope for compensation, but hope that compels one to keep going, a hope that presses into the kingdom and takes spiritual Canaan by force. This is a hope that becomes contagious whereby the flock learns to hope against all hope. Certainly, endurance is sustained by a certain hope and this hope is one that does not disappoint. It is a hope that Christ is immutable and unchangeable, that His Word persists in just the way it was iterated. It is a hope that confesses His promises to be true and realized in us, "the hope of glory" (see Col 1:27). I would argue that one cannot endure as a good soldier without some semblance of hope pulsing in one's spiritual veins, vivifying the soul. Abraham hoped against all hope though his body was as good as dead. His faith did not waiver to believe that he would indeed be father to many nations. This faith was a catalyst that created a deposit of righteousness to his spiritual account. He believed and it was credited to him as righteousness (see Rom 4:18–22).

So it is that endurance of affliction for the sake of others is contingent on an exclusive obedience to the kingdom and an active disentanglement from the affairs that color carnality. It is a lawful and patient obedience in the same direction as one trains in mastering one's soul to wholly follow Christ. It is a partaking of a dogged and determined hope that cannot be chipped away, penetrated, or dismantled. Christian endurance, pastoral endurance, is one that sows and then reaps a kind of hope that believes for the impossible.

Suffering Soteriology

Paul was appointed to suffer. Imagine being commissioned with the following: "I myself will show him how much he must suffer for the sake of my name" (Acts 9:16). This was Paul's commission, and the appointment was for the enduring salvation of the gentiles. We have already noted the typology of the shewbread in foreshadowing affliction as a part of the election process. Paul continues to describe this election for affliction or hardship with other metaphors and ironies. Indeed, the greater his chains, the greater the gospel's freedom (see 2 Tim 2:9). Paul became a prisoner of Christ insomuch as this was evidence of God's grace in and through him (see Eph 3:1). Paul noted his bonds as a direct result of defending and confirming the gospel, which is inexplicably correlated with including others in the partaking of grace (see Phil 1:7). Suffering hardship creates the context for others to experience grace. The mystery of Christ can result in bonds, and it is Paul's plea that these bonds be remembered by the church at Colossae (see Col 4:3, 18). Indeed, he ends his letter to the Colossians with this request. But why would he ask such a thing? Why would he end his epistle with an urging that the church remember his bonds? Perhaps the humanity of Paul is best purported as a reason for his request. Perhaps he too longs for the kind of love that is embodied in one noting and recognizing his suffering and empathizing with Paul in his chains. Perhaps Paul becomes the very object and illustration of what the author of Hebrews intends when he writes, "Remember those who are in prison, as though you were in prison with them, those who are being tortured, as though you yourselves were being tortured" (Heb 13:3).

When one member of the body is chained, we are all chained. This is the fellowship of genuine Christian community! It is not merely meeting on Sunday or Wednesday. It is the affective oneness of those who suffer. It is the kind of oneness that journeys with another as if it is my journey. It is remembering and aligning with others in their chains. It is becoming an Onesiphorus who diligently seeks out the suffering to refresh them in their bonds (see 2 Tim 1:16–17). The one who remembers doesn't wait for a chance happenstance to associate with the suffering but seeks them out until they are found, lifting any pretense of shame and refreshing the afflicted. One is afflicted so that one can also be refreshed. The affliction is for soteriological endurance, the agent of refreshing is for the courage to endure.

The pericope of 2 Timothy 2:3–10 is an inclusio beginning with a charge that Timothy suffer and ending with Paul's own suffering as a legacy he imparts to Timothy. Paul will also bring a nuance to his endurance that has soteriological significance. For example, how does he endure for the elect's sake? Paul's endurance, or ὑπομένω (*hoop-om-en'-o*), is to sustain a load of miseries, adversities, persecutions, or provocations in faith and patience.[3] The concept of ὑπομένω in correlation with soteriology is manifold, but usually refers to one's own endurance to the end for the sake of one's own salvation, not necessarily for the elect. Thus, Paul is introducing a nuanced definition of soteriological endurance. In Matthew's gospel, Jesus is quite clear that "you will be hated by all because of my name. But the one who endures to the end will be saved" (Matt 10:22). Paul's use of ὑπομένω in Romans 12:12 intimates a kind of patience in tribulation as patience and endurance appear to be synonymous in Paul's expression when thinking of persecutions or tribulations. Perhaps this is why love includes this very verb tense in 1 Corinthians 13:7. Love is a requirement for ὑπομένω. Love endures all things for love can never fail. Now Paul will create a parallel in the credal hymn attached to the end of 2 Timothy; he states that if "If we endure, we will also reign with him" (2 Tim 2:12). Thus, Christian suffering is not solitary suffering; it cannot be, for it is with Christ that one suffers. It is a joining in the fellowship of suffering first inaugurated by Christ Himself.

But again, this kind of ὑπομένω still implies an act that is done on behalf of the individual, not on behalf of the elect. We do get an echo of this sentiment of vicarious suffering when the author of Hebrews states that Jesus, ". . . for the sake of the joy that was set before him endured the cross, disregarding its shame, and has taken his seat at the right hand of the throne of God" (Heb 12:2). However, of course, the obvious difference is that Christ is the agent of vicarious suffering. He endures the cross with a sense of joy for the salvation of the world. Thus, we must ask whether ὑπομένω is also a vicarious suffering of one of us for the elect. Is there soteriological significance for the community when one suffers with or

---

3. Zodhiates, *Key Word Study Bible*, 1765.

in Christ? As Christ was one who suffered for all, does the Christian appointed to suffering recapitulate this where he or she suffers for all? Does the elect obtain salvation when one suffers in Christ? Is ὑπομένω used in this sense only here in Paul's second epistle to Timothy?

Vicarious Suffering

Although ὑπομένω is not used in the same sense, it has become a synonym of a philological *hapax legomenon*[4] in Colossians 1:24, where Paul refers to the notion that he is "rejoicing in [his] sufferings for your [the Colossians] sake, and in [his] flesh [he is] completing what is lacking in Christ's afflictions for the sake of his body, that is, the church."

Jerry Sumney, writing in *Catholic Biblical Quarterly*, takes on this theological dilemma by exploring Paul's vicarious suffering for the church and what this exactly means. He begins by stating that Paul suffers in a vicarious way but not in an expiatory fashion. "That is, his suffering confers benefits on the Colossians but does not function as a means of forgiveness."[5]

Indeed, Sumney refers to three forms of vicarious sufferings that have been entertained when attempting to understand Colossians 1:24, which is also related to our text in 2 Timothy 2:10, as both instances intimate a vicarious endurance in suffering for the sake of the body of Christ. Sumney conveys expiatory and mimetic sufferings and briefly explores eschatological sufferings as types of vicarious sufferings that have distinct roles within the body. For example, Sumner rejects the idea that Paul's sufferings are expiatory as this would contradict the all-sufficient sufferings and death of Christ, which is Paul's polemic throughout the letter of Colossians.[6] Sumney asserts that Paul's sufferings are a type of

---

4. This is a Latin phrase referring to the sole use of a term found only here in Colossians and nowhere else. In Colossians, the word used solely here is ἀνταναπληρόω, which has a lengthy translation by the online Greek Bible as "what is wanting in the afflictions of Christ to be borne by me, that I supply in order to repay the benefits which Christ conferred on me by filling up the measure of the afflictions laid upon me." See http://www.greekbible.com/l.php?a)ntanaplhro/w_v-1pai-s—_.

5. Sumney, "'I Fill Up What Is Lacking,'" 665.

6. See Sumney, "'I Fill Up What Is Lacking,'" 665, where he states the central assertion of his article: "I argue that Colossians envisions as genuinely vicarious, but not expiatory; that is his sufferings confers benefits on the Colossians, but does not serve as a means of forgiveness (an understanding of Paul's sufferings that would run counter to the place Christ is given throughout the rest of the letter)."

"mimetic reactualization," a term he borrows from Seeley when he refers to Seneca's account of the death of Socrates.[7] In this way, Paul's sufferings are exemplary in that the sufferings themselves are a type of proclamation that others would be encouraged to likewise endure for the sake of the gospel. Obedience will therefore initiate sufferings to some degree as obedience is in the pattern and likeness of Christ, which can create context for suffering (see 2 Tim 3:12).

I would like to assert that Sumney's dismissal of an eschatological framework in interpreting Colossians 1:24, although an attempt at arriving at one unified reading, may miss a particular nuance of the text throughout the Pauline corpus, and underrealize the power imbedded in the virtue of Christian suffering. He states that an eschatological view of Paul's suffering is a reading into the text notions that Paul himself did not envision. However, I would like to assert that Paul's inclusion of a vicarious suffering for the elect in his second epistle to Timothy suggests that he contributes to the Parousia of Christ on behalf of the Christians to whom he writes, while at the same time creating a mimetic vicariousness to which he encourages all Christians to imitate as a fruit of enduring in one's salvation.

Moreover, we find a kind of quantitative vicarious suffering that fills the cup of Revelation 6 and therefore contributes to bringing near the Parousia of Christ. Rob Dalrymple also writes of this text in Colossians as a correlation to the messianic woes Jesus explicates in the Gospel of Matthew, which are to be "endured by the people of God until they have accomplished the full measure of that suffering."[8] This implies that Christian suffering, including vicarious suffering, has a contribution in the consummation of the kingdom. Dalrymple further asserts that whenever God acts in accordance with His covenant in moving closer to a new age, the people of God suffer the "birth pangs" of this coming kingdom.[9] These messianic woes and the suffering of God's people are aptly summarized in Matthew's gospel when Christ associates the birth pangs with the inauguration of persecution and even martyrdom:

> ... all this is but the beginning of the birth pangs. "Then they will hand you over to be tortured and will put you to death,

---

7. See Seeley, *Noble Death*, 114.
8. See Dalrymple, *Understanding the New Testament*, 125.
9. Dalrymple, *Understanding the New Testament*, 125.

and you will be hated by all nations because of my name. (Matt 24:8–9)

I do agree with Sumney that Paul's vicarious suffering cannot be expiatory and that only Christ's suffering provides forgiveness of sins. However, I would like to provide two brief excursions to illustrate the mimetic and eschatological quality of vicarious suffering when Christians like Paul suffer for the sake of the elect.

Mimetic Suffering

First, although not cannon, the story of Eleazar in 4 Maccabees provides a historical anecdote that helps to elucidate a type of mimetic vicarious suffering. The author of Maccabees appears to first lay the groundwork for what we would know today as cognitive behavioral therapy. That is, his central thesis is "whether pious reason is sovereign over the passions" (4 Macc 1:1).[10] He will provide several allusions to Old Testament scripture to validate this thesis but will utilize an intertestamental account as the main point of affirmation. Cognitive behavioral therapy is similar in that one is to raise awareness in another thoughts that may be distorted that produce manifold emotions that can be unhealthy and contribute to disorders such as depression or anxiety. If one can insert or substitute a thought that is more consistent with reality than one's perception, one is able to modify one's emotional response, as the emotional response is less noxious to thoughts rooted in reality as contrasted to distorted cognitions rooted in a false perception.

The author of 4 Maccabees also has a secondary thesis, which asserts that clear and godly thinking also provides a framework by which certain virtuous emotions or behaviors can be displayed, such as courage and justice. At the same time, these virtues mitigate those emotions that oppose justice and courage, such as "malice," and "anger, fear, and pain" (see 4 Macc 1:4). After utilizing the first three chapters as an introduction, the author of 4 Maccabees is prepared to illustrate clear and godly thinking as a means by which the courage of vicarious suffering is enacted through Eleazar's story.

We find ourselves within Israel. Onius is the high priest and, according to Maccabees, was "a noble and good man (4 Macc 4:1). However,

---

10. Please note that all references to Maccabees are taken from the New Revised Standard Version Updated Edition.

Simon was a political opponent of Onius and sought to supplant Onius as high priest, an office that was conveyed as a lifetime appointment. Simon made several attempts to damage the reputation of Onius, making false allegations in order to influence his removal. However, when unsuccessful, Simon turned to the governor of the region, Apollonius. Simon alleges the following:

> I have come here because I am loyal to the king's government, to report that in the Jerusalem treasuries there are deposited tens of thousands in private funds that are not the property of the temple but belong to King Seleucus. (4 Macc 4:3)

Apollonius then reports to King Seleucus the false claim, which engenders an invasion of Jerusalem seeking to confiscate the reported silver within the temple treasury. Simon and Apollonius lead a military troop into the heart of Israel.

In truth, the offerings within the temple were free-will offerings from the people of Israel for the maintenance of the temple, not portions of tribute or taxes that were withheld. Therefore, there was a city-wide protest. Onius and all the priests together stood within the temple court, interceding as Apollonius approached the temple treasury. Then, and quite miraculously, a mighty host of angels appear within the temple itself to defend the temple from Apollonius' troop. In fear, Apollonius repents of his deed and pleas that Onius would intercede that he should not be killed by this angelic army. Onius intercedes for Apollonius and reports back to Seleucus all that had occurred.

After the death of Seleucus, his son Antiochus comes to reign in his stead. Antiochus replaces Onius with Jason, who secures such an appointment by bribing the newly installed king with 208,620 pounds of silver every year as a tribute. Jason ignores the maintenance of the temple and begins to inculcate Greek culture within Jerusalem by erecting both a Greek school and athletic complex.

While at war with Ptolemy of Egypt, Antiochus is informed that Israel may have celebrated when a rumor of Antiochus' death had circulated. As a punitive measure, Antiochus forbids any practice of Judaistic law. He enforces this ordinance with persecution and even death. The author of Maccabees illustrates the holy defiance of such an ordinance when he describes the following:

> ... even to the extent that women, because they had circumcised their sons, were thrown headlong from heights along with their

infants, though they had known beforehand that they would suffer this . . . (4 Macc 4:25)

The force of Antiochus' persecution intensifies as he systematically orders each Jew to eat pork and other foods sacrificed to idols as a measure of enforcing his ordinance that Israel abandon the law. Anyone who defies this order would be tortured to death by being stretched upon a wheel. Eleazar is first chosen to eat forbidden food in the company of Israel. Eleazar is aged by this time and from a priestly family, also having become a legal expert in the Mosaic code.

Antiochus compels Eleazar to obey the ordinance first by insulting his age and his adherence to a religion that Antiochus deems "vain opinion concerning the truth (4 Macc 5:10). Antiochus taunts Eleazar in the following manner:

> Before I begin to torture you, old man, I would advise you to save yourself by eating pork, for I respect your age and your gray hairs. Although you have had them for so long a time, it does not seem to me that you are a philosopher when you observe the religion of the Jews. (4 Macc 5:6–7)

It appears the enemy's strategy is the same in all epochs of time: insult and undermine God's authority as irrelevant, unwise, and unintelligent. The other strategy is to ignore God's holiness by placating the human desire that to indulge in sin and vice will only be met by pardon. This is Antiochus' final argument for Eleazar when he says,

> For consider this: if there is some power watching over this religion of yours, it will excuse you from any transgression that arises out of compulsion. (4 Macc 5:13)

Eleazar is granted permission to reply, and in his lengthy reply he refers to a piety that overcomes self-preservation and a determined adherence to the law that would suffer even death rather than break the law by defiling his integrity.

> You scoff at our philosophy as though living by it were irrational, but it teaches us self-control, so that we master all pleasures and desires, and it also trains us in courage, so that we endure any suffering willingly; it instructs us in justice, so that in all our dealings we give what is due; and it teaches us piety, so that with proper reverence we worship the only living God. (4 Macc 5:22–24)

Again, the author is emphasizing this historical anecdote to emphasize the virtue of self-control, depicted not only by Eleazar's holy defiance but also through his instructive monologue. Eleazar's speech is also a type of mimetic vicarious suffering, for in being given a platform to speak, he instructs all of Israel and then models a holy adherence to God's law in the face of suffering, torment, and death. In this way, we will see if he suffers on behalf of Israel and whether his suffering spares others.

As Eleazar is tortured, beaten, and bruised, he is asked to feign consuming the defiled food and even here he declines though it would save his life. Half-dead, he provides remarks that are illustrative of mimetic vicarious suffering. He knows that this event is setting a pattern for the next generation to follow; he will not be defeated in the ensuing legacy, but is determined to triumph to death. For in his death is a victory of legacy, vicariously suffering for all of Israel, so that the future Israel will also be emboldened to suffer for the sake of their faith. Eleazar replies to the guards, who compel him one last time to save his life,

> For it would be irrational if, having lived in accordance with truth up to old age and having guarded the reputation of a life lived lawfully, we should now change our course and ourselves become a pattern of impiety to the young by setting them an example in the eating of defiling food. (4 Macc 6:18–19)

As Paul's suffering is for the elect of the gentile church that they might endure in salvation despite marginalization and persecution, Eleazar also suffers for the youth of Israel so that they would follow the law in its entirety. Both illustrate a concern for a future generation, for endurance of soteriology, and even perhaps a kind of suffering that is preventative in nature. That is, perhaps Paul and Eleazar suffer so that others may be spared.

What if this is also the role of a pastor? What if a pastor is meant to suffer in mimetic and vicarious ways to illustrate a pattern of genuine faithfulness to God despite the outcome so that others may be spared? This suffering may be physical, as a pastor endures chains and imprisonment on behalf of a congregation, but it also may be mental anguish. If being a pastor emulates the pattern of Christ, then indeed one should anticipate suffering. And more so, I would like to argue that one can envision such suffering as having redemptive qualities. These redemptive qualities are certainly not expiatory but offer a mimetic pattern for a burgeoning generation of pastors who are watching the current generation. Moreover, the suffering may also spare others from physical, mental, or emotional suffering by becoming the object of human wrath.

The other type of vicarious suffering that Eleazar conveys is a function of intercession, a priestly role in calling on the Lord that mercy be applied to His people. Thus, this identifies yet another function to vicarious suffering, the function of intercessor. As intercessor, the one suffering on behalf of those who will remain pleads for their redemption and preservation. Not only is this mimetic in that it models a kind of selflessness for other priestly agents to emulate, but it also contributes to the mystery of suffering, yet another nuance to vicarious suffering. The one suffering is given a platform of intercession so that God would intervene to spare those for whom the sufferer prays. Eleazar's parting words are intercessory and priestly:

> You know, O God, that, though I might have saved myself, I am dying in burning torments for the sake of the law. Be merciful to your people, and let our punishment suffice for them. Make my blood their purification, and take my life in exchange for theirs. (4 Macc 6:27–29)

Here is the mystery of vicarious suffering; it is essentially intercessory. The sacrifice or death can have a sanctifying effect on the community. Eleazar is not only standing as an example in a mimetic way, but also praying that his death would spare the death of all Israel. His plea is that Israel would be saved in and through his death. This is the outcome of vicarious suffering—it is to spare, preserve, save, and forebear. It is both immediate and eschatological, sparing in the present while also contributing to the suffering appointed for future ages.

Eschatological Suffering

Let us now underscore the role of eschatological suffering with another anecdote of history—that of Perpetua and Felicitas. We turn to the passion narrative first, with confirmation of mimetic suffering as the biography states its purpose with the following: "for these too will someday also be venerable and compelling for future generations."[11] The future generations are you and I. We are both charged and comforted with the kind of passion we are commended to emulate.

---

11. Heffernon, *Passion of Perpetua and Felicitas*, 125.

Perpetua was a young woman of twenty-two years with a nursing infant when she was arrested and placed in jail for her faith. She worried for her child, who was still quite vulnerable and who required frequent feedings. And yet, the Lord would console her in these apprehensions. She began to see her imprisonment as her "palace, so that I wanted to be there rather than anywhere else."[12] The Greek text of the *Passion* employs the word *praetorium*, which was a description of a military commander's tent and was the very place where Christ was mocked in Matthew's gospel (see Matt 27:27).[13] The prison is henceforth translated to "palace," for it is the very headquarters of Perpetua's spiritual fight and last stand in the faith. It would also become the waiting ground for her future glory in Christ.

So, when does suffering or mental anguish become joy? This is the question I sought to answer within the context where my wife suffered from mental anguish. If I were to remain as pastor, her suffering would ensue and yet I had an opportunity to deliver her and myself by taking another job. In essence, I had the ability to work in a different town, away from those who persecuted us both. But were we fleeing the providence of God in moving away from our persecutors? Or were we shaking the dust from our feet, having been given a place of respite and refreshment from the Lord? It is difficult for me to discern whether the opportunity to resign was God's providence or a temptation to flee. It sometimes becomes too much to bear to interpret our departure as a running from God. In many ways I must believe that it was a running to God. Otherwise, I might despair. However, is this not the same struggle of any pastor who is seeking God's will for him or her and their family? There is the inclination that one remains and suffer the reproach as Christ suffered reproach. There remains also the inclination to protect one's family from ensuing persecution, hurt, and slander. Only God can answer this question and we must honor the notion that each situation is highly nuanced and contextualized, distinct from other situations.[14]

---

12. Heffernon, *Passion of Perpetua and Felicitas*, 126. See also where Tertullian situates suffering under the rubric of God's providence for the early church. He remarks persecution should be endured because it comes from God, the source of all good, and thus persecution is itself a good, since it too comes from God. He points out that in our flight from persecution, we may unwittingly flee from the providential good and hence from God (Heffernon, *Passion of Perpetua and Felicitas*, 159).

13. See Heffernon, *Passion of Perpetua and Felicitas*, 166. See also Tertullian, who defines *praetorium* in *Cic. Verr.* 4.65.

14. I later discuss Paul's exit and deliverance from certain cities and how to discern

LEGACY OF ENDURANCE 69

We find later that Perpetua was asked by an anonymous Christian brother if she discerned what would be their destination while imprisoned—would they be freed or would they suffer? Perpetua sought the Lord in prayer and was given a curious and eschatological dream that very night.

> I see a bronze ladder of great length, reaching up to heaven, but so narrow that people could only climb up one at a time. And on the sides of the ladder, iron implements of every kind were attached. There were swords, lances, hooks, knives, and daggers, so that if anyone climbed up carelessly, or not looking upwards, he was torn to pieces and his flesh clung to the iron weapons.[15]

The dream is reminiscent of Jacob's dream of a ladder reaching to heaven whereby angels were ascending and descending. Jacob's dream was eschatological as Jesus refers to it when he typifies the ladder as representing Himself (see Gen 28:10–17 and John 1:51). The ladder appears to represent each Christian's journey to heaven, which is ascended one at a time. That is, every person must make his or her choice for Christ as an individual soul. Moreover, once someone chooses Christ, there are obstacles and threats on either side of that choice. One must continue to look heavenward, to the kingdom, and press into this kingdom with every rung of the ladder, or one will be caught within the snare of the enemy (see Matt 7:14).[16]

Perpetua continues her dream:

> . . . and there was a serpent of great size lying at the foot of the ladder, which would lie in wait for those who climbed and deterred them from climbing. And the first to go up was Saturus. (Because he had been our teacher and because he had not been present when we were seized, he later voluntarily handed himself over for our sake.) And he reached the top of the ladder and he turned back to me and said: 'Perpetua, I am waiting for you, but be careful that the serpent does not bite you.' And I said: 'In the name of Jesus Christ, he will not hurt me.'[17]

---

when one may need to shake the dust from one's feet.

15. Heffernon, *Passion of Perpetua and Felicitas*, 127.

16. See Heffernon, *Passion of Perpetua and Felicitas*, 168, where he also notes that Perpetua's dream is "a conflation of Jacob's ladder, Jesus's remarks on the difficulty of attaining the path to eternal life, the dragon of Revelation, and the prophecy in Genesis that the woman will bruise the head of the serpent (Gen 3.15, 28.12; Mat. 7.13; Rev 12.3)."

17. Heffernon, *Passion of Perpetua and Felicitas*, 127. The dream is a fusion of eschatological and mimetic vicarious suffering, for it also provides exhortation to the

The dream continues its eschatological fervor as Perpetua sees a great serpent lying at the bottom of the ladder. The serpent is no doubt an allusion to Satan, who awaits any who would stumble from the ladder, but also appears to deter any Christian from even beginning the journey upward (see John 10:10). Perpetua's teacher has gone before her to the uttermost length of the ladder, implying that her teacher will die a martyr's death before her. The teacher encourages Perpetua to continue her journey but also warns of Satan's looming attack. Sarturus is a part of the great cloud of witnesses who have served the Lord until the end. He charges that all Christians face what they must and remain faithful in the journey to Zion (see Heb 12:1). We have the writings of the Torah, Wisdom Literature, Prophets, Gospels, Epistles, and Apocalyptic Literature, all of which encourage us on our journey to persist, to move forward, to press into the kingdom though it be a forceful pressing and though we face hardship on every side (see Matt 11:12 and 2 Cor 4:8). The witness of the saints and ultimately the witness of Christ compels us forward like a cacophony of marching orders sent in love to encourage our faith!

Perpetua approaches her enemy after claiming victory through the Lord.

> And from beneath the ladder itself, the serpent slowly stuck out its head, as if it feared me, and I stepped on its head and climbed up, as if it were the first step.[18]

Perpetua re-enacts the prophecy from Genesis, participating in the eschatological fulfillment that began with Christ's victory upon the cross and will be consummated with the second Parousia. The head of the serpent is and will be crushed (see Gen 3:15 and Rom 16:20)! In Perpetua's dream, there is an allusion to militant participation in the crushing of Satan's head. That though the seed of woman is a prophetic foreshadowing of Christ, it is we, all who join Christ, who, also within the rubric of His authority, crush the head of the serpent. Indeed, the Christian journey begins with a crushing as one overcomes the deceit and intimidation of the enemy in trusting Christ as Savior and King!

Perpetua's dream continues with her ascent up the ladder:

Christian community that one is to live one's faith in Christ without wavering. See also Heffernon, *Passion of Perpetua and Felicitas*, 168, where he provided further commentary on mimetic suffering.

18. Heffernon, *Passion of Perpetua and Felicitas*, 127.

> And I saw an enormous garden and a white-haired man sitting in the middle of it dressed in shepherd's clothes, a big man, milking sheep. And standing around were many thousands dressed in white. And he raised his head, looked at me, and said: 'You are welcome here, child.' And he called me, and from the cheese that he had milked he gave me as it were a mouthful. And I received it in my cupped hands and ate it. And all those standing around said: 'Amen.'[19]

Perpetua encounters the Good Shepherd, an allusion envisioning Christ. His white hair is reminiscent of John's apocalyptic vision (see John 10:11 and Rev 1:14). The garden is reminiscent of paradise, which was the initial impetus of creation, lost through sin, and redeemed by Christ (see Gen 2:4). The assembly of those dressed in white is an allusion again to John's apocalyptic vision of the multitudes from every tribe and every tongue dressed in white (an allusion to consummate sanctification) and having palm branches (see Rev 7:9).[20] The palm branches are a recapitulation of Christ's first Parousia and triumphal entry into Jerusalem, and here marks the entry of the second Parousia to rule the earth.

Christ encourages Perpetua by providing a reassuring remark that she is indeed welcome in heaven. It is similar to Christ's words to all believers who are steadfast in their faith when he says, "you good and faithful servant, enter into the kingdom" (Matt 25:21). The eating of the cheese milked from the sheep by the Shepherd's hand is a curious image. Could it be the words of prophets and saints that have gone before her, both in terms of Scripture and other encouraging writings? Could it be the witness, testimony, and perhaps even suffering of other saints that now give her strength for her journey? Could it be a eucharistic metaphor as Perpetua was a catechumen, a rather new disciple who was still awaiting the privilege to partake in the Eucharist and the *agape* feast?[21] The vision no doubt conjures up images of the promised land, Canaan, a land flowing with milk and honey (see Exod 3:8), also an allusion of

---

19. Heffernon, *Passion of Perpetua and Felicitas*, 127.

20. There is also an allusion to "those who had been slain for the Word of God" (Rev 6:9). This would validate the eschatological premise of vicarious suffering, in that others who have contributed to the quota of martyrdom are awaiting Perpetua's contribution to hasten the return of Christ. See Heffernon, *Passion of Perpetua and Felicitas*, 181.

21. See Heffernon, *Passion of Perpetua and Felicitas*, 183, for Tertullian's remarks of early Christian baptism: "when we are taken up [from the baptismal pool] (as newborn children), we taste first of all a mixture of milk and honey, and from that day we refrain from the daily bath for a whole week" (*Cor.* 3; cf. 1 Pt 2.2).

heavenly paradise (see Luke 23:43). Perpetua does not indicate any other meanings besides her polemic that she would suffer and enter a martyr's fate. Indeed, the Greek text of Perpetua's rendering speaks of the necessity of suffering—καἰἐνοή σαμενότι δέοι παθεῖν ("And we knew we would suffer")—emphasizing a kind of eschatological telos where suffering has a certain kind of apocalyptic purpose in the economy of God's kingdom.[22]

While still imprisoned and after her hearing and conviction to be sent to the arena to her death, God had given Perpetua a vision concerning her deceased brother, Dinocrates. The vision consisted of him being hot and thirsty and being unable to reach a pool that was just out of reach to quench his thirst. Her brother had died at seven years of age from a terrible cancer that procured an obvious wound on his face. This may have been an aggressive skin cancer that was incurable at the time. There was a great gulf between her and Dinocrates in Perpetua's vision. She interpreted this vision as a call to intercede for Dinocrates' suffering. The role of vicarious suffering again here translates into vicarious intercession. Even as Perpetua suffers, she intercedes for her brother who suffers. Suffering thus begets intercession, and perhaps in an eschatological/metaphysical manner.

The fact that her brother is hot and thirsty is a parallel to the rich man who was engulfed in flames and who pleaded with Abraham to provide a drop of water for him. The great gulf between Perpetua and Dinocrates is perhaps an allusion to the great gulf between the poor man Lazarus and the rich man who suffered eschatologically (see Luke 16:19–31). It is also possible that the chasm represented the great gulf between the dead and the living. And yet, the obvious cannot be ignored; is it possible for Perpetua to intercede for someone who is deceased?[23] Is it possible that this

22. Heffernon, *Passion of Perpetua and Felicitas*, 184 and 193, where Heffernon acknowledges the Carthage church as one elevating suffering as a mysterious fulfillment of salvation. He states, "even the threat of death did not prove to be a deterrent to joining the sect, as such a humiliating end became the heroic path through which they achieved heavenly salvation."

23. The apostle Paul hints at postmortem intercession when he prays that God would grant Onesiphorus mercy though he is by this time deceased (see 2 Tim 1:18). Moreover, Perpetua would have had a thoroughly classical Christian teaching in similar didactic manner as Tertullian provided. "Tertullian certainly believed prayers for the dead were efficacious and urged married women to pray for the repose of their husband's soul so that they might be joined together at the first resurrection (*pro anima eius orat et refrigerium . . . et in prima resurrectione consortium*, De Monog. 10.5). He urged his followers to say prayers in honor of the faithful dead on the anniversary of their death (Cor. 3; see also Cypr. Ep. 12.2.57)." Heffernon, *Passion of Perpetua and Felicitas*, 216.

intercession could alleviate the eschatological suffering of Dinocrates? Is it possible that while Lazarus, Abraham, or Perpetua could not cross the great chasm, that Christ could preach the gospel to the souls in Hades (see 1 Pet 3:19)? Is postmortem repentance even possible? Perpetua does not answer this looming question but certainly raises more eschatological questions and tension with her vision and subsequent intercession for her deceased brother. She certainly intimates that her desire to intercede did not originate with her but was a divine impetus so that her intercessions perhaps would alleviate Dinocrates' suffering.[24]

It is also clear that her intercessions are described as groans, a double lamentation if you will, seeking the relief of her brother. She is in desperate straits for her brother's deliverance.[25] We might also interject a possible metaphorical interpretation of Perpetua's dream. That is, though the identified object of the dream is Dinocrates, could it be that he symbolizes the plight of her father and/or her son? That is, we already know that her father pleaded with Perpetua to reject the faith, and the implication is that he is not a believer. Her son, still an infant, is not aware of the gospel. Does she intercede for their sake? Is Dinocrates an eschatological sign for her family who are yet estranged from the kingdom?

Moreover, this is where we might raise awareness for the pastor or any other Christian that suffers vicariously for another—can one's suffering have multimodal effects? That is, can vicarious suffering serve to alleviate, encourage to persevere in, or ascertain eschatological relief of another's suffering perhaps in ways that are beyond finding out?[26] I would argue that we perceive intercession in far less important terms than God does. Though we cannot see the wind, we feel the effects; though we may not see the Spirit's work through our intercession, the effects can be felt by others a lifetime away (see John 3:8).

24. Indeed, "there is an intriguing textual variant in MSN which reads *pati* instead of *petere*, and thus has Perpetua say that she knew she was worthy to 'suffer' for him." Heffernon, *Passion of Perpetua and Felicitas*, 213.

25. See Heffernon, *Passion of Perpetua and Felicitas*, 213, for the force of the language describing Perpetua's groans. This is akin to Augustine's description of his mother's groans for his salvation. The Latin emphasizes the element of sorrow more than the Greek does, as the Latin uses two participles, *gemens* and *lacrimans*. Thus, the force of lamentation is given double emphasis. See Heffernon, *Passion of Perpetua and Felicitas*, 227.

26. See Heffernon, *Passion of Perpetua and Felicitas*, 128–29, where Perpetua intercedes for her brother postmortem that he may receive a gift. Though she does not describe this gift, perhaps it is the gift of grace, forgiveness of sins, and eternal life. Most likely, it is the relief of Dinocrates' suffering.

Finally, she intercedes that Dinocrates would receive a "gift." Is this an allusion to *charis* or grace? It is pressing theological orthodoxy to consider postmortem reception of grace and so this point must be left to mere speculation regarding Perpetua's intent here. Moreover, we can run the risk of heterodoxy if we seek to engender doctrinal statements from Perpetua's vision. On the other hand, curiosity and pressing on certain dogmas can enable us to envision a greater efficacy to intercession.

We have further extrapolation of the "gift" when Perpetua is given yet another vision. Dinocrates' wound was healed and there remained only a scar. The rim of the pool containing the water was lowered and he was drinking relentlessly.[27] A golden cup of water that never dried was also provided for Dinocrates, from which he also drank. He was refreshed and began playing in the pool of water as any child might.[28] Not only does this picture realize a sort of baptism, but also a sort of consumptive regeneration. The play that Dinocrates never had in life, he has, purportedly, in the eschaton. Baptism, thus, can be envisioned as a return to the garden in an existential manner, and a restoration of childlike play, which is often stripped away by wounds that engender cynicism. The drinking of the cup also has eucharistic undertones, perhaps referring to the power of the blood of Christ in the sacrament of Eucharist to render restoration of the child who was lost. And isn't this return what the Lord intends for us? That is, a return to a type of childhood? For if one is to enter the kingdom, one must become like a child (see Matt 18:3).

Perhaps baptism is a reconfiguration of birth. As an infant, we pass through a deluge of water emerging from the birth canal to take our first breath. In baptism, we emerge a new spiritual child with the same wonder and joy as the pre-fall creation. I suppose one lesson of Perpetua's eschatological vision is that the same waters that can be for the healing of our souls can be the waters that liberate our souls to relentless joy and play. And this begs the question, do we have the slightest knowledge of how to enjoy the Lord, life, or play? Perhaps Jesus is ever leading us back

---

27. Could this have been a reference to water baptism? Early African congregations often coincided both spiritual and physical healing at the event of water baptism, as a metaphor of the pool of Bethesda (see John 5). "Tertullian argues that water was the first element to contain life, and he states that it is the water of baptism that cleanses the faithful and that signs of physical healing actually betoken spiritual healings (*De Bapt.* 3.6.5)." Heffernon, *Passion of Perpetua and Felicitas*, 222.

28. See Heffernon, *Passion of Perpetua and Felicitas*, 234, where he states, "*Traho* is used here in the sense 'to draw into one's body' the healing water without ceasing; it suggests Dinocrates is reveling in the water, rather like splashing in it."

to this existential paradigm as it portends kingdom life. And perhaps we pastors may emulate a pattern of childlikeness by inviting our children into our liturgy, celebrating the digressions they may introduce to any confines of our supposed order.

Not only is play included in Perpetua's vision of Dinocrates, but play is recapitulated once more in Sarturus' vision of heaven and the martyr's entrance thereof. It is worth noting that the injunction to play follows the "sign of peace," which was likely a greeting with a holy kiss as in Paul (see 1 Cor 16:20). In our world, where everything is sexualized and where gestures of love can be envisaged with corruption, the kingdom sign of peace is difficult to imagine within our current Christian communities. However, the holy kiss of the kingdom is without guile, pure, and without other agendas. The communal gesture of love was prompted by the tender stroke of the Lord Himself upon the faces of the would-be martyrs. We should not be surprised by such a greeting in an eschatological vision, as this was doubtless also a liturgical greeting within the early Christian community.[29]

We also have the anecdote of the sinful woman whose display of lavish love is offensive to the Pharisee. The women, a sinner, loves much as she is forgiven much. She anoints the feet of the Lord; she wipes His feet with her hair, and if this were not enough to complete the full measure of her affection, she kisses His feet without ceasing (see Luke 7:45). As a pastor, I could not imagine how I would react if I were to witness such a display of affection within our church. I would imagine most pastors would be uncomfortable with this public display of affection. And I am not necessarily advocating that we encourage differing genders to kiss one another's feet in our liturgy, but I am advocating a return to a type of love that may push the envelope of our own limited thinking when conceptualizing our communal gatherings.

It is the kiss and the divine stroke upon the face that precipitates the divine injunction that they go and play.[30] What if suffering is meant to bring us back to childhood? What if suffering is meant to open our minds and hearts to carefree play, unfixed schedules, and enjoyment of the now? What if the task can wait, the assignment can be modified, and the work transformed? What if we pastors could create a gathering where the

---

29. Heffernon, *Passion of Perpetua and Felicitas*, 289–90.

30. See Heffernon, *Passion of Perpetua and Felicitas*, 290, where he defines "play" in the following manner: "in the present instance the imperative suggests a mélange of meanings—'be at rest,' 'be merry,' 'be well,' 'be at peace.'"

imagination is once again unleashed? What would this look like within our churches? What would this look like for the world? Sarturus' vision again underscores the triumphant victory of the martyr by envisioning the fruit of this victory being peace, refreshment, and rest or play! As a pastor, I often scolded my children for playing hide-and-seek within the chair isles of the sanctuary. Perhaps if I had this to do again, I would join them. I have now transitioned from pastoral ministry and find that it is still very difficult for me to play with my children. Having eight children, one would think that play is all around me, and it is. But the question remains: Do I join the play? Do I join the childlike wonder of a discovery in the woods? Do I join the joy of putting a puzzle together? Do I play with my children when they laugh in a raucous manner?

Do we invite children to the altar? Do we have a time in our liturgy specifically designated for them? I can recall attempting to have the children stay within our church services throughout worship with a time of prayer for them at the end of our time of worship. I can recall many complaints concerning the children's behavior during the services. I sometimes wonder if our children's behaviors are not necessarily the problem, but our own. Perhaps once we have suffered enough at our own hand in our own adult world, do we finally realize that there is a kingdom secret just waiting to be unraveled by our children and by our paying attention to them.

After a litany of complaints, we eventually returned to separating our children in their own service for the entire service. We had an occasional family service, approximately four times per year, as a means of including the children and creating a time for them to participate in the sermon for that day. However, I always wondered if this continued to capitulate a culture where children must have some type of amusement park church service, being unable to tolerate a conjoined time together despite the twists and turns this might introduce to our firmly fixed schedules. Children no doubt teach us about divine interruptions, and O how we need these in our American churches, where synchrony, screen, and social media appeal loom like idols over our pulpits.

One of the highlights of my time as a pastor included one such interruption. A boy of about twelve years of age interrupted our altar service to request that he pray for me. Surprised and humbled, I allowed for this role reversal. He laid his hands on my head and began praying. A congregant captured this with a photograph, and this remains in my mind a seminal moment for my pastoral tenure. Why? I think the Lord is attempting to bring me back to childlike wonder and play. He is reminding me of the more salient features of the kingdom. He reminds me that my children are more important than I can imagine. Is it more important that I leave a legacy of rigid schedules or divine interruptions? Pastors, who has more influence over you? Is it the rich donor or the child who comes to you with the affirmation that he or she is praying for you?

I remember another child, who would come on several occasions and ask that I bend down and give him a small moment of my attention. His statement was simple but had a profundity and sweetness that rose above the complaints and slander. "I am praying for you pastor," he would say. I now reflect and wonder if it was his prayers that sustained my wife and I during the tumultuous time of religious ire, secret consorting, and plans to undermine authority.

I can recall one other incident when we had a foot-washing service. Very few had come for the service as it was on Maundy Thursday and not a typical day for gathering at church. What I cannot erase from my mind is the kind of enthusiasm and eagerness my children displayed as they sought to wash each other's feet and the feet of others who had attended, including my own. They were so very excited and though it almost became a game to them, it was a didactic in the kind of joy that comes with play. We can hold together the tension of holiness and play; these principles need not be mutually exclusive. When was the last time you enjoyed washing the feet of another? When was the last time you allowed a smile to dress your countenance? When was the last time you belly-laughed—you know, the kind of laugh that shakes your insides with a kind of warmth that spreads over your entire body? Pastors, when was the last time you modeled this kind of joy for your congregation?

Here is my charge to the American church: let the children back into your meetings. Make a way somehow and bring them right into the center of the liturgy. Be open to divine interruptions and navigate your liturgy with flexibility. Relax the order of service, and you might find a kind of laughter, joy, and peace that has long been delayed and removed because it was deemed inappropriate to the holiness of the liturgy. We could use a little more wonder and play in all of us! If we do suffer, then we can anticipate, perhaps, the fruit of childlike play, not only for us but for the ones we vicariously suffer for.

In summary, Perpetua interprets this vision to mean that Dinocrates' suffering had ended and thus perhaps the gift she mentions prior is simply the relief of his postmortem suffering. Let us ask again, can vicarious suffering create a context of potent intercession to the extent that eschatological relief can be procured?[31] Moreover, should we take Dinocrates' restoration literally or figuratively? Many dreams hold symbolic power and are potent metaphors describing a wholly alternative phenomenon. For example, one could consider that Dinocrates is a representation of Perpetua. Dinocrates' position in a place of confinement and suffering could represent Perpetua's imprisonment. His relief within the pools of baptism and refreshing, birthed through intercession, may represent Perpetua's glorious transition from the suffering of this life to the cure of heaven. Her intercession, thus configured, could be for her own courage to persevere unto death. The stocks could not indefinitely hold her for liberation was on the horizon.

There can be little doubt that the dreams and visions of Perpetua and her company had an eschatological fervor with illustrations of heaven and glimpses of spiritual warfare. Perpetua's vision of struggling with an Egyptian in the arena she interprets as her struggle with the devil and her subsequent triumph through being steadfast in her death. Sarturus, a member of the confined faithful, also had a vision of entering by escort of angels what appears to be the garden of the Lord, where he meets those who have already given their lives for the Lord and ushered him to meet with the Lord Himself.[32] We should also note that the visions of the martyrs being greeted by prior martyrs is curious and raises the point that I have heretofore been attempting as a polemic. There is a company of martyrs recognizably distinct in the kingdom. And as such, there appears to be a type of eschatological quota where suffering for one's faith contributes to the eschatological clock navigating the second Parousia of Christ. God will vindicate when those appointed to suffer have completed their appointment (see Rev 6:10–11).

Felicity, yet another young woman among the company of those who refused the idolatrous sacrifice to the gods of Rome, was pregnant, nearing term at eight months. While imprisoned, she gives birth to a daughter, which opened the opportunity for her to suffer with her company, as it were, because there were no public punitive measures meted out to one who was pregnant. She makes a remark that heralds back to a prior thesis that vicarious suffering is mimetic, which bears mentioning

---

31. Heffernon, *Passion of Perpetua and Felicitas*, 129.
32. Heffernon, *Passion of Perpetua and Felicitas*, 129–30.

here. While the prison soldiers mock and scorn her for her difficulty in giving birth, she replies with the following:

> Now I alone suffer what I am suffering, but then there will be another inside me, who will suffer for me, because I am going to suffer for him.[33]

She gives birth to a daughter, who is given to Felicity's sister to raise. Felicity appears to instigate a prophetic unction concerning her child. That is, her child will emulate her example of suffering as a result of Felicity's suffering for the Lord. This mimetic quality is the posterity she passes on to the next generation as her legacy of fidelity.

As Perpetua and her company neared the day of the games, they became more endeared to the guards who kept watch over their captivity. And perhaps what follows is yet another validation concerning Paul's remarks that he is suffering for the elect's sake, that they may obtain salvation in Christ Jesus. For in Perpetua's resolve and courage, one of the prison guards, "the adjutant in charge," no doubt, becomes a believer in Christ. This is yet another validation that vicarious suffering can result in the salvation of souls. There is an indelible impact and potential transformation of the soul mediated by the Holy Spirit as one witnesses the resolve of another in the face of incredulous suffering. So, Paul suffers for soteriological endurance, and Paul suffers perhaps for soteriological emergence as well. Perhaps suffering for Christ both engenders and perpetuates a context for salvation. The unwitting prophecy of the high priest concerning Christ is aptly described here when he says, "You do not understand that it is better for you to have one man die for the people than to have the whole nation destroyed" (John 11:50).

Again, it should be re-emphasized that a Christian's suffering is not expiatory as Christ's suffering but appears to create context for the soul to receive the expiation of Christ. We find this again reiterated when a crowd came to have one last look at the martyrs-to-be on the day before the games. After an admonition by Sarturus, we find that "the crowd left the prison stunned, and many of them became believers."[34]

---

33. Heffernon, *Passion of Perpetua and Felicitas*, 132. "The idea owes something to Justin's notion of the pre-existing seed of the Logos, which exists in everyone but which Christians share more fully because they worship and participate in the life of the Logos (2 *Apol.* 7.1)." Heffernon, *Passion of Perpetua and Felicitas*, 309.

34. Heffernon, *Passion of Perpetua and Felicitas*, 133.

We find yet another mimetic quality when Perpetua, marred by the trampling of a cow, speaks to her brother, "Stand fast in faith and love one another, and do not lose heart because of our sufferings."[35] She is herself bold until her death, encouraging the same kind of unwavering fidelity to the cause of Christ. Somehow Christ is glorified because of their deaths, and she would share in His suffering and in His glory (see Phil 3:10).

In conclusion, we have explored the enigmatic phrase Paul administers when he cites his suffering as vicarious for the soteriological endurance of the Ephesian church. I have polemically called for two kinds of vicarious suffering as an illustration of Paul's statement. First, that vicarious suffering has a mimetic quality encouraging future generations to endure their own salvation even at their own material and physical peril. Second, I have argued that there is an eschatological quality to vicarious suffering that contributes to the second Parousia, engenders vision or revelation, and perhaps mysteriously spares other souls from similar suffering. This is illustrated in table 2 below. As Origin has noted, the martyr's "baptism in blood" intercedes for one's own or communal post-baptismal sins through vicarious suffering.[36]

Table 2: Types of Christian Suffering

Type of Suffering	Result of Suffering	Resulting Fruit	Benefactors
Expiatory	Forgiveness of Sins	Redemption	For the World
Mimetic	Courage for Others	Fidelity to God	For Believers
Eschatological	Sparing of Others	Childlike Play/Rest	For the Lost

Perhaps this was known to the early church so that they were able to paradoxically enter the joy of suffering for the name of Christ (see Acts 5:41). Perhaps this kind of joy is missing in the American church.

Or to be more personal, perhaps this joy is missing in me. For a pastor who was wounded and has exited pastoral ministry, I reflect on

---

35. Heffernon, *Passion of Perpetua and Felicitas*, 134. And see p. 352, where he notes the use of the Greek σκανδαλίζω ("to cause to stumble, give offense or scandal to anyone"). Thus, Perpetua exhorts her brother with her final words that he need not be scandalized or give himself to apostasy.

36. See Heffernon, *Passion of Perpetua and Felicitas*, 359, and *Exh. Mart.* 30.1–7. However, Origin borders on an argument that the death of the martyr is expiatory, from which I would differ. Only Christ's death is expiatory.

times of relentless intercession for the church that may not have come without the modality of suffering. For the pastor who does transition, perhaps one can derive consolation from the premise that one's suffering may have spared the same kind of suffering for the next pastor. Perhaps God used your example, your preaching, your intercessions to work on the hearts of those who slandered and wounded you so that repentance was the fruit. There are still times that I pray for the church I pastored. That prayer burden has been difficult to ignore, and maybe it is not to go away. A pastor, called to be a pastor, does not stop becoming a pastor because he does not pastor a local church. The call to love the people through intercession remains a pastoral call. So, I pray when prompted and hope that both meaning and fruit emerge from what was a tumultuous time, and trust God with His bride.

Pastors, any suffering you endure for the sake of Christ, love, and calling has meaning and purpose in the kingdom. It may be the case that a type of legacy may be undone when a pastor transitions (i.e., the dismantling of certain ministries). However, one can take consolation in a legacy that remains—you are now numbered among the many countless servants of God who have also been opposed. Take comfort that this is also a good legacy, for it has provided an example that one can still love and be steadfast in the faith when under the stoning of accusation. Suffer for the sake of the next generation of pastors. Suffer to spare other souls from such a fate.

Chapter 6

Legacy of Honor

> In a large house there are utensils not only of gold and silver but also of wood and clay, some for special use, some for ordinary. (2 Tim 2:20)

AFTER EXPLORING THE LEGACY of suffering, Paul pivots to the next lesson for Timothy, regarding a legacy of honor. We have already explored the mimetic, eschatological, and intercessory power of suffering, which is transmitted intergenerationally. Now we will explore the scope of Paul's emphasis on honor within the church community itself. Indeed, the honor here bestowed is one rooted in an esteemed recognition within the house of God itself. Therefore, it is a position that is rooted in the pragmatic operations of the church, and we should note that Paul has already accepted the fact that there will always be vessels of honor and vessels of disrepute within the body of Christ. Thus, pastors should expect to interact with vessels of disrepute at any parish and during any work. It is as if Paul recognizes this mixed aspect to ministry and is unveiling this aspect to ready Timothy's expectations as pastor of Ephesus.

In retrospect, I believe I had erred in believing otherwise. That is, I had anticipated interacting with vessels of honor within my own community, with an expectation that I would be marginalized by those outside of the body of Christ. However, I became aware rather acutely that there remain in every church vessels of dishonor who make robust attempts to dishonor others. Perhaps if I had expected the legacy of inheriting both sets of vessels within the house of God, I may have had differing responses when interacting with vessels of honor versus vessels of dishonor. So, for those beginning pastoral ministry, please hear this stark warning and brace yourself for encounters with both vessels of honor and those of dishonor. Go into any work expecting to be exposed to both. Moreover, seek to maintain your integrity as a vessel of honor even as the poison of slander is spewed in your direction. You must leave a legacy of honor, which is important here to Paul and important to pastoral ministry.

Let us begin with a literary structure for 2 Timothy 2:14–26 that will elucidate why honor appears to be the central theme of this pericope and how honor is inextricably tied to our words. Paul quite commonly uses chiastic structures to communicate a polemic, and this short but potent diatribe is no exception. He implements a modified chiastic structure in the following manner:

> A—Words of Strife (2:14)
>> B—Word of Truth (2:15)
>
> A'—Words of Virulent Ungodliness (2:16–18)
>> B'—Word of Christ's Name (2:19)
>>> C—Vessels of Honor vs. Vessels of Dishonor (2:20–21)
>> B"—Word of the Lord's Name (2:22)
>
> A"—Words of Strife (2:23)
>> B'"—Word of Instruction (2:24–26)

We can see from the structure above that the great distinction between vessels of honor and those of dishonor is underscored with a discussion of words acting as bookends to the central statement. Vessels of honor are illustrated by the Word of Truth (2:15), Word of Christ's Name (2:19), Word of the Lord's Name (2:22), and Word of Instruction. Truth and instruction form the first and last premises describing a vessel of honor. In this manner, the vessel of honor is one that aptly and continually instructs with the Word of Truth. There is also a double emphasis placed on the holy name of God (Christ and the Lord) as a reiteration that the pastor instructs while appealing to the name of Christ on all occasions. Perhaps this is a prayerful appeal, or perhaps it is an authoritative appeal. In this way, the pastor speaks truth, speaks God's Word, and does so in prayerful appeal to the divine name and divine authority. This is the legacy of honor Paul transmits to Timothy and which Paul would like Timothy to transmit to the Ephesian church.

In contrast, the vessels of dishonor are couched with words that engender strife and ungodliness. Notice that where Paul gives double emphasis to the divine name when describing vessels of honor, he gives double emphasis to words of strife when describing vessels of dishonor. This is an important rhetorical device as the double emphasis provides a more potent contrast and drills down into Paul's polemic for the hearer. Words of strife, therefore, are given an important place in the mind of dishonorable vessels and become a sort of litmus test of identifying such vessels in the body. Paul provides, in a literary structure of chiasm, a pathognomonic trait in diagnosing the disreputable vessel—division and strife.

Pastor Brad made several attempts to preserve the reputation of so many who were dividing the body of Christ with their words. The strife they created was splintering the body. He did not want to believe that these were vessels of dishonor but sought to conceptualize them as seeking what was best for the body of Christ as they saw it. And some of this may have been true. But if the modality of expressing their vision, direction, or perspective is to engender strife publicly by shaming a member of the church or by sending community-wide emails or letters with scourging words intent to wound and divide, then be aware pastors—this is a vessel of dishonor within the church. Paul seeks to emphasize the contradistinction by the A-B format, striking a greater juxtaposition between the two vessels.

Finally, the structure is complete by providing a last word. There are more B statements than A statements. That is, the last word will always be the word from the vessel of honor. Where the kingdom is concerned, we can rest assured that the last word is not slander, strife, division, and accusation, but the Word of Instruction. I believe Paul is intentional in creating a greater weight for the words of honor as opposed to the words of dishonor, and more than this, a finality.

That is, the final word will come from a vessel of honor in any house of God. It may not be within our desired time; it might not even be while we are present as pastors. That is, if a pastor transitions from a certain work and does so with vessels of dishonor still present and still deriding the exiting pastor, know that God will not disavow such an honorable vessel. He will in the appointed time come to defend His servant. He will do so with a meekness that confounds the strongest of rhetorical figures. He will deal with the opposition with a kind of wooing to repentance that is mysteriously disarming. He will do so to recapture the vessels of dishonor from the captivity of the devil.

You see, the vessels of dishonor, the ones opposing the work of the Lord and engendering division, are captured by Satan. It is difficult to conceptualize a seasoned Christian as being caught within the prison of Satan, but this is possible. It is a possibility of one's own who clings to strife. Strife is the bedrock that splinters a church. Slander is the tool of strife. Accusation is the medium that moves strife along. Spiros Zodhiates has recognized the etymological nuance of the Greek here for strife, λογομαχέω (*log-om-akh-eh'-o*), as coming from two Greek words. The first Greek word is *logos*, literally rendered "word," "words," "speech," "reasoning," or "computation," and the word *machomai*, which is rendered "to war," "quarrel," or "dispute." Zodhiates also goes on to add a sense of context when he asserts that this word alludes to a kind of conflict that disputes subjects of trifling importance.[1]

That is, there is a sense of triviality to the strife being engendered. For example, Pastor Brad attempted to call a certain church member to discipline, and this church member emailed all the leadership and staff stating that he was lacking in transparency because he would not participate in a church disciplinary process over email. Pastor Brad informed the church member that he preferred to address the conflict of having been accused of appealing to the demonic in person. He should have realized that one accusation would lead to the next as strife became the aim of this vessel of dishonor.

Pastors, be aware that within your church right now are vessels of honor and dishonor. Expose and discipline the vessels of dishonor with meekness and instruction. Leave the rest of the work of calling the vessel to repentance to the Lord. Also, be encouraged that the Lord will always have the last word. Be confident that He is sovereign over His church and will act when the time is right. As for you, guard your words and speak only truth with appeal to the name of Christ. Leave a legacy of honor!

Paul uses the metaphor of a common house to illustrate his honor/dishonor polemic. He states that in any house there are vessels not only of gold and silver but also of wood and earth. He identifies gold and silver with honor and wood and earth with dishonor. Both vessels remain in any house and so it is with the house of God. But Paul provides a mechanism whereby one can be purged of the dishonorable and inexorable words that mitigate the advancement of our soul—sanctification.

---

1. Zodhiates, *Key Word Study Bible*, 45.

Sanctification, Sincerity, and Honor

The Greek ἁγιάζω (*hag-ee-ad'-zo*) is rendered as "to hallow," which is in distinct contrast to *koinos*, which means "to be defiled" or "common." It is a perfect word to illustrate the juxtaposition between common and sacred, honor and dishonor, free and captive.[2] The phenomenon of ἁγιάζω cannot be apprehended without there first being a separation. That which is filthy cannot be made clean until first it is set apart or consecrated. The agent of separation appears to begin with the self. That is, one first wills to be separated unto God's service. This act of holy movement then creates a context for the cleansing aspect of sanctification, which is performed by God. The one seeking sanctification separates him- or herself from the devices, programs, sins, wickedness, pursuits, and mechanisms of the world. In doing so, the one seeking sanctification withdraws from fellowship with the world. One does this by first entering into fellowship with God.[3] Fellowship with God is the beginning of sanctification. This relationship is itself a sanctifying phenomenon, for one's affections are transformed because of the inherent relationship. Therefore, sanctification is defined by relationship that creates a context of consecration. The fellowship with God inculcates a kingdom ethic that is distinguished from the ethics of this world and directs one to the path of being a vessel of honor. And though the impulse to move into relation with God is volitionally left for the individual to accomplish, sanctification is not a unilateral act guaranteeing one's separateness. It is a participation one has with God, who becomes the purging Agent, the launder's Soap, and the refining Fire. We respond to an invitation unto honor and the more we respond, the greater the sanctification. A vessel of honor is holy, with sacred intentions, and sincere, without duplicitous motivations.[4]

This latter definition is one often associated with ἁγιάζω but not necessarily attached to the word itself, but stands as a meaning for ἁπλότητος (*haplotetos*). These synonyms are important as ἁπλότητος can help us with a certain nuance for ἁγιάζω. If we are to assert that these two constructs are synonyms that aid in lexical understanding, we would then also come to understand sanctification as simplicity, purity, sincerity, faithfulness, and plenitude.[5] This would then imply that sanctification is a synecdoche,

---

2. Zodhiates, *Key Word Study Bible*, 1680.
3. Zodhiates, *Key Word Study Bible*, 1680.
4. Zodhiates, *Key Word Study Bible*, 1680.
5. Zodhiates, *Key Word Study Bible*, 1691.

that it is a part of the Christian walk that represents a consummate relationship with God. The part represents the whole; the fellowship begins a seed that grows into bouquet of intimacy; the one separated is the one embraced. The fellowship breaks bread together, discusses matters of the heart, and enjoys a closeness that is often rejected by vessels that seek to remain in dust, mire, and worldly power struggles.

The New Testament employs ἁπλότητος in a moral sense as standing as an antonym to duplicity. Sincerity is a type of description where one is genuine in how he or she carries his or her disposition with God and others. There is an obvious expression of love and affection. It stands opposed to one who is affectionate in person but slanderous behind closed doors. This would be duplicitous and act as a mitigating factor to sanctification and snare to one's sanctifying fellowship with God. There is also the notion of faithfulness when describing ἁπλότητος. One who is faithful is one who genuinely assists another without an agenda for promotion or because it is politically expedient. Sanctification is manifested by how we relate to God and to one another. Its fruit is manifested in how we respect authority, show kindness to subordinates, speak of others, and love the world. One could argue that sanctification is a result of an ever-increasing and fiery love for God and neighbor.

Paul utilizes ἁπλότητος in 2 Corinthians 8:2 when using the literary device of irony to describe the Macedonian churches. He states, "For during a severe ordeal of affliction their abundant joy and their extreme poverty have overflowed in a wealth of generosity on their part."

The word rendered "generosity," which is here the word ἁπλότητος, could also be rendered "simplicity." Paul's use of irony creates a healthy tension that draws the reader to conclude that it is possible to have abundant joy in affliction and be quite generous in the context of abject poverty. Indeed, sanctification purges us of the need to hoard, amass, draw unto oneself, and build larger storehouses. Sanctification walks in a Christian paradox of suffering that procures great joy, and whose poverty ironically creates a posture of liberal giving. Simplicity is the birthing stool of liberality. It is also the disposition of divine fellowship. Genuine and simple reliance upon the Lord because of radical trust enables one to let go of the normal anxious acts of this world that typically operate to validate and nourish self-preservation.

Paul will once again employ ἁπλότητος when describing giving in the next chapter: "You will be enriched in every way for your great generosity, which will produce thanksgiving to God through us . . ." (2 Cor 9:11).

This premise is within the context of a quote from the Psalms where God has dispersed seed abroad and given to the poor. His righteousness remains forever (see Ps 112:9). Paul preaches from this text that God provides seed to the sower and by doing so provides bread for one to eat. He also is the agent that increases a harvest and multiplies the fruit of one's righteousness. This righteousness and multiplicity are for the purpose of generosity, so that ἁπλότητος is a nuance of sanctification that involves a kind of liberality that remains the fruit of transformation. As a pastor, I would often provide a recurring phrase when discussing our tithes and offerings: "It is about the heart." Our gifts are not necessarily about an amount, but about the condition of our hearts in proximity with our Savior in fellowship. The sanctified soul is freed from the trappings of this life, which acts as a catalyst to liberality in giving, whether it be of service or goods. Liberality ought to have simplicity and purity as a bedrock. In utilizing ἁπλότητος as a possible definition of ἁγιάζω, we have discovered a certain nuance to sanctification that emphasizes motive and sincerity. The sanctified give, act, speak, and behave with proper motives, which are engendered by a transformed heart.

Sanctification creates a vessel of honor, and it is a vessel of honor that becomes useful for the Master's work in the kingdom (see 2 Tim 2:21). And it is the Master who creates from the same lump vessels of honor and others of dishonor (see Rom 9:21). Now this statement from Paul to the church in Rome betokens a type of sovereignty that causes one to question one's choice in the matter. But certainly this discussion is also helpful, for it enables us to investigate how Paul is conceptualizing the church body when he writes to Timothy.

Election and Honor

Paul writes in Romans 9 concerning the election of Israel. Paul will provide a new way of looking at Israel's election. He beckons the hearer to move beyond simple genetics and genealogy and conceive an idea of spiritual heritage. That is, not all Israel is Israel, though one claims to be the son or daughter of Abraham. But the true Israel is the people of promise, the seed that embraces the promise God has fulfilled in the sending of Christ. He pivots to Isaac as the son of promise to illustrate that the true Israel is the children of Isaac, and more so, children with Isaac, becoming the promised son or promised daughter.

Paul continues his diatribe on the seminal family of Abraham, Isaac, and Jacob. He will now discuss the controversial statement from God that he loved Jacob but hated Esau (see Deut 32:4 and Rom 9:13). This pertains to Paul's theology on election, that God calls and the vessels respond. Our works are contingent upon God's call. He appeals to Moses' encounter with God when God said to him, "I will have mercy on whom I will have mercy, and compassion on whom I will have compassion" (see Exod 33:19 and Rom 9:15).

Paul has already used many examples and citations to tie honor and dishonor into election but will cite one more that will make his case concerning a vessel of dishonor. He cites Pharaoh as a vessel that was called by God to have a hardened heart, for it was the hardened heart of Pharaoh that created a context for the power of God to be on display and for His wonder to be declared throughout the earth (see Rom 9:17). Paul then modifies the statement from Moses. Where Moses emphasized mercy with a statement on compassion, Paul draws a contrast between the mercies of God and the hardening from God (see Rom 9:15, 18).

Paul then employs a *reductio ad absurdum* (reduction to absurdity) argument to illustrate the futility in questioning God's intent in creation and attempting to refute one's inability to resist God's elected will. That is, it is absurd to question God's elected will. And so, Paul follows with the verse of interest, which provides corroborating nuance to his thinking for Timothy in the second letter: "Has the potter no right over the clay, to make out of the same lump one object for special use and another for ordinary use?" (Rom 9:21).

The vessel of honor and vessel of dishonor are derived from the same source. The lump of clay is fashioned one way to be a vessel of honor and another to be a vessel of dishonor. There seems to be a utilitarian implication here. That is, what makes the vessel honorable or dishonorable is how the vessel functions within the community. Certainly, this imagery of the potter conjures up allusions to Jeremiah's vision of the potter (Jer 18:1–17). Whether Paul is intending to draw a parallel is uncertain; it is altogether possible that Paul was quite familiar with Jeremiah's vision.

If indeed Paul is alluding to Jeremiah's vision, it enables yet another nuance to his thinking on honor and dishonor in terms of God's election in forming a vessel. For example, one should note that the potter in Jeremiah's vision was able to "remake" a marred vessel that the potter himself had marred. That is, the implication here is that a marred vessel was intended to be marred, and then of course is noted to be held within the grasp of the potter. The word *shacath* is used by Jeremiah to describe the vessel as made by the potter. This word is first used in Genesis 6:11–12 to connote the corruption that precipitated the worldwide destruction of the flood. Humankind was *shacath*, corrupted and marred and fitted for destruction, with Noah as an exception to carry on the covenant promises of God.[6]

The Psalms have a collection of *shacath* sayings appealing to God for mercy so that He will not destroy (see Pss 57–59, 75). The "Destroy Not" title of these hymns may have been a singular tune that was superimposed upon the text of these psalms and sung as a form of prayer and liturgy.[7] It appears from Jeremiah's vision that God's mercy can triumph microcosmically over judgment. There is likely no other example as familiar as Nineveh that illustrates this point. God relented His judgment upon a people elected for judgment in response to their repentance to Jonah's message. However, we find that Nineveh was still destroyed generations later in fulfillment of God's original decree. The Potter is able to remake or refit a certain lump of clay (see Jer 18:4). He responds to repentance and thus can reassign a clay from destruction to life when repentance is fulfilled. Is not this the call in Jeremiah 18? Is it not that Israel would repent, turn from idolatrous vanity, and turn back to the "snow of Lebanon"?

Jeremiah 18:7 appears to correlate to the vessel made to be marred, and indicates a nation destined to plucked up, pulled down, and destroyed. The vessel that was remade appears to correlate to the nation that is built and planted (see Jer 18:9). The impetus of this remaking phenomenon is centered on repentance and return. This implies that humankind plays a role in its elected destiny through the means of repentance. The vision of the potter is yet another prophetic illustration of this quintessential call for God's people to return to Him.

The people's response to this vision yet again provides further nuance when considering election and honor. They respond, "But they say, 'It is no use! We will follow our own plans, and each of us will act according to the stubbornness of our evil will'" (Jer 18:12).

Hopelessness is an antithesis of kingdom virtue that mitigates genuine repentance. Hopelessness appears to also facilitate the hardening of a vessel into a state of dishonor. Hopelessness is often assessed

---

6. Zodhiates, *Key Word Study Bible*, 1667.
7. Zodhiates, *Key Word Study Bible*, 1667.

as a risk factor for suicide, as one who has no hope can often entertain a desire to end one's life. Hopelessness leads to a kind of single path whereby one becomes rigid and unable to see that there may be other ways, other options, or other solutions. Hopelessness hardens the heart. Hopelessness solidifies in a sense what may have been the beginning of a vessel of dishonor. I would like to argue that when one includes Jeremiah's vision with Paul's allusion to a lump of clay in Romans, together with his discussion on vessels of honor and dishonor to Timothy, we participate in election through the positive means of repentance and the negative means of hopelessness. These human responses provoke God's responses to the human vessel most obviously in a microcosmic fashion. How these human responses may affect God's macrocosmic election is yet another debate not intended for our time here. I would argue that in many ways, macrocosmic election remains a mystery.

Hope, Repentance, Election, and Honor

The verb *ya'ash* is used only six times in the Old Testament scriptures and is usually rendered "to despair" or "abandon."[8] The first use is by David, who describes Saul's *abandoning* the search for David if he were to flee to the land of the Philistines (see 1 Sam 27:1).

The second use is by Job, who describes his condition as *ya'ash* or desperate, abandoned, hopeless when describing his own state as the wind (see Job 6:26). This is a curious example, as Job does not agree with his friends' argument that he had somehow sinned, but relentlessly and doggedly adheres to and defends his righteousness. And yet, he describes his situation with despair. It is as if Job represents a paradox, one who both hopes and despairs. He hopes that he will not bow to the lie of his friends and yet despairs that he may be beyond recovery. Hope and despair can exist concomitantly, even if quite ironically.

The third use is by Solomon in Ecclesiastes when he despairs that his lifelong work and legacy will be given to another at the point of his death. He despairs that he cannot control the choices of this future steward and wonders if his legacy will be unraveled in the context of foolishness (see Eccl 2:20). He causes his heart to despair, which is a precipitating cognitive state to conclude that all is vanity and even concludes that this passing of leadership to someone else can be a great evil (see Eccl 2:21).

---

8. Zodhiates, *Key Word Study Bible*, 1617.

Pastor Brad often has entertained the temptation to envision his tenure as a practice in vanity. That is, most of all the investment and toil over a five-year period had been undone by the determinate counsel of the church board and ensuing pastor. When he thinks of this, he often extends his hands to heaven and asks the universal existential question, "Why, God? Why would You send me to a people who would reject me after only five years? Why would You send me with a revival mandate, only to see it overturned by competing visions of people with greater influence? Why would I work so immensely for a counseling center, sacramental community, and community missions, just to see it dissolve and fizzle within months of my departure? Why did I become the brunt of slander, opposition, and animosity? What good ever became of my time as pastor?"

But in time, within the context of quiet prayer, he is moved to individuals whose hearts were changed. He thinks of the counseling interns who matriculated through their internship through the ministry of the church. He thinks of the men and women called to ministry who were able to obtain their credentials with his encouragement and weekly meetings to explore the heart and vision of ministry. He thinks of the prayers that do not go unnoticed by our Father, who bottles up the tears of intercession for a timely outpouring of revival upon the land (see Ps 56:8). He thinks of one soul who heard quite audibly the Lord provoke him to lay down his life of drugs, sex, and hedonism and find Christ, and who quite serendipitously stood up in service to march to the altar to receive Christ. He thinks of a small group of Vietnamese Christians who began receiving the baptism of the Holy Spirit and who, without speaking English, could sense a type of belonging among the fellowship, to grow in the work of the Holy Spirit. He thinks of the souls saved in a poor town of Africa, perhaps forgotten by the world but remembered by God. He thinks of the hours working as a counselor to serve with great joy those who were suffering. He remembers the look on their faces when that evening thousands responded to the invitation to receive Christ. He thinks of his children experiencing the Eucharist, Seder supper, and foot-washing in a way that he had never imagined was possible when he was a child. He thinks of the pastors he counseled who experienced emotional recovery to be the shepherds God called them to be. He remembers the tears shed, the joy of laughter, the human interactions that make life so rich, the initial obedience to respond to the call, and the comfort of the Holy Spirit to hold him in grief.

It is those remembrances that hold back the waves of despair that seek to penetrate his soul. Every pastor, and in particular, those who have transitioned, would do well to erect stones of remembrance of lives and relationships rather than programs or events to keep the spark of hope alive in his or her heart.

The fourth example is used by Isaiah in a scathing rebuke of Israel for their idolatry. He likens the people to a harlot who seeks the nudity of other nations, kings, and customs. He reveals that by seeking to prostitute themselves, they have denigrated their previous covenant with Yahweh and sought another covenant with idols of stone, infanticide, sexual perversion, and sorceries of all kinds. He employs *ya'ash* in a positive light, emphasizing that the children of Israel ought to have explicated that there is no hope in idols. In contrast, rather than awakening to the despair of idolatry, they found their livelihood in hell, a stone that they could hold to debase their souls (see Isa 57:9–10).

The fifth example of *ya'ash* is found in Jeremiah and is quite like Isaiah's use. He utilizes a metaphor stating that Israel is akin to a wild donkey following the pleasure of an aroma when in heat no matter the sinister source of the odor. The donkey turns no lover away and Israel has sought lovers in stones and trees, and likewise will turn no lover away, no matter how foreign, false, and fickle. Jeremiah goes on to lament, "But you said, 'It is no use, for I have loved strangers, and after them I will go'" (Jer 2:25).

Despair is a prototype for idolatry and an obstacle to repentance. One ceases in *metanoia* just as the turn is beginning to occur when despair enters the soul. So, one throws his or her hands to oblivion and decides that idolatry is the path of least resistance. Like a donkey in heat, one seeks out lovers without discretion.

The final example of *ya'ash* is the exposition of Jeremiah's vision at the potter's house. Jeremiah again laments in the context of Israel's despair, "But they say, 'It is no use! We will follow our own plans, and each of us will act according to the stubbornness of our evil will'" (Jer 18:12). The potter has made a pot fitted for destruction, a vessel that has been marred and tainted by incessant idolatry. We can see the parallel between Jeremiah 18:4 and 18:11. Israel has been destined for destruction, a vessel of dishonor, having itself participated in its own election unto judgment. Jeremiah 18:12 provides an opportunity for the potter to remake the vessel into one of honor, but the response further legitimizes the marring of the vessel and thus the destiny, as illustrated by the final word of the Lord,

"I will scatter them before the enemy. I will show them my back, not my face, in the day of their calamity" (Jer 18:17).

Therefore, what I have attempted to show through a small scriptural excursus is that a vessel of dishonor or honor is primarily identified by his or her words or speech. Out of the heart, the mouth speaks (see Matt 12:34). And so, a vessel of honor speaks from a pure heart, while a vessel of dishonor speaks from a hardened heart. The hardening of the heart is a divine action that hinges on the personal response to God's message. If repentance is the response, the heart is softened, and the vessel is well on its way to being one of honor. If hopelessness manifested as defiance is the response, the vessel is well on its way to being one of dishonor and fitted for calamity.

Election, Mercy, and Honor

But there is more to Paul's premise of election as illustrated by the pottery metaphor. Election is inextricably wedded to God's mercy. Karl Barth provides greater nuance and clarity to honor and dishonor within the rubric of God's mercy when he states,

> In these ways of his—as they have been realized and revealed in the history of Israel—he is free and has the right to make and to use vessels of honor and vessels of dishonor i.e, to raise and to introduce witnesses to the fulfillment of his divine purpose and witnesses to human incapacity as regards to this purpose.[9]

God's mercy and divine will makes use of both honor and dishonor to accomplish His purposes upon the earth (see Rom 9:15, 18).[10] On one hand, the vessels of honor display God's mercy in purity, and on the other hand, the vessels of dishonor accomplish God's mercy in depravity. Both are displays of God's mercy, one that illustrates the splendor of God's grace at work in a yielded vessel, the other to illustrate the utter need and desperation of humanity for a Savior at work in a defiant vessel. Israel needed

---

9. Barth, *Shorter Commentary on Romans*, 74.

10. See Barth, *Shorter Commentary on Romans*, 74, where he asserts that Paul's rhetorical polemic to the question in Romans 9:19 is predicated on his thesis in 9:15, one of God's mercy. He states, "He spoke of the right of God's mercy, and that is why the expression is as it is expressed in the counter-question in 9:20, 'O man, who are you to remonstrate with God?' For you are the man, Paul wants to say, who as the object of God's mercy, are not at all in the position—you have no voice and no word—to ask God whether he has reason to find fault with you."

Pharaoh for the miracles to ensue. Pharaoh is the *prima facie* of a hardened heart and thus a vessel of dishonor. Without Pharaoh and arguably the pharaohs that follow, humankind is forever tempted to build its towers of Babel. Even the vessels of dishonor in our churches help all to become aware of their own sinfulness and to come to the acute realization that all our righteousness is like filthy rags before our Sovereign.

Vessels of dishonor are destined and present in every congregation to illustrate God's mercy and our depravity, and to move us corporately into an impulse of repentance. Barth also is aware of the *reductio absurdium* Paul raises when he cites the question of human pride, which states that one cannot resist God's will if God has indeed predestined that he/she be a vessel of dishonor. This question, as Barth rightly asserts, "Desires to turn the shield with which God protects us into a shield for us to protect ourselves from God, from God's goodness."[11]

I once remember sitting in a theology class with Dr. Hollis Gause, and he made a statement that has ever since prodded my own secure reflections. His thesis was that God, as love, cannot act in any other way as this is His essence and substance. So even in hell, God's love is manifest and present in the form of judgment. Now, I am not sure if this was taken from Barth, but it sounds like a statement that perhaps Barth would make, and he does so here to help us understand that election, honor, and dishonor are predicated on God's mercy. Mercy and miracles are the manifestation of both honor and dishonor, and God in His wisdom can make good use of both to display His wonders. When we question God's mercy, it is not to get one over on God, but it is to justify our dishonor, sinfulness, and wickedness so that we need not be accountable to Him. God's shield of mercy we distort into our shield to rhetorically justify our frailty and, worse, to glorify it.

Indeed, one could argue that the question in Romans 9:19 originates from the evil one, who seeks to deceive humanity into hopeless depravity. For in the question is imbedded a resistance to the hope of repentance. Indeed, even if the vessel is one of dishonor, and one who accentuates human impotence, it does not abrogate him or her from responding to the honorable witnesses of God, to join the unified anthem underscoring God's mercy. Barth rightly asserts this as well:

> It does not permit him [Pharaoh] to play off the divine negation under which he stands against the divine affirmation that is

---

11. Barth, *Shorter Commentary on Romans*, 74.

after all put before him by the existence of the positive witnesses of God's goodness—as was done, for instance, by Moses, before Pharaoh, right to the end.[12]

The central theme of mercy continues through Paul's diatribe on vessels of honor and dishonor, vessels of mercy and hardening. He endures the vessels of wrath, delaying such wrath for the express purpose of showing His glory through the vessels of honor (see Rom 9:22–23). God's glory is His and cannot be shared. He has elected that this glory be revealed not only directly through vessels of honor, but also indirectly through his enduring patience with the vessels of dishonor and wrath. Even here His great mercy is on display. The fact that vessels of dishonor remain, disrupting our congregational life, persecuting God's servants, and assassinating the character of His vessels, is because of His mercy! God's mercy is beyond finding out; it is extravagant and mysterious. His mercy endures, is new, is manifest one way in one situation and yet another way in an altogether different situation, but it is mercy nonetheless.

His wrath is deferred, delayed, purposefully put on hold for His glory to be revealed. The children of Israel remained in bondage for four hundred years. Was this not the delay of wrath upon the vessels of dishonor, an incredible breadth of opportunity for the Egyptian dynasties to repent? And yet, in the fullness of time, God's wrath was rendered upon the oppressive system of Egypt, the vessels of dishonor. Pharaoh is as much a display of God's mercy as Moses. It is the very endurance of dishonor that leads to the revelation of His glory in vessels of honor (see Rom 9:23).[13]

C. K. Barrret notes this as well in his commentary on Romans when he states, "Pharaoh is regarded as standing within God's purpose, which is a purpose of mercy. His place in it may be an ignoble one, but it is within and not outside it."[14]

Barth and Barrett are writing within the same thread of thought and act as an amen to one another. Pharaoh's no is one that aligns with God's mercy just as Moses' yes also aligns with God's mercy. Both the obstinate no and yielded yes stand in the sphere of election as distinct but teleological manifestations of God's mercy. The aim of both the "yes" and "no," though contradistinctive, find the same aim in historical

---

12. Barth, *Shorter Commentary on Romans*, 74.
13. Barth, *Shorter Commentary on Romans*, 75.
14. Barrett, *Commentary on the Epistle to the Romans*, 188.

redemption. God can endure the no so that the yes can display the splendor of His glory. Indeed, it is the yes that becomes more emphatic in the context of a stronger no. The greater the force of obstinance, the greater the magnitude of God's glory in the yes.

The Old Testament writers are keen to use the word *kabed* for the description of Pharaoh's heart and this begs greater exploration in understanding the hardened heart as a primary attribute of a vessel of dishonor. The word essentially refers to a heaviness, so that a literal rendering would be that "Pharaoh's heart was heavy." This heaviness is used in the Old Testament to confer a dysfunction of sorts, that is, a mitigating factor in reception from outside stimuli or appeal. For example: the heavy (*kabed*) tongue stammers and stutters (see Exod 4:10); the heavy (*kabed*) ear is unable to hear (see Isa 6:9–10); the heavy (*kabed*) eye cannot see (see Gen 38:10). In this way, the Old Testament understanding of the heart can be envisioned as an organ of reception that when heavy (*kabed*) is dysfunctional to the extent that it is unable to sense or receive signals or messages from an outside source.[15]

In this sense, we might understand a heavy (*kabed*) heart as a mental state that entertains internal narratives alone. The internal narratives may be distorted but become the only truth that one can perceive or adopt. Perhaps Pharaoh's internal narrative of self-divinity was an entrenched cognition, further concretized when challenged as his mental state was heavy and unable to receive outside stimuli or alternative narratives. Pharaoh's ambivalence may also give us insight into a soul who receives the signs of God with an initial change of heart, but who quickly reverts to an old script. The signals from God Himself are as seeds that fall to the wayside, without fertile ground from which repentance can spring.

And yet the hardening of Pharaoh's heart takes on a greater nuance in Old Testament literature as *kabed* is not the only construct to describe the hardening motif. The word *hazag* is also used, adding yet another variance to the story. The word has come to be used in both a positive and negative sense. The literal rendering is "to be firm" or "strong" (see Judg 7:11). Other scriptural narratives have employed the word to connote courage (as in Deut 31: 6, 7, 23). The *hazag* heart is unswerving, steadfast, resistant to change, and unmoving. In a positive manner, it is used to describe the faithful adherent to Yahweh (see Ps 27:14). In another way, it

---

15. See Wilson, "Hardening of Pharaoh's Heart," 22, for his discussion on a definition for *kabed*.

can be used to describe the stubbornness of one to relent to the signs and messages of Yahweh (see Ezek 2:3–4).[16]

Therefore, the hardening of one's heart can indicate that one's heart, like an organ that ceases to respond to outside signals, has either an inability or an inhibited ability to respond to God's outside messages. As a result, the hardened heart becomes inculcated in its own perception and internal narratives, becoming immovable. This is a heart that is unable to receive a counterargument. The constructed schema has become impenetrable to other possibilities, even divine ones.

A church board member called Pastor Marcus and stated she would like to "clear the air" between them. Pastor Marcus received this invitation as a possibility for a moment of reconciliation. However, he was disheartened with a surprise assault of grievances she listed, one after the next, without adequate space given for him to address these grievances. As soon as he began to provide a different perspective, she quickly turned to the next grievance that she had accumulated over two years. Because she had conceived these perspectives as the only possible explanation, she was sure that Pastor Marcus had no integrity, that he had manipulated certain hires, that he was attempting to destroy the church, and that he should have been sued in litigation because of the method in which he hired. With each example, Pastor Marcus attempted to provide greater nuance to her conclusions concerning the history, of which she did not participate, and his intentions within these examples that she was providing. However, in the end, she would hear none of these. The result was an hour of constant accusation and desire to confirm her suspicions concerning Pastor Marcus by cutting off his explanations as a means to validate that her resignation from the board was an ethical call to action because of a corrupt pastor.

In the end, it appears that her "clearing the air" was in truth a desire to justify her distorted conclusions about Pastor Marcus so that her departure could be seen as a righteous one. There is little doubt that she had consorted with disgruntled staff members in order to draw her conclusions without any real consideration of Pastor Marcus's explanations of these events. However, one who has hardened one's heart to a unilateral

---

16. See Wilson, "Hardening of Pharaoh's Heart," 23, for his discussion on the rendering of *hazag*. Moreover, he notes that there is still yet another term to describe the hardening motif of Pharaoh. The term *qasa* is yet another way to describe a hardened heart, which most often is translated "stubbornness."

view of any situation has difficulty receiving any messages that may contradict such internal schemas.

Now, herein lies the rub for pastors. Do you find your heart hardening to other perspectives? Do you find the wounds accumulating to the degree that you cannot tolerate a different perspective, a nuance, and narrative that may assist in making your own narrative more beautiful and perhaps more comprehensive?

The temptation is for your heart to become heavy because you yourself have encountered so many heavy hearts in your congregation. Perhaps your staff has also undermined your authority and you double down with a hardness that becomes a wall of stone. Your internal schemas become immovable and an "only way" motif develops that prevents your own heart from outside messages, even divine ones. The great temptation of every pastor is to overreact to resistance, in particular sinister resistance, so that all suggestions are overlooked, all helpful nuances to a vision are shut down, and all community and true friendships are suspected. Pastors, purge yourselves of the things that turn your heart to stone. Quiet your heart once more to hear the message of God for you, the embrace of God loving you, and the face of God shining upon you!

We must acquiesce to the thought that it was Yahweh that hardened Pharaoh's heart (see Exod 4:21), and that this hardening mysteriously placed Pharaoh within God's elective mercy (see Rom 9). However, we also have raised a polemic that there is human participation in God's election. Paul exhorts Timothy to become a vessel of honor by purging himself of the contents within vessels of dishonor (2 Tim 2:21). I have also sought to argue that Pharaoh is a prototype of a vessel of dishonor, with other future ignoble vessels following in the same spirit, such as Alexander, Hermogenes, and Phygellus. I would like to explore more fully the precursors for Pharaoh that created a context for the heaviness of his own heart. Perhaps this exploration will help us as pastors to reject such signs and precursors that could lead to our own heaviness of heart.

Harbingers of a Hardened Heart

We find the first harbinger of Pharaoh's hardening was likely the wound of an invasion. In Exodus 1:8, we find that a new king had come into power over Egypt. The statement "who did not know Joseph" is also key here to a beginning of corrupt discourse and journey. It is quite possible that this indicated the invasion of the Hyksos people into Egypt. The phrase "arose over Egypt" could also be easily translated "arose against Egypt," which thus could be a literary allusion to this invasion and hostile takeover.[17] In this case, the Pharaoh that did not know Joseph was a Hyksos king who subjugated the Israelites to great bondage, fearing their numbers would undermine their recent authority in the region.

Another theory is that the Hyksos reigned in Egypt for approximately 150 years (i.e., 1730–1570 BC). At the end of this reign, a new line of Egyptian natives had driven out the Hyksos, establishing Ahmose I as a new dynasty, who also may have been the Pharaoh that did not know Joseph. If this theory is accurate, the Hyksos would likely have treated the Israelites with kindness as they themselves were also foreigners in a land that they had ironically come to reign.[18]

In the latter case, one of the possible precipitants to a hardened heart is a suspicion of aliens, immigrants, foreigners, and "others." This suspicion of the other can be skewed as a threat to self-preservation and a dissolution to identity. Perhaps it was Ahmose who wanted to consolidate his reign by oppressing any non-Egyptian to protect against a future takeover, as was the plight when the Hyksos invaded Egypt.

This overreaction to preservation can have oppressive consequences. When we suspect an outsider, one who may have a different vision, culture, or perspective than what the collective identity has become accustomed to, the church can exclude from membership the one seeking access from the outside. Moreover, the tighter we hold on to our collective past criteria for membership, the greater the heaviness of our hearts to reject anything new.

Moreover, this heaviness of heart seems to me to also result from fear—fear that I will be oppressed, fear that I will be rejected, fear that my identity will be lost. This fear of rejection often leads unknowingly to rejecting others. Perhaps this is done unaware, outside the realm of consciousness, so that one rejects in the name of preservation when one is really rejecting out of fear that he or she might be rejected or even feels rejected in the moment. Fear is a strong emotion that can lead the heart on a trajectory of *kabed*. Perhaps this is why the only antidote to fear has been divinely constructed as perfect love (see 1 John 4:18).

---

17. See Zodhiates, *Kew Word Study Bible*, 78, for an alternative translation of Exodus 1:8.

18. Free, *Archeology and Bible History*, 77.

Walter Brueggemann writes of exclusivism but in a way that has one reflect on the power of Sabbath, which is the collective gathering of the community for worship and the cessation of all work. He also notes the exclusivism that Israel executes not long after leaving Egypt. Again, there is a strong effort to preserve one's identity and to prevent yet another epoch of oppression and bondage. Moses provides a short litany of community membership in Deuteronomy 23:1–8. What is interesting to note here is the treatment of Egyptians. One would suspect that the fear of being held in bondage by Egypt would prompt Moses and the entire community to exclude such persons from Israelite identity on the grounds of preservation and protection.[19] But listen intently once again to the instruction:

> You shall not abhor any of the Edomites, for they are your kin. You shall not abhor any of the Egyptians, because you were an alien residing in their land. The children of the third generation that are born to them may come into the assembly of the LORD. (Deut 23:7–8)

The criteria for Egyptian inclusion are based on an ironic formula of Israelite otherness in the land of Egypt. And yet, there remains still a component of exclusion as there is a delay in membership inclusion. So, it becomes a policy of both exclusion and inclusion. The legal code has imbedded within it a certain jurisprudence of remembrance. By including the Egyptians, Israel is to remember their own otherness. And what if this is the central gestalt of membership? What if we are to include the other not only as a means of transforming the other soul into a son or daughter of God, but also to remind the ones already included of their own hearts of destitution, their own *otherness*—that they were also once excluded on the grounds of their own sin and *lostness*. Inclusivity breeds self-reflection and allows us to recall our former slavery and our constant need for a Savior.

Perhaps this is why Isaiah adds to this tension of exclusivity vs. inclusivity by broadening the brush of inclusion with the following:

> Do not let the foreigner joined to the LORD say,
> "The LORD will surely separate me from his people,"
> and do not let the eunuch say,
> "I am just a dry tree."

---

19. See Brueggemann, *Sabbath as Resistance*, 46–57, for a discussion on Sabbath as resistance to exclusivism.

> For thus says the Lord:
> To the eunuchs who keep my Sabbaths,
> who choose the things that please me
> and hold fast my covenant,
> I will give, in my house and within my walls,
> a monument and a name
> better than sons and daughters;
> I will give them an everlasting name
> that shall not be cut off.
>
> And the foreigners who join themselves to the Lord,
> to minister to him, to love the name of the Lord,
> and to be his servants,
> all who keep the Sabbath and do not profane it
> and hold fast my covenant— (Isa 56:3–6)

Israel was faced with the same dilemma of membership after the Babylonian captivity as when they were freed from Egypt. Isaiah inserts his prophetic impetus into the debate of membership criteria. Brueggemann also notes the parallel and juxtaposition of both times within the spiritual history of Israel. He is keen to note that the criteria in Isaiah is distilled to Sabbath and covenant keeping, whereas in Moses the criteria is more specific. However, if we note the inclusion of eunuchs, the promise is quite remarkable. Eunuchs are not only included, but they are given a name and a home, "better than that of sons and daughters." Now, this is radical inclusion and unexpected. I would imagine some bristling of the Israelite community in response to Isaiah's prophetic utterance.

I would also imagine an eruption of tears from a eunuch listening intently to Isaiah's message, for it is proleptic of the gospel. For a eunuch has no tangible means of preserving a posterity unto himself or the leaving of a legacy to his children. That he would have a name and a house within the framework of Yahweh's enduring community is a profound decree with enormous possibilities. One could argue that a legacy is created from what was no legacy at all. The unaccepted becomes accepted, the inadmissible is admitted, and the fruit that enables admission is Sabbath keeping and covenant embracing. As Brueggeman notes,

> The community welcomes members of any race or nation, any gender or social condition, so long that a person is defined by

justice, mercy, compassion, and not competition, achievement, production, or acquisition.[20]

Thus, I would like to further this proposition that an unresponsive heart begins with the seed of suspicion. A hardening is birthed by suspecting others as being sinister in their intentions. The seed of suspicion then conceives fear, which leans into developing systems of oppression meant to keep one's identity through the exclusion of all "outside" threats by any means necessary. The hardening of a heart is a synergistic participation, involving the divine election of God in creating a vessel of dishonor with a heavy heart, but also one in which the individual fully participates in his or her dishonorable disposition, not as outside but still inside God's covenant community, to further perpetuate His mercy and redemption in an ironic sense.[21] What a paradox that God can make and use vessels of dishonor to show His wonders!

Indeed, Israel likely could follow Paul's argument when Pharaoh is the object of dishonor, hardening, and subjection to God's wrath. But when Paul also places Israel as a community of dishonor and hardening, I can imagine the stones being grasped to reject such a message. Israel is proleptic, for in God's elective will and mercy, Israel becomes hard as a stone so that the hearts of gentiles would become ablaze for God. Indeed, perhaps God is enduring the obstinance of Israel even now for the worldwide opportunity for the Gentiles to respond to the call of God (see Rom 11)!

If we extend this to Timothy's context, the vessels of dishonor at Ephesus, namely, Phygellus, Hermogenes, and Alexander, are certainly uniquely fitted for destruction, but this destruction is deferred so that the glory of the Lord might be revealed in Timothy. Moreover, there is a participation in the molding of the vessel by the vessel itself. Timothy can "purge himself" of attributes that lead to greater hardening and thus greater dishonor (see 2 Tim 2:21). Timothy is appointed to illustrate a contrast from the vessels of dishonor for the glory of the Lord to be revealed at Ephesus. The greater the vessel of dishonor, the greater the contrast between God's kingdom and the kingdom of this world. For a summary of these harbingers of hardening, please see figure 4 below.

20. Brueggeman, *Sabbath as Resistance*, 55.

21. See the Exodus story where Pharaoh's heart is cited as being hardened twelve times (Exod 7:13–14, 22; 8:15, 32; 9:7, 12, 34–35; 10:20, 27; 11:10; 14:10). On some occasions the reference identifies Yahweh as the agent of hardening and at other times Pharaoh is identified as the agent of hardening.

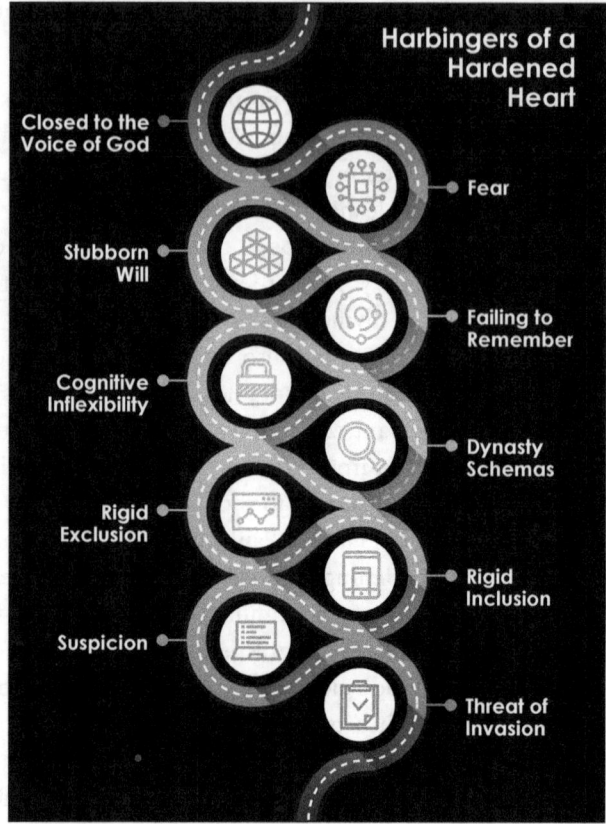

Figure4: Harbingers of a Hardened Heart

Pastors, there is a Pharaoh, Phygellus, Hermogenes, and Alexander in your congregation right now. These agents seek to oppose the vision you have for the church; they slander your reputation, leverage their influence in the church to create division, and accuse you of manipulation, feigned salvation, and demonic entertainment. They engender attempts to ruin your character in public and they oppose the truth. Pastor Marcus was surprised by some of the vessels who sought his destruction and removal in the name of their own vision for the church. And when these agents sought to coerce the vessels of honor, who refused to participate in character assassination and who supported their pastor in prayer and unity, what was a subtle contrast became quite conspicuous. Crisis has a way of revealing the noble from the ignoble, the pure from the political, the humble from the proud, the rigid from the malleable.

To illustrate further, let us explore another example with Pastor Marcus, who was pastoring a congregation for a little over five years. When budget cuts became necessary, some staff positions were eliminated. A certain member of the church had objected to the staff changes and so wrote an email to the entire leadership of the church and to Pastor Marcus's regional pastoral supervisor. And if this was not enough, the letter was also addressed to the head bishop of the entire church. The content of the letter was filled with character assassination, accusing Pastor Marcus of a lack of transparency and as such implied that he needed to be deposed as pastor. Amid staff changes, a crisis within the congregation ensued and ignoble purposes were revealed.

The intent was for Pastor Marcus's destruction. The dishonorable vessel was used of God to show us all the reality of human depravity and the need for a Savior. The question remains: What does Pastor Marcus do in this situation? Does he defend himself, remain silent, or correct the record? Moreover, this opportunity is yet another merciful example from God to reveal the heart of Pastor Marcus. For though he decided not to retaliate to preserve the reputation of this church member, he conceived all sorts of conversations or declarations in his heart. Glory be to God, who uses vessel of dishonor to reveal hearts. Pastor Marcus realized his own depravity and desperate need for a Savior. God used the vessels of dishonor in the church he was pastoring to unveil the ignoble places in his own heart so that he could repent and draw near to the blessed Savior. Perhaps in doing so, Pastor Marcus was crafted all the more into a vessel of honor.

Pastors, deal firmly with the vessels of dishonor. It is not if but when they will come to oppose the truth, your prayerful vision, your difficult decisions, and seek your destruction. As Moses with Pharaoh, be relentless in your message; do not cease to utter the refrain, "Let my people go!" However, know that when you do, their opposition will escalate to character assassination, and be prepared to weather a vitriolic storm. Trust that God is revealing the vessels of dishonor and honor within the congregation. And more importantly, He is using the vessels of dishonor to search out your own heart, to remove even the conceived seeds of dishonorable intentions. Purge yourself from the ignoble that God reveals in your own heart as He uses vessels of dishonor to perform such work. Be gentle, teach, be patient, forbearing the reproach for as long as you can with God's help. Let meekness be a virtue you embrace during your own tumult. Leave a legacy of this fruit and the vessels of honor will take it up and run with it because of your example. And in the end, if you do depart, if the tumult is tearing your family apart and you must leave for the sake of your family, know that in doing so you left a legacy akin to Paul and Timothy's legacy. Somehow, meekness is a catalyst for deliverance. In God's mystery, meekness becomes a key to the prison doors that hold the vessels of dishonor imprisoned. The devil has taken the vessels of dishonor to perform his will of division and strife and does so by continuously striking at the shepherd (see 2 Tim 2:25–26).

During Pastor Marcus's tumult, he eventually departed to protect his spouse and children against any further slander from church members. Not long after he had departed, a seasoned pastor in his state called him and congratulated him, which at first glance may seem rather odd. He clarified his congratulations by stating that Pastor Marcus had fought well and as such received his "combat boots" in the kingdom. The victory is not necessarily in the expulsion of such vessels of dishonor, although this may be God's ultimate plan as well, depending on His elective will in any congregation, but also in the way God orchestrates ignoble vessels as well to bring us to His heart!

Finally, I would like to make an attempt, albeit if only a frail attempt, to answer the question raised above as to what Pastor Marcus ought to do when faced with false accusation. One leans into the virtue of meekness. God has given meekness, in ironic fashion, as the strategy for victory. If meekness, then, is so important in standing firm against the onslaught of such vessels of dishonor, what could be said of this virtue?

Meekness as Victory over a Hardened Heart

Meekness is a cardinal virtue of ancient Near Eastern culture and a paradigm for those who live in and love their community and neighbors. Often, it is a forgotten virtue in a modern culture of self-promotion and strength. We are immersed in a culture that is forever pulling us into postures that display strength, not weakness. And although meekness may look like weakness in an external fashion, it produces fruit of great inner strength as the meek remain tame in a world that is spiraling into chaos.

Most modern definitions will render the construct for meekness (πραΰς) with terms such as "gentleness" or "humility." In some ways, this helps us remove the connotation of weakness from the disposition of meekness. In some ways, our culture can adapt to gentility and humility more readily than if we were to move toward a paradigm of weakness. At the same time, we should not always view meekness as antithesis to might. Perhaps weakness is the very path to might when viewed through the lens of the kingdom.[22]

There is a component of life where one's definition of meekness may be on greater display, and this is conflict. Conflict is inevitable in our walk, not only as Christians, but as people. Conflict is the great luminary of our character. Our responses to conflict have the potential to create frustration, bitterness, and anger. The meek have the uncanny ability to accept undesirable circumstances both actively and deliberately as a part of the larger picture of God's providence at work among them.

As the apostle Paul says on two occasions:

> By contrast, the fruit of the Spirit is love, joy, peace, patience, kindness, generosity, faithfulness, gentleness, and self-control. There is no law against such things. . . . Let us not become conceited, competing against one another, envying one another. (Gal 5:22–23, 26)

And:

> With all humility and gentleness, with patience, bearing with one another in love, making every effort to maintain the unity of the Spirit in the bond of peace. (Ephs 4:2–3)

There is no law against meekness, indeed, for the meek uphold the law and submit to authorities God has placed in the land (see Rom 13). But more than this, meekness is a catalyst for unity, peace, and perseverance. Meekness is not a passive resignation to fate, or a reluctant submission to events. Rather, meekness is the patient and hopeful endurance of trial, persecution, and difficulty where one may seem externally vulnerable and weak, but is inwardly resilient and strong. Therefore, the kingdom does not describe the meek as weak, but rather describes them as strong even as our culture continues to uphold the false virtue of self-aggrandizement and conspicuous strength.

So, meekness is really a description of the strong who are placed in a position of weakness and they persevere without giving up. Beloved, never give up! If you find yourself in a position where you feel the most vulnerable and weak, without love, support, strength, or escape—persevere! Ask God for the meekness that He gave Moses: "Now the man Moses was very humble, more so than anyone else on the face of the earth" (Num 12:3).

Jesus continues to ask us to emulate His character, which by very nature was gentle and humble in heart, as He says, "Take my yoke upon

---

22. Zodhiates, *Key Word Study Bible*, 1751.

you, and learn from me, for I am gentle and humble in heart, and you will find rest for your souls" (Matt 11:29).

To all who are weary of striving, working, ensnared with anxiety—Jesus says to us all—yoke yourself to Him, Beloved. He is gentle, meek, and humble in heart—and in joining Christ in this way, we also become like Him in character.

The definition of meekness is of course culminated in Jesus' total surrender to the cross and the laying down of His life for the sake of the world He so unceasingly loved. He entered this world in the condescension of a manger. He entered Jerusalem, gentle and riding on a donkey (Matt 21:5). He entered the Garden of Gethsemane submitting to the cup His Father had prepared for Him. He entered the cross pleading for the forgiveness of those who knew not what they were doing. He stood in the trial of accusation, and silent before his accusers. He is the one who perfectly displays the meekness of heaven. The gentle *Paschal* Lamb who surrendered to death, which is the seed of His might, will be on display as the Lion of Judah when He returns in great triumph as our King.

You may find yourself in this moment having stumbled into a vulnerable and even weak place. Pastor Marcus was in the same place, at the center of controversy and wondering how he could endure a moment where meekness was required. What if it is this very display of restraint and weakness that God plans for you, so you can better trust Him? So, trust God in the difficulty, Beloved. Believe that He is always at work behind the scenes for your benefit and for the fruit of the Spirit to be birthed in your life. Paul would boast in his weakness, knowing that God's strength was made perfect in Him (see 2 Cor 12:9). God's strength looks so very different to the strength of our culture. Thus, a vessel of honor will leave a legacy of honor through the means of meekness. Be patient, endure, and love well, and let us once again resonate with the hymnist when he writes,

> Loving Jesus, gentle Lamb,
> In Thy gracious hands I am;
> Make me, Savior, what Thou art,
> Live Thyself within my heart.[23]

---

23. Wesley, *Hymns of Worship and Service*, #458.

Chapter 7

Legacy in Perilous Times

> You must understand this, that in the last days distressing times will come. (2 Tim 3:1)

CHARLES DICKENS GIVES US an apt beginning to his novel *A Tale of Two Cities* with a description that alludes in parallel fashion to Paul's description of the last days. Dickens begins with:

> It was the best of times, it was the worst of times, it was the age of wisdom, it was the age of foolishness, it was the epoch of belief, it was the epoch of incredulity, it was the season of Light, it was the season of Darkness, it was the spring of hope, it was the winter of despair, we had everything before us, we had nothing before us, we were all going direct to Heaven, we were all going direct the other way . . .[1]

In so doing, Dickens creates the synopsis that is the tapestry for the entire tale that he is about to tell. He creates a jarring juxtaposition of characteristics inherent in the French Revolution that gives us a sense of tension. The times were perilous indeed, but Dickens, with some semblance of hope, creates an epoch narrative that will be a caricature that is timeless in describing the human condition. The human condition is to live in tension. We navigate perilous times, calamity, and deplorable conditions, and yet no matter how dark the times become, imbedded somewhere in the crevice, unbeknownst to many, is a thread of redemption.

---

1. Dickens, *Tale of Two Cities*, 1.

Dickens may be an unusual source to draw from for theological reflection, but reflect we will with an excursus into the life of Sydney Carton, a character that ultimately fulfills the dialectic of worst and best, foolishness and wisdom, incredulity and belief, darkness and light, despair and hope, hell and heaven. The character will aid us perhaps also in reflection of 2 Timothy 3:1–9 as Paul describes a perilous epoch of humanity notable as the "last days." This will hopefully culminate in a polemic for this chapter, which is a modification of Dickens: *the worst of times creates context for the best of times*. Or rather, *the worst of humanity creates opportunity for the best of humanity*.

This is the opportunity of perilous times! It is an opportunity for heroic actions of sacrifice, for greater fidelity to God's Word, for chivalrous acts of immense love, and for a forbearance that is beyond description. When peril comes—and it will—how will you react? What kind of legacy will you leave? How will your name be remembered? Sydney Carton, as we will see, has a name that is given posterity as the tale unfolds. If we were to reduce 2 Timothy 3 into such a rubric that runs parallel with Dickens, we might use the following literary structure:

A. The worst of humanity (2 Tim 3:1–9)

B. The best of humanity (2 Tim 3:10–17)

Sydney Carton begins as a representation of his time, a reign of suspicion, debauchery, and hedonism. He escapes through revelry of drink and loathes his participation in the England of post-American Revolution, or rather the world of his own making. He gives intimation to this when intoxicated with wine and is rather impulsive with his honest remarks: "As to me, the greatest desire I have, is to forget that I belong to it (the terrestrial scheme). It has no good in it for me—except wine like this—nor I for it."[2]

Carton is insolent and bitter in his disposition. He considers his work as a lawyer a game and life, whether sentenced to death or freedom, a frivolous pawn in the scheme of a vain and meaningless world. Carton dines with Darnay, a prisoner that he has aided to acquit by being his legal counsel in cooperation with his partner, Stryver. As Carton becomes more and more intoxicated with the newly freed prisoner before him, he seems to become more honest with his feelings. He gives a remark that seems to illustrate the perilous times the apostle Paul

---

2. Dickens, *Tale of Two Cities*, 83.

speaks of: "I am a disappointed drudge, sir. I care for no man on earth, and no man on earth cares for me."[3]

Carton is vulnerable with Darnay in a state of disinhibition. Perhaps it is because Darnay illustrates what Carton is not. Perhaps it is because in physical stature and likeness Darnay very much resembles Carton, but in virtue and character they are diametrically opposed. Carton suggests this when reflecting on himself: "A good reason for taking to a man, that he shows you what you have fallen away from, and what you might have been!"[4]

Carton goes on to describe Darnay as having won to some degree the affections of a bright young maiden by the name Lucille Mannette. He then gives a last word before he passes out in a drunken stupor: "Come on, and have it out in plain words! You hate the fellow."[5]

I would like to advance the polemic that perilous times illustrate a type of humanity that typifies a secondary affect of self-love but with a primary affect of self-loathing. Paul describes the perilous times as men who are "lovers of themselves" (2 Tim 3:2). But what if this love of self is a compensation for how a man or woman hates the self? The ego is fragile in this regard, thus propped up by self-adulation, and the pain coped with by drunkenness of all sorts. Carton cares for no one else because he does not care for himself. He projects hatred for himself, status, position, and disposition upon others. Finding another soul of virtue is only a painful reminder of the potential for himself, and the fact that he does not live a life of honest and respectable affection. Thus, night after night, drunkenness helps him forget how much he hates himself. If he can hate someone else (i.e., Darnay), then perhaps he will hate himself less, and indeed continue to live a false love for himself that is shallow and feigned.

Paul begins by placing Timothy in the context of what will become a degradation of humanity. Furthermore, there seems to be a double entendre in the "last days" comment that serves as our introduction. For it appears that Paul warns of something that Timothy will face in his lifetime with a future view also in place. That is, the consummation of what follows are the "last days" just prior to the second Advent of Christ. Thus, for us to anticipate anything else other than perilous times in the last days, as we approach the second coming of Christ, is to ignore the warnings of Scripture.

3. Dickens, *Tale of Two Cities*, 84.
4. Dickens, *Tale of Two Cities*, 84.
5. Dickens, *Tale of Two Cities*, 84.

As I write, a novel coronavirus (i.e., COVID-19) is sweeping the entire world in a pandemic. Communities have shut down and isolated themselves. Unemployment has soared. There are more than one hundred thousand deaths in the US alone. A white police officer was caught on video murdering a black man he was arresting by placing his knee on the neck of the hand-cuffed and disarmed victim. This has unearthed chaos, riots, and looting. Statues are toppling, blocks of cities are being unoccupied without the rule of law, there are calls to defund the police, and the whole world seems to have searched their own souls in terms of race relations. There is a recapitulation of the civils rights era. And this can be related to what Paul writes to Timothy concerning the "last days."

Kairos Can Transform *Chronos*

Paul uses what I believe is an intentional emphasis on a certain kind of time when he uses the Greek καιρός (*kairos*) to describe the "last days." There are two words in the Greek that describe time, one being χρόνος (*chronos*), the other καιρός. Chronos is used to signify a timeline or a regular interval of passing history. It is where we get the Englisih word "chronology." Thus, where used, it describes the linear passing of time. Such instances of *chronos* would be the revolution of the Earth's orbit and the regular turnover of days, weeks, months, and years.

However, where the word *kairos* is used, there is a different sense of time. The English term most similar to the Greek *kairos* might be "opportunity." That is, *kairos* is not necessarily the linear passing of time as *chronos* indicates, but rather an opportunity for the accomplishing of some task.[6] These kinds of moments beg for something to take place that can change the way *chronos* proceeds.

So, when Paul says that there will be perilous times in the last days, it is for the direct purpose of accomplishing some prophetic task. The question then remains, what kind of prophetic task? I would thus like to propose that the prophetic opportunity of perilous times is exposure (see 2 Tim 3:9). That is, the covert vulnerabilities and corruption of our human institutions become exposed in the wake of perilous times. I would argue that the means of this exposure are disarming acts of valiant love, as we will see to be the case with our case study, Sydney Carton. Love has a way of exposing our hearts and disarming our hatred.

---

6. Zodhiates, *Key Word Study Bible*, 1726.

Paul would write in the following pericope concerning hopeful endurance. The endurance of suffering, prophetic utterances, and sound teaching also are means of exposure—but all must be done in love. Perilous times can certainly create feelings of apprehension, but also provide context for the rise of love that is transformational and just might catalyze reformation.

Thus, just as Martin Luther King Jr. emerged as a voice of love one for another amid his own perilous time, the *kairos* moment is ripe for yet another voice to lay down his or her own aspiration and comfort, to act in a way that loves, preaches, teaches, and models a kingdom ethic that foils the Jannes and Jambres of our day! For indeed, there are many who are throwing their staffs in the ring to become serpents and who are practicing enchantments to deceive the populace.

The warning has been issued, and we should note that this is not the first time Timothy has heard this warning from Paul, and the warning is repeated so that we as Timothy feel the full force and gravity of the prophetic situation. In 1 Timothy we hear of a similar refrain: "Now the Spirit expressly says that in later times some will renounce the faith by paying attention to deceitful spirits and teachings of demons . . ." (1 Tim 4:1).

The warning is for the believer. The Spirit confirmed to Paul and Timothy that some will depart from the faith in the latter times (*kairos*). They will believe the narrative and doctrines of demons. This narrative elevates happiness over holiness, self over God, and creature worship over worship of the Creator.

We are warned so that we do not fall ourselves. In the last days, there will be a doubt concerning the return of Christ. Some, if not many, will scoff at the faithful who look forward to his coming. Listen to the prophecy in 2 Peter:

> First of all you must understand this, that in the last days scoffers will come, scoffing and indulging their own lusts and saying, "Where is the promise of his coming? For ever since our ancestors died, all things continue as they were from the beginning of creation! (2 Pet 3:3–4)

So, we have the scoffers, who chase their own diverse lusts led from anticipation of our Lord to making themselves lords. They see the *chronos* of time continuing without interruption. However, what may be indiscernible to the scoffers is this: there is a *kairos* coming, an opportunity for an interruption in *chronos*. Peter continues by saying it like this: "The Lord is not slow about his promise, as some think of slowness, but is patient with you, not wanting any to perish but all to come to repentance" (2 Pet 3:9).

Thus, *kairos* is one opportunity following another, all like the movement of a great symphony arriving at its finale in the second coming of Jesus Christ. Within the ever-escalating movements are tender mercies of God granting space for repentance, for the salvation of all who turn from darkness to light. Perilous times come time and again for the opportunity for exposure through mighty acts of love.

The perilous times are present for the sinner to repent. The perilous times are couched into *chronos* so that people will see the frailty and ineptitude of humanity and look to the very present Help in time of trouble (see Ps 46:1). When all is perilous and society is altogether evil and wicked, there is a hope, and that hope lies upon the bedrock of the resurrection for it is the sign that He is coming back. Jesus is coming again. He is coming and beckoning His saints to travail for redemption on the earth. Do not miss the opportunity of perilous times—for it is an opportunity for us in this very hour!

Even when peril enters the church, it is an opportunity for the pastor. The opportunity affords travail; the travail anticipates the coming of Jesus. Perhaps peril has come to you, pastor, as a mechanism to heighten your awareness of the second coming of the Lord. Perhaps it is for you to preach concerning the return of Christ; perhaps it is to believe that His return is imminent; perhaps it is for you to expose the wickedness behind closed doors; perhaps it is to dig a hole in the wall to learn of vile idolatry (see Ezek 8:8). Perhaps it is for you, in your seeming exile to Patmos, to behold the Lord in all His glory and find a renewed eschatological fervor. Peril also has its merits if we choose to seek them out. *Kairos* is the opportunity for the pastor to peer into the grander future of a better society, to have a holy discontentment of the now and preach the people forward in God's kingdom.

It is here where Paul decisively acts to provide a litany of adjectives to describe the nature of the degradation that will happen to humanity in the last days. First, there are attributes that describe the human's obsession with the self. That is, there will be an elevation of pride and diminishing of humility. Boasting will be praised. What may have been deemed confidence will be replaced with shameless self-aggrandizement. These efforts, I imagine, are the smoke screen endeavors of a self-loathing generation.

Second, there will be a loss of virtue and holiness. A people who are implacable, refusing to halt hostilities. Truce-breakers and ones who derive joy from stoking the flames of irreconciliation.[7] Sexuality will be distorted. Lying will be commonplace. Good will be called evil and evil will be lauded as good.

Third, pleasure will be exalted and pursued, betrayal will be common, and a sense of entitlement will prevail. However, there is a subtle but sober warning in this litany of vices that will deceive many—the form of godliness.

The manifestation of the wicked above will not be through an obvious or conspicuous medium. No, rather, wickedness will be shrouded in a form of godliness that is devoid of power.

The travesty is that many will be deceived with this form, and not know or experience the true power of God. The Greek word όρφωσις (*morphosis*) is employed to describe form and it is how we obtain the word "morphology" or the topographical picture of a thing or person. So in this context, όρφωσις is an external form of Christian life with no inner power, the mere appearance or mask of pious conduct.[8]

This may be represented in the definition of love we entertain in our society, a love devoid of correction, devoid of discipline, and devoid of true concern for one's soul. We often forget that the Lord disciplines those He loves (see Heb 12:6).

Perilous times ought to compel us to lose the mask, to remove the form and with sincere authenticity seek the Lord in travail. We cannot be satisfied with a mere form of piety; we need true holiness! We ought not be content with something that merely appears right; we need the signs of the kingdom and the fruit of the Spirit bearing witness! I am not hungry for a form, Beloved; I am not able to continue waiting for the form to somehow correct on its own. I am hungry, ravished, and indeed desperate for the true authentic outpouring of the Holy Spirit in such a magnitude that changes *chronos* time! We need a *kairos* moment, an opportunity in peril to see the kingdom come with signs following those who believe (see Mark 17:17–18)!

---

7. Please see Trentham, *Studies in Timothy*, 122, where he defines "unforgiving," in 2 Timothy 3:3 as a word that "originally meant 'without libation or drink offering.' "It came to eventually mean 'without truce,' which was sealed by libation. Finally, it came to mean 'implacable,' 'refusing to halt hostilities.'"

8. Zodhiates, *Key Word Study Bible*, 1739.

The warning and charge are clear: turn away! But how do we turn from the insidious counterfeit to genuine godliness with power? Perhaps it is the commingling of truth with prayer! Perhaps it is our awakening that we our prayerless and thus godless; we are sinful and thus in need of a Savior! Perhaps perilous times are the very looking glass through which to see the true intent of our hearts, who curry favors with others, love luxury and comfort, and seek every opportunity to see ourselves in an article or on a screen. Wesley Duewel would describe prevailing prayer in the following manner:

> God's cause creeps forward timidly and slowly when there are more organizers than agonizers, more workers than prevailing prayer warriors. We need prayer warriors who have seen the heart of God, who have experienced the power and glory of the cross, who know the Bible meaning and significance of the day of judgment, heaven and hell. We need prayer warriors who feel the slavery, the absence of any eternal hope, and the doom of the unsaved; who feel the transforming power, joy, and glory from Christ of the saved. We need prayer warriors who pray as though God is God and as though Satan is Satan.[9]

Duewell is right not to secure the ends of prayer without first securing the means of prevailing prayer, that being the will of God upon the earth. The intercessor discerns the will of God upon the earth and prays until this breaking in from above is upon the earth. It is an offensive posture, taking the initiative to wage war, to begin the battle, to fight for the faith itself. A prevailing intercessor does not relent, does not shrink back, does not give in, does not retreat, but heads sometimes recklessly forward for the prize of the high calling. Perilous times are not without a kingdom response, that response being mighty prevailing prayer in the context of travail to the ends of apocalypse. Prayer is a means of exposure! Prayer is a noble legacy to leave in times of peril!

Later we will explore the reference to Jannes and Jambres, two figures from Pharaoh's Egypt. This reference is notable and brings us also to what preceded God's intervention through His servant Moses. God was responding to the travail of Israel. Their cries came to His ears, and He responded by sending a prophetic deliverer in the person of Moses.

Likewise, God hears the travail of those suffering amid perilous times. Perilous times create an environment of travail. Pastors, we would

---

9. Duewel, *Mighty Prevailing Prayer*, 23.

do well to call regular travail meetings in response to the peril we face in our churches and in our communities. Pastors, in perilous times model travail, weeping, and birthing pains so that deliverance becomes the fruit. Perhaps it is deliverance that comes from the ashes of calamity.

Match the number of riots we now face with the number of prayer meetings for mercy and healing. Match the toppling of statues with prayer meetings toppling the strongholds of animosity in our society. Match the number of deaths attributed to COVID-19 with the number of cries unto the Lord to look upon and heal the land. Match the number of black lives dead at the hands of hatred to the prayerful groans of a people who know no other solution to our fractured society but to call upon our Lord for healing to come to every heart who suffers!

I recall one instance where a cause for travail erupted within our congregation in response to the sorrow of lost babies through the murder of abortion. We have sacrificed so many babies on the altar of convenience (approximately sixty million babies in the US alone), and a travail erupted that consumed the congregation—this is travailing prayer!

Paul moves from adjectives to behaviors as he begins to describe the societal ramifications of human degradation. Captivity is certainly noted here in terms of sexual immorality. Thus, we see that many who perhaps are ignorant of the warnings, naïve to the truth of God's Word, or disenchanted by the perilous times may indeed fall into the trap of captivity.

This is the ignorance of a people who move from one fancy to the next, one charismatic figure to the other, heeding every whim or entreaty of such figures, but without really encountering the already-revealed truth of Christ. Perhaps Paul is prophetic in describing a fad culture and generation. Pastors also fall prey by moving from one fad to the other, hoping that at some point the fad will take hold and draw the crowds. If we can just get that speaker, or implement that program, or hold that event—the crowds are sure to come in. We are "always learning, never [able] to come to the knowledge of truth because [we] would rather flit to some new fancy than face the moral demands of the truth already revealed to [us]."[10]

---

10. See Trentham, *Studies in Timothy*, 124–25.

Freedom For vs. Freedom From

We must be careful not to enter captivity because of our desperation, but with longsuffering await the deliverance of the Lord. It was after the fallout of World War I when perilous times came to Germany, and out of the wake of that desperation a tyrant and villain was born who performed unimaginative atrocities in his time. And how could we not define the times of the Nazi regime as anything but perilous? But it was there where Dietrich Bonhoeffer discovered opportunity. For even as he would march back into Germany and there be put to death for his resistance, he paved a way for the deliverance of subsequent generations.

Thus, where there were perilous times, there was also an opportunity for Christ. Was it not Christ Himself who bound Himself to a historical point in time that was perilous and full of unrest? Bonhoeffer comments more on this when he says,

> It is a question of the freedom of God, which finds it strongest evidence precisely in that God freely chose to be bound to historical beings and to be placed at the disposal of human beings. God is not free from human beings but for them. Christ is the word of God's freedom.[11]

Now, I want us to be clear, for I think Bonhoeffer has stumbled upon something that has to do with our text. To say it another way, Christ bound himself to a place in time that was perilous in nature and there was the very source of deliverance—by being free *for* them, not being free *from* them. Bonhoeffer follows this notion by binding himself to the perilous times in his own country to bring the Christ of freedom for the people rather than being freed from them. He could have enjoyed a teaching tenure in the United States or England but chose rather to be a voice crying in the wilderness, "Prepare the way of the Lord" (see Isa 40:3; Matt 3:3; Mark 1:3; Luke 3:4).

Therefore, freedom is not being free from perilous times but being free through perilous times for our neighbor. In this way, we are inextricably bound to our neighbor. Thus, we must surrender to being disposable. This is the more painful aspect of perilous times. When we trust Christ enough to surrender to the pain that comes with perilous times, we are surrendering to freedom when we surrender to our own disposal.

---

11. Bonhoeffer quoted in Amos, *God for Now*, 85.

To return to Sydney Carton, we find that Miss Mannnette invokes a sense of affection in Carton that enables him to dream of virtue once again, even if despair remains as to its attainment. After confessing his love for Miss Mannette, who is already betrothed to Darnay, he gives the following remarks:

> I wish you to know that you have been the last dream of my soul. In my degradation I have not been so degraded but that the sight of you with your father, and of this home made such a home by you, has stirred old shadows that I thought had died out of me. Since I knew you, I have been troubled by a remorse that I thought would never reproach me again, and have heard whispers from old voices impelling me upward, that I thought were silent forever. I have had unformed ideas of striving afresh, beginning anew, shaking off sloth and sensuality, and fighting out the abandoned fight. A dream, all a dream, that ends in nothing, and leaves the sleeper where he lay down, but I wish you to know that you inspired it.[12]

Sydney Carton is experiencing a revolution within his own soul. There is an opportunity in the perilous moment of the French Revolution and growing English tensions for Carton to change course, to move upward, to fight a fight that had long been abandoned. The new inspiration comes from a love he has experienced for Miss Mannette. And yet, this love is not reciprocated —but the return of a dream still ensues. Carton is being stirred for something beyond sensuality and slothfulness. He is being stirred into valor, courage, moral resolve, and, as we will see, surrender. Love has a beautiful way of sparking light in what is a dismal landscape. Carton finds that his dream is unreachable in his mind of despair, and yet, however calamitous his own view of his future, there is something changing within. Ironically, the change comes through the medium of peril and a sense of loss.

Carton's exchange is a jarring contrast from his disposition heretofore observed in the text. His confession is complete when prior to his departure from Miss Mannette he offers the best of himself for her and for the ones she loves. Listen intently to the sacrificial language; it is perhaps Carton's Freedom Day. He is becoming free through freedom for Miss Mannette, not from Miss Mannette.

---

12. Dickens, *Tale of Two Cities*, 144.

> For you, and for any dear to you, I would do anything. If my career were of that better kind that there were any opportunity or capacity of sacrifice in it, I would embrace any sacrifice in it, I would embrace any sacrifice for you and for those dear to you. Try to hold me in your mind, at some quiet times, as ardent and sincere in this one thing . . . think now and then that there is a man who would give his life, to keep a life you love beside you![13]

A man who loathes himself and thus comes to loathe all is transformed by the pure and simple virtue of a young maiden for whom he has tender affection. The virtue of sacrifice seems to spring forth from the earthen soul seeded with love. This love is not merely romantic, but one that longs to see the lifelong good of another. Carton is indeed transformed as he is willing to sacrifice on behalf of Miss Mannette's family. He foresees a husband and children for whom he can someday labor for the preservation of her posterity and joy. Darkness may prevail for a season, but within it are rays of light that pierce even the hardest of hearts to become the most honorable of knights. This is the potential irony of perilous times; there are few who may find love and light in a shrouded epoch of humanity. This transformation will find a legacy in acts of bravery and valor. The legacy will be told and retold. Pastors, we all know and long to heed the warning of Jesus that lawlessness will arise and the hearts of many will grow cold. It is in those perilous times that your heart must be softened by the glow of love so that a legacy of endearment, the washing of feet, the service of affection, and the fruit of the kingdom may secure a legacy to be told in the shroud of darkness.

At the height of woundedness, a pastor can often wonder if he or she ought to surrender to the pain of being cast away, asked to resign, asked to leave as not a *good fit* for the church. Pastors, this is where the pain is palpable. What if you do take the risk of submitting to a people who will eventually hurt you, a people who will inflict the wounds of criticism? What would surrender like that look like? Can we retain our identity as free sons and daughters when submitting to such vitriolic storms? Do we take the risk and give ourselves to the disposal of another?

Paul goes on to describe the perilous times to Timothy. We find a time where there is much learning but inability to ascertain the truth. One would imagine that learning ought to lead one into truth, but not in the age of perilous times. During the last days, learning will rise like

---

13. Dickens, *Tale of Two Cities*, 146.

never before. Higher education will be in a golden age of *Pax Romana* and trust in the knowledge of the global scholarly network will appear to be without question.

However, the warning is this: such learning, divorced from truth, is learning divorced from the source of truth, God Himself. That is, in perilous times, one may apprehend the complex equations of planetary revolution, or the myriad wonders of medical science to cure, or the mathematical foundation of the most exquisite structure, yet miss the essential truth of all—the revelation of our Lord Jesus Christ, Himself the author and substance of truth.

This then begs the question, what is the opportunity herein? What is the *kairos* moment in a society that draws all knowledge to itself except the knowledge of the truth? I would again argue that it is imbedded in the last line of Paul's diatribe on perilous times: "their folly will be manifest to all" (2 Tim 3:9). Exposure is the end of perilous times. Love will manifest the foolishness of those who have sought power, wealth, influence, and titles with no thought of truth, love, mercy, forbearance, or justice.

Imagine that one function of perilous times is that we come to the truth that we are indeed helpless without the intervention of God Himself. What if the opportunity of captivity, the opportunity of deception, is the very manifestation of God to deliver us from such heinous traps by exposing their futility?

When you have labored through with all human ingenuity and skill to convince the world of truth, to deliver the captive to freedom, without avail, fall upon your knees, travail, and watch the deliverance of the Lord through the means of exposure!

History has shown us that God's presence is strongest when the church faces the most heinous of perilous times. Pastors, we must help the flock see the perilous times as an opportunity for a great manifestation of God's glory to expose! Remember the promise of joining Christ in weakness so that we may join Him also in His resurrection (see 2 Cor 13:4)! If He parted the Red Sea during the calamity of Egypt, who knows what He may do in the perilous times that are here and certainly coming in greater magnitude. Pharaoh's no was manifested as foolishness in the face of the plagues and completed by the crossing of the Red Sea.

Paul finally closes the section on perilous times with an interesting allusion to the sorcerers of Pharoah's court during the time of Moses. Paul's allusion is for the purpose of comparing the perilous times ahead to Pharoah's court. The comparison is made to illustrate the resistance to truth and the prophetic ministry. But it is also to illustrate the opportunity of perilous times, the opportunity of exposure, which is our polemic for perilous times.

Exposure in Perilous Times

Now, we should stop here to fully realize the comparison. That is, we have already noted that the perilous times will be an age of learning but one also of forsaking the truth. So, we should not be surprised if there is an abandoning of truth in the last days, especially in structures of higher learning. We have been warned.

However, I think Paul's allusion is also to note the resistance to the prophetic when he compares the sorcerer's attempts to withstand Moses to the resistance of the prophet and the prophetic in the latter days. Jannes and Jambres represent for us today the bidding of the principality that was behind Pharoah—the enemy of our soul, the great serpent, the devil himself. We find that manner by which Jannes and Jambres resisted Moses in Exodus 7:11: "Then Pharaoh summoned the wise men and the sorcerers, and they also, the magicians of Egypt, did the same by their secret arts."

So, we find inherent in prophetic resistance lying signs and wonders, signs quite unequivocally consumed by the Lord's manifestation. Just as Pharaoh's court resisted truth and attempted to legitimize this resistance through emulating the prophetic signs, the perilous times will do the same.

The resistance to God, to the prophetic, to the prophet, to the truth will be a movement emulating on display lying signs to maintain the status quo, keep the people blind, and squash the proliferation of truth!

It is true that Jesus died, it is true that He was raised from the dead, it is true that He sent the Comforter who is at work today, and it is true that He is coming back. We must hold to this confession, for it will be resisted and broadly affronted by a Pharaoh's court, bent on the silencing of truth and the feverish efforts to legitimize its regime. We cannot remain silent in the face of such resistance. Moses was not silent, and today we must capture His refrain once more: "Pharaoh, let my people go!"

Moses did not relent; he did not shrink back; he did not forget to ever state the same refrain, "Let my people go." And in his obedience God's glory was on display at Pharaoh's court to delegitimize the regime, humiliate its authority, and illustrate who was the true and living God!

So, what is the opportunity of perilous times? Exposure! When we stand our ground, when we, like Moses, stand in Pharaoh's court unwavering in our confession, God exposes the darkness, the folly, and the weakness of human and idolatrous powers in perilous times and shows all a better way.

Just as Jannes and Jambres were shown to be fools without true power, the one who brandishes so much of his or her knowledge, power, and authority all built upon wicked imagination will also be exposed. God will expose; He will deliver; He will make known His glory!

> The magicians tried to produce gnats by their secret arts, but they could not. There were gnats on both humans and animals.... The magicians could not stand before Moses because of the boils, for the boils afflicted the magicians as well as all the Egyptians (Exod 8:18; 9:11).

The madness of human degradation can be transformed to the soundness of human flourishing again under the auspices of unfeigned repentance and a coming to the knowledge of truth. We have an opportunity to say with Moses, "Let my people go."

And doesn't this need to be the constant refrain in our songs, liturgy, prayers, and preaching? This is the light exposing the hidden darkness of static triumphalism.[14] The freedom of God is the central tenet of the pastoral ministry, showing God to be the *solus Deo* and the gods of this age a farce. We must reappropriate the narrative of heaven, "Let my people go!" We must fear God and break free from the approval of human innovation and criticism. We must expose Pharaoh's magicians, for Jannes and Jambres very much exist in our parishes. Walter Brueggemann further comments,

> The Egyptian empire could not! The gods of Egypt could not! The scientists of the regime could not! The imperial religion was dead! The politics of oppression had failed!... [The] false claims to authority and power cannot keep their promises, which they could not in the face of the free God.[15]

14. See Brueggemann, *Prophetic Imagination*, 17, where he coins the term "static triumphalism." Brueggemann asserts that we will never understand prophetic imagination if we do not first realize that the religion of static triumphalism is wholly connected to the politics of oppression and exploitation.

15. Brueggemann, *Prophetic Imagination*, 20.

The promise of oppression is upended by the freedom of God. The rules of tyranny are nullified by the greater authority of grace. The status quo of slavery is brought to desolation by the prophetic cry of the prophet. The ruse of charm within every congregation is exposed by the rod of God. The plagues of God turn upon the enemies of His freedom as chastisement upon the empire that defies His newness, doubling down on the austerity of oppression. "Make more bricks," our enemy says, not knowing that the blood of the Lamb is even now on the doorpost of our hearts to deliver us from death. God is waiting to throw the rider and the chariot in the sea, waiting for the pastor to stand and say, "Let my people go!" Will you preach this, O servant of God? Will you do so even when ice hangs over your branches and it feels that this may be the only phrase you can utter? Will you preach this when barren, alone, rejected, and hurting? Will you take the loneliness of the wilderness, as Moses, and let it fuel the passion ever more to be a mouthpiece for our Sovereign?

As I sit here and write, I wonder about the next time I will preach, the next time the fire will find its expression, the next time that freedom will dawn in the declaration of God's everlasting truth. And just perhaps I have it wrong. Preaching is not merely a pulpit phenomenon. I preach daily to my children, my colleagues, my friends, and my acquaintances. I am already confronting Jannes and Jambres. We must all leave a legacy of exposure, transparency, and constant refrain of freedom. Leave a legacy where love is the opportunity in perilous times! Take up courage as a mantle and do not fear, lavishly sacrificing ambition and convention for the greater virtues of love and surrender.

I would like to return to our case study as a final word, the conclusion of Sydney Carton. I have argued that perilous times are cyclical seasons (*kairos*) for an opportunity to change *chronos* time through prophetic acts of truth and love. I have argued that perilous times come again and again to illustrate the futility of our regimes and institutions—to expose the corruption, injustice, and idolatry imbedded in these structures. We have looked herein at a description of the "worst" of humanity that creates context for the "best" of humanity. I would like to return to our unconventional theologian, Dickens, as a capstone statement illustrating a transformation from worst to best motivated by love in the context of peril.

Dickens begins his last chapter of his tale with a provocative lesson:

> Crush humanity out of shape once more, under similar hammers, and it will twist itself into the same tortured forms. Sow

the same seed of rapacious license and oppression over again, and it will surely yield the same fruit according to its kind.[16]

The French Revolution is in full swing; nobles are being executed by revolutionaries because of their status. Their crime was the family and status in which they were born. As nobles oppressed the poor, now the poor oppress the nobles. There is no change really. The same degradation of humanity exists under the guise of vengeance with more palatable narratives of justice, which is no justice at all. The seeds of animosity bear the same fruit, whether rich or poor, black or white, French or English, noble or common. Dickens is astute to note the same politics of oppression simply with a new name.

He goes on to illustrate a passing down, if you will, of a culture of oppression and death through federal and generational animosity for neighbor.

> Change these back again to what they were, thou powerful enchanter, Time, and they shall be seen to be the carriages of absolute monarchs, the equipages of feudal nobles, the toilettes of flaring Jezebels, the churches that are not my father's house but den of thieves, the huts of millions of starving peasants![17]

Dickens realizes the cyclical nature of perilous times and oppression. An appeal is given to time and history as the revelation of human depravity. Although Dickens does not use the term *kairos* as the apostle Paul, he illustrates the very substance of Paul's etymological force. Perilous times have come and still more are yet to come.

We are on the brink of yet another revolution in our own nation. In the name of justice and freedom, we wound one another with the same oppressive sentiment of the regime we attempt to disentangle ourselves from. A compound in Seattle has proclaimed itself autonomous from law enforcement and policing as a reaction to an unjust and heinous death at the hands of a police officer, only to have yet another killing occur within its borders. The human soul cannot be heretofore liberated from its murderous intent without a divine encounter. It is encounter with divine love and affection that destroys the internal schemas of suspicion, hatred, and power. Without the kingdom of God, we are lost. Our kingdoms are grossly insufficient in the face of God's. The den of thieves is still in operation within the framework of the politics and liturgy of oppression.

16. Dickens, *Tale of Two Cities*, 346.
17. Dickens, *Tale of Two Cities*, 346.

Carton has been able through wit and opportunity to change places with Darnay, who was imprisoned for being an emigrant of noble genealogy. He languishes in prison awaiting the guillotine. His wife, Lucille Mannette, and daughter have secured safe passage back to England. However, all are heartbroken in anticipating the pending death of a dear husband and father. This is now the prophetic opportunity in perilous times, and the vessel through whom such valor will be performed is none other than Sydney Carton. The once-drunk becomes engulfed with passion; the once apathetic and uncaring soul becomes a knight of sacrificial love and devotion.

Carton smuggles Darnay out of prison, also securing safe passage for him to England to be restored to his family. Carton takes his place in this prison, bearing a striking resemblance to Darnay. Carton will face the guillotine in Darnay's stead. Carton will make good on his oath, solemnly pledged to Lucille some ten years prior. Carton will love her and her family not as her husband, but as her brother. Carton will penetrate the peril with virtue and something redemptive will be born.

The last lines of Dickens's tale reveal that after Carton's death, Darnay and Lucille have a son. This son will carry the name Sydney, to carry a legacy of abounding affection, to remake a name for the late Sydney Carton, to be a son that Carton never had, a figure to live in the light of a path well chosen. Somehow, Carton knows this intuitively, perhaps even proleptically, just before he dies. Listen to his own narrative of this altogether redemptive component in dark times.

> I see that child who lay upon her bosom and who bore my name, a man winning his way up in that path of life which once was mine. I see him winning it so well, that my name is made illustrious there by the light of his. I see the blots I threw upon it, faded away. I see him, foremost of just judges and honoured men, bringing a boy of my name, with a forehead that I know and golden hair, to this place—then fair to look upon, with not a trace of this day's disfigurement—and I hear him tell the child my story, with a tender and faltering voice.[18]

What is the opportunity in perilous times? It is the laying down of dreams, aspirations, and even one's life in the name of virtuous, untainted, and genuine love for another. The hope was a baby birthed with the same name with an opportunity to redeem the history and legacy

---

18. Dickens, *Tale of Two Cities*, 351.

of the man whose own transformation made possible the coming of a new life, and who would carry the legacy of love to another generation. The story will be told.

Pastors, your story will be told after you have submitted to the animosity, attempted to love, and understood when stones were being thrown. Your story will be told when you have done all that your soul could withstand when enduring the slander and false accusations. Perhaps you feel like Carton, on your own way to certain demise. If so, let his story encourage your own—there is yet another baby to be born, another dream to emerge, another hope to pierce the darkness of peril. The reign of terror creates opportunity for the injection of love and hope. The darker the times, the greater the opportunity! This is the legacy you leave!

Rejoice in the departure, in the persecution, in the opportunity God gave you to persevere for a season. You leave behind stories that will continue to be iterated in the lives you have touched with the tender grace of God. And though your grave may be a metaphor and not the concrete demise of Carton, perhaps, just perhaps, God is also delivering you from the peril by bringing you to a place of rest—rest from your labors for just a time, a place for healing, a place for redemption, a place for wholeness. Perhaps the wounds of a warrior will find their balm in a new country, a new identity, where the empires of the past will no longer hold you in their grip. And as Carton, you may also say, "It is a far, far better thing that I do, than I have ever done; it is a far, far better rest that I go to than I ever have known."[19]

---

19. Dickens, *Tale of Two Cities*, 351.

Chapter 8

Legacy of Deliverance and Departure

> Now you have observed my teaching, my conduct, my aim in life, my faith, my patience, my love, my steadfastness, my persecutions, and my sufferings, the things that happened to me in Antioch, Iconium, and Lystra. What persecutions I endured! Yet the Lord rescued me from all of them. (2 Tim 3:10–11)

WHEN DOES ONE KNOW when to shake the dust from one's feet (Matt 10:14; Acts 13:51) and move to the next city? Do we receive this answer in prayer? Can we even hear clearly in the pain? Is it when a loved one is suffering from the weight of loneliness, rejection, and slander? Is it to prioritize a spouse, one's family, one's Sabbath? Is it because a "greater" opportunity came to us or because we have "taken the church as far as we can"? Is it because the church is declining? Is it when the church rejects your ministry as a majority or simply when a church board calls for your resignation?

The answer is full of nuance and complexity that has no simple solution. Pastor Jordan prayed deliberately for several months prior to his resignation. He consulted with those who loved him and those who were over him in the Lord. He and his wife fasted, prayed, and spent many sleepless nights agonizing over the decision. He waited longer than those who loved him most had advised.

Pastor Jordan first remembers submitting a reorganization plan to his pastoral coach and consultant sometime prior to submitting it to the church board. This was a radical reorganization of both personnel and budget and so he longed for counsel on the matter. He had obtained a church coach from a church-consulting organization, who had been assisting him over several months prior with team-building, organization, and staff culture motifs. He had also submitted the plan to his state supervisor and pastor and a trusted co-laborer who also pastored in another state. All did not hesitate to encourage him to submit the plan, albeit radical; it merited discussion as a way of moving the church into the next chapter. He did not receive a word of apprehension and no one conferred that he should rethink the plan. He hoped that the plan would spur them as a board to consider several possibilities for stewarding their resources well.

It was this plan that created various false accusations that he wanted to close the church. In actuality, the plan was an effort to conserve finances while allocating funding to youth and children's ministries. The plan also included the possibility of a church replant that would serve to alleviate the debt of the church by selling the building, which would allow more freedom in serving the community and the world through the financing of ministries. However, this must have been something of a sacred cow as this spurned any affections or relational equity that he had built with the church board. This led the council to redefine the narrative of the dwindling finances as a direct result of Pastor Jordan's failure to grow the church.

So, the question remains, when does one shake the dust from one's feet? When does a pastor choose to resign? And I will not be writing about the typical reasons why a pastor may resign or transition, such as what is often captured in the media as moral failure. Rather, I believe Paul's instructions to Timothy in chapter 3 of his second epistle provide some guidance on the matter.

As I have mentioned in *The Coming Winter*, Paul associates with the doctrine that he is preaching (2 Tim 3:10). By inserting the personal pronoun "my," he is indeed aligning his entire character with the gospel with which he has been entrusted. He appeals also to his manner of life, purpose in vocation, faith in prayer and in mission, and his patience, love, and longsuffering to encourage Timothy into emulating his pattern.

He then offers Timothy a reminder of the persecution he has faced in three cities. It is to these three cities that we now turn to discern the circumstances wherein we are to shake the dust from our feet as pastors.

Envy

Let us begin with Antioch. We can find the narrative of Paul's journey in Antioch in Acts 13. As was his custom, Paul and his company visited the local synagogue in the city to preach the gospel. Indeed, it was the ruler of the synagogue that first implored that Paul provide a word of exhortation (see Acts 13:15). Keep this in mind pastors, as the very leaders who call upon you to preach may later ask you to resign. It is important to be discerning in this regard. However, even in this, do not let the opportunity to preach the gospel pass. You must simply expect persecution in the work of the Lord.

Paul begins a sermon that is rooted in a Judaistic metanarrative. He invokes all the major figures of the Torah, moving quickly to the recent events of John the Baptist and Jesus Christ. He cites the Messianic Psalms as substantiation and concludes with the good news, that there is indeed forgiveness of sins in Jesus Christ. The Jews depart from the synagogue once the sermon is complete, but the gentiles seek yet another sermon from Paul. They appeal for him to return to preach the next Sabbath (see Acts 13:42).

And when the crowd was yet small and there was no garnering of influence in Antioch, the Jewish leaders of the city seemingly did not take note of this Pharisee-turned-Christian. However, when some Jews converted to the grace of Jesus Christ and when nearly the entire city came for the hearing of the word, there was a conspicuous turning of events, or should I say a turning of hearts (see Acts 13:43–45).

Now let us take note of one key reason for leaving a church: those with influence begin to envy. Envy, as I have written before, is a gangrenous sore beginning as a blemish on the soul, fed by pride that consumes the very soul of an individual until the rancor can no longer be hidden. Envy grows with a formidable force in the human heart and manifests as blasphemous words. For it is from the heart that the mouth speaks (see Matt 12:34). So how does one discern the dissemination of envy? Simply mark the words that are being said. Let us quote Acts 13:45 and underscore this as a reason to take ministry to another community: "But when the Jews saw the crowds, they were filled with jealousy, and blaspheming, they contradicted what was spoken by Paul."

Envy is manifested by contradicting and blasphemous words. It is a direct opposition to the work of God through you and to the very office God has placed you. As a pastor, you have authority from God to shepherd the flock. As those influential in the flock contradict, revile, and oppose you as a minister, this may be a possible sign to shake the dust from your feet. I have written in *The Coming Winter* that to blaspheme is not only to reproach God, but can also mean to disparage and revile the character of God's servant. David Peterson has interpreted this verse with the following: the Jews "began to contradict what Paul was saying and heaped abuse on him."[1] Pastors are often abused, and it is the abuse that can become a mechanism to discerning that a departure is imminent. The abuse is the fruit of envy. Envy and jealousy create potential for the worst of human behaviors. Often, the one perpetrating the abuse is unable to recognize envy as the motivation, for it is often misconstrued as having a righteous origin. Many who abuse pastors do so in the name of God or prophecy. Peterson goes on to remark,

> Jealousy at the success of others is sadly a common human failing, and religious leaders are especially vulnerable to such behaviour.... The final expression of jealousy is organized persecution, resulting in expulsion from the region.[2]

After presenting his budget, Pastor Jordan was the object of character disparagement and reviling. His salvation was called into question, and he was accused of calling on demons. These accusations and narratives also found their way into the speech of certain staff members and began to disseminate throughout the body. This was an all-out assault on the identity of a child of God and a sinister undermining of his identity and office as a pastor. This was not from God, but from Satan, who is the accuser of the brethren. When this occurs, it is time to pray about whether God is leading you to take the good news to another city.

The servant of the Great Awakening Jonathan Edwards takes up the subject of envy by offering his own definition. He states, "Envy may be defined to be a spirit of dissatisfaction with an opposition to the prosperity and happiness of others as compared with our own."[3] Comparison saps what sprinkling of joy we have in this life, replacing it with callous bitterness and cynicism. It is the one hot on the heels of power and authority, and if at all threatened with the success of another, it pursues a line of character assassination to restore the shallow happiness of authority regained. Often, it is distorted as a belief that one's

---

1. Peterson, *Acts of the Apostles*, 397.
2. Peterson, *Acts of the Apostles*, 397.
3. Edwards, "Christian Love," 91–92.

current post or opinion is the divine one, and thus must be realized at any cost, including the sin of blaspheming another.

Edwards would go on to provide greater nuances in this regard as well:

> The thing that the envious person is opposed to and dislikes, is, the comparative superiority of the state of honor, or prosperity of happiness, that another may enjoy; over that which he possesses.[4]

There is no rest until the other's "comparative . . . state of honor, or . . . happiness" is destroyed to restore the state of happiness of the one propagating destruction. In the end, this state of happiness pursuant to the destruction of another is no genuine happiness at all. That is, envy cannot create or restore happiness lost. Indeed, envy further perpetuates a state of discontentment with oneself. But envy is coy in that it can convince another that a return to Eden is possible vis-à-vis the destruction of another. Indeed, the envious can further be deceived that the very happiness enjoyed by another is rightfully his or her own, and ought to be reclaimed through any means necessary.

Envy "is a disposition natural in men, that they love to be uppermost; and this disposition is directly crossed, when they see others above them."[5] Envy is the natural disaffection of the fall. It requires unnatural intervention from the divine to replace the natural bent of the human heart with humility. If the disaffection of prominence is affronted, and the soul is not yet crucified of its natural bent to superiority, then sinister schemes become the labor of such a soul to shoulder oneself to prominence once again. In many regards, it is envy that can both hinder and abruptly stall a revival in the body of Christ. God's appointed structure is dismantled by envy, and in the vacuum of lawlessness everyone does what is right in his or her own eyes.

Charles Finney, one of the vessels used by God in the Second Great Awakening, takes up the topic of those sins of commission that hinder a revival. He identifies one of these sins as envy. Finney does not mince words when he comments,

> It has been more agreeable to you to dwell upon their faults, than upon their virtues, upon their failures, than upon their success.

---

4. Edwards, "Christian Love," 92.
5. Edwards, "Christian Love," 92.

Be honest with yourself, and if you have harbored this spirit of hell, repent deeply before God, or he will never forgive you.[6]

Envy seeks the injury of others to elevate the self. If one is honored or advanced beyond what one believes he or she ought to be, or if one envies the honor or praise of another, the temptation is to bring such an honorable vessel down into the mire of the one envying through the mechanism of slander. Slander also has a way of halting a revival as it introduces a mean-spirited nature to the body of Christ, and as people are prone to believe vice rather than virtue, the whole church can bemoan with slander. Listen to Finney's admonition of slander as well:

> The times you have spoken behind people's backs of their faults, real or supposed, of members of the church or others, unnecessarily or without good reason. This is slander. You need not lie to be guilty of slander—to tell the truth with the design to injure, is slander.[7]

Ironically, Finney is not as much concerned with truth or lies as he is with motivation. What is the motive and intent of one speaking evil of another? If it is to injure beyond recovery, to run another's name into the ground, to conspire against another's integrity and character, then one is slandering and thus mitigating any seed of revival from sprouting. In this environment, it is fitting for the servant of God to shake the dust from his or her feet and transition.

Deceit of the Devout

We find later in our narrative another possible sign to resign one's post and seek another assignment in the kingdom. The Jewish opposition stirred up devout and honorable men and women to raise a persecution against Paul and Barnabas (see Acts 13:50). O, how one seed of envy can dislodge an entire ministry from God for a community. The season of refreshment was cut short; the revival of souls was abruptly stalled; the good news could not be heard over the noise of devilish envy. It is tantamount to Jesus not performing many miracles in Nazareth because of the unbelief there (see Matt 13:58). Now those who were devout and honorable believed the likely distorted accounts of the covetous Jews.

---

6. Finney, "How to Promote a Revival," 367.
7. Finney, "How to Promote a Revival," 367.

The word "devout" (Acts 13:50) is from the Greek σέβομαι (*sebomai*), meaning "to fall back on" or "before." It is a posture of generating respect for another or being impressed by the loftiness of another. It is often used in the book of Acts and the New Testament altogether to refer to gentile proselytes (see Acts 13:43).[8]

And is this not what envy summons? There are casualties caught unaware in the crossfire of dissension who, ignorant of the truth, align with the envious and join the persecution of the servants of God. It was honorable women of the city and the chief men of the city who joined the throng seeking Paul's expulsion (see Acts 13:50). Robertson cites the language here as a forcible expulsion that is often done when someone is considered a public nuisance. The aorist active indicative tense brings a connotation of coercion, and so Robertson comments, "just a few days before they were heroes of the city and now!"[9]

There were no doubt honorable men on the church board who had served for years, but who remained silent when slander reared its head and were so influenced by stronger wills that they joined the recitation to see Pastor Jordan removed.

The silence of good, devout, and honorable men permits the handiwork of the devil to remain. One member of the finance committee, simply there to present the budget, not to discuss or vote on it, was the sole person who defended Pastor Jordan. He reminded the board that something similar had happened more than twenty years earlier to another pastor of this same church and it nearly destroyed him. "Destruction," a word that seems fitting—and yet I wonder if the destruction, albeit wounding, was also for Pastor Jordan's good. Perhaps it was there to teach him the lesson of when to leave a certain community for another.

When the devout and honorable men and women of the community are either silent or complicit with the influential members stirring up dissension, it is OK, pastors, to shake the dust from your feet. There is yet another city that is waiting to receive the ministry of Christ through you! But before you go, do not hesitate to deliver messages dripping with boldness; let the audacity of the Holy Spirit bring warning and admonition to the opposition. Paul's word was stern and plain: "Then both Paul and Barnabas spoke out boldly, saying, 'It was necessary that the word of God should be spoken first to you. Since you

---

8. Zodhiates, *Key Word Study Bible*, 1756.

9. Roberston, "Robertson's Word Pictures of the New Testament," https://www.biblestudytools.com/commentaries/robertsons-word-pictures/acts/acts-13-50.html.

reject it and judge yourselves to be unworthy of eternal life, we are now turning to the gentiles" (Acts 13:46).

Do not fear speaking the truth and to even expose those that have hindered the truth. Pastor Jordan did provide admonition that we ought not to slander one another but did not expose the opposition or those that had sinned in slandering his reputation.

We find the phrase in Acts 13:51 that we have been borrowing from throughout this chapter: "they shook the dust off their feet." The concept appears to be somewhat related to the Jewish custom of hospitality where one would receive foot-washing upon entering a town or home. This was a common gesture of hospitality at the time, given the long journey of a pilgrim and the dust that would accumulate along the way. It is like offering a bathroom to wash hands prior to supper.

We know Jesus transformed this common practice of hospitality into a sanctifying act of teleological love. So it is that when Jesus instructs His disciples in Matthew 10:14 to "shake the dust from your feet," it is as if to say, "We no longer have a share with you concerning the truth, seeing that it is altogether rejected."

The disciples were not received; their feet had not been washed, so that even the dust that had accumulated in the city was no longer tolerated to cling to their feet. The irony here is the fact that it was joy that accompanied the departure. Paul and Barnabas were able to suffer for the name of Christ. The Holy Spirit had enabled joy in the context of rejection (see Acts 13:50–52).

However, this was not Pastor Jordan's reaction to his own rejection, but perhaps it is because it was his first exposure to such opposition. He thus postulated that as one can experience the joy that accompanies persecution, one is better able to withstand such rejection, knowing that it is not the individual being rejected, but rather the ministry through him or her.

The Holy Spirit enables joy. Thus, I wonder if this is the purpose of persecution, to bring us ever closer to divine joy and satisfaction. When Jesus cites the mourning of the blessed ones in Matthew 5:4, He uses a word that can be rendered as "satisfaction."[10] The mourning precipitates the comforting, and the comforting is what mediates satisfaction, so that mourning is required for comforting. Without pain, we would not mourn; without mourning, we would not know the satisfaction of divine

---

10. See Zodhiates, *Key Word Study Bible*, 1734 where he defines μακάριος, the Greek word for blessed to mean "fully satisfied."

consolation. Therefore, pain is a necessary means of Christian formation, for in such pain we know the kind of consolation we can then bring to others' pain through the ministry of empathy.

Disaffection

Next, we explore the signs of departure found in the narrative of Acts 14 and Paul's journey to Iconium, the same he recalls to Timothy in 2 Timothy 3. The sign of a shaking is found in Acts 14:2, "But the unbelieving Jews stirred up the gentiles and poisoned their minds against the brothers."

The unbelieving Jews once again stirred the gentiles, and perhaps even the new believing gentiles, to think that Paul and Barnabas had evil intentions in Iconium. Their minds were "poisoned" as noted above—from the Greek κακόω (*kakoo*), meaning "to harm" or "do evil." It can convey the act of maltreatment in excess to the extent that one is plagued or injured.

However, the closest meaning given the current context of this narrative is that the unbelieving Jews convinced the gentiles and Jews of the city to have adverse affections toward Paul and Barnabas. That is, their affect was changed by the course of conversation. Whatever idiom, phrase, gossip, slander, or false accusation that had been communicated was successful in changing their affect or affections toward Paul and Barnabas. Affections are primary human attributes, typically illustrated through emotions or mood. One's affections or mood can have a powerful influence on one's cognitions. One can engage in emotional reasoning, which can defy logical conclusions. The one operating from emotional reasoning does not entertain the reason of experience, logic, history, or truth. Truth becomes lost in the affect. And when truth is lost in the affect, it becomes difficult to recover such truth. It as if affections must once again be modified to recover logical thinking.

Although a dated paper, G. H. Bower wrote on his investigations into this phenomenon through a series of experiments with university students.[11] He simply used recall of either melancholy or exuberant events

---

11. For more recent investigation of mood's influence on cognition, please see Peterson, "Clinical Characteristics." In his investigation, data from 137 depressed patients and 103 healthy controls, including neuropsychological test scores, self-reported cognitive difficulties, and ratings of mood, were pooled from two studies, one conducted in Copenhagen, Denmark, and the other in Christchurch, New Zealand. Cognitive

from the lives of these students to observe what kind of future possibilities could be entertained when amid either affect. What he found was that mood can affect cognitions in the following domains: (1) free associations, (2) themes of fantasies (T.A.T. stories),[12] (3) snap judgements of people, (4) judgements of event likelihood, (5) interpersonal judgements, (6) self-perception, and (7) self-confidence.[13] That is, depression or joy colored impressions that were simply free or spontaneous thinking, ruminations or fantasies, how we perceive or judge other people, whether we think an event is likely in the future, how we see ourselves interacting with others, our view of the self, or confidence in our own ability.

Mood is a powerful mediator either positively or negatively in the way we think of ourselves and others. So, when the Jews essentially disaffected the people of the city, they were able to change their mood so that their cognitions were adversely affected. That is, their thoughts toward Paul and Barnabas became more suspicious; they could foresee a negative influence upon their town or community because of these two individuals remaining. Indeed, disaffection can perpetuate a kind of nefarious rumination that becomes a projected reality.

When one board member accused Pastor Jordan of having a false Christian walk and essentially living a façade, he later asked to see him and apologize. His initial intention appeared sincere and so he agreed to meet with him. He apologized and used the word "projection" to describe the dynamic that had occurred between them. "Projection" is a term we employ in psychological science to describe an interpersonal dynamic where one sees in others what one is truly feeling in oneself.

That is, in this case, perhaps he was calling Pastor Jordan's walk a Christian façade, utilizing examples such as the omission of miracles and kingdom signs, because he himself had not experienced the miracles and kingdom signs and thus projected his personal doubts upon Pastor Jordan. Perhaps this was coming from a place of grief, as he was praying and

---

discrepancy scores were calculated using a novel methodology, with positive values indicating disproportionately more subjective than objective difficulties (i.e., "sensitivity") and negative values indicating more objective than subjective impairments (i.e., "stoicism"). Patients with more depressive symptoms and of younger age overreported cognitive impairments across all illness states.

12. See Bower, "Affect and Cognition," 157, where they utilized the Thematic Apperception Test (TAT stories) to demonstrate the influence of mood upon the generation of stories from a series of several pictures. The pictures are standardized illustrations from the TAT.

13. Bower, "Affect and Cognition," 395.

believing for a certain member of the church family who was suffering from cancer to be healed. This member would eventually die from cancer during the grumblings and ramblings about the future of the church, when the future of the church was coming alongside a dying man, taking his hand, and pouring out love upon him. The future of the church may be more simply envisioned than one might think. Perhaps presence is the future of the church—the presence of Jesus in every human interaction of compassion and love we have with the days God gives us.

Thus, for this member to say he had projected his own feelings upon Pastor Jordan was to say, "My feelings of insecurity and wonderings of whether my Christian walk is genuine, I displaced onto you." This displacement is often a coping mechanism to alleviate the emotional angst that one would experience if one owned such feelings. Pastor Jordan may never understand why, after such a tender exchange, this person continually called for his resignation in subsequent meetings. Perhaps the insight he displayed in that moment of reconciliation could not be reproduced. Or perhaps he had been disaffected and his cognitions thus reflected his mood concerning Pastor Jordan.

Bower goes on to conclude that through his research, a myth was unraveling. This "strongly held myth is that people are rational creatures, that they are well-functioning information-storage devices who can set aside their passions, look at the facts objectively, and can arrive at their evaluations and decisions rationally and without bias."[14] Bower asserts that all his university student subjects were assessed on whether they believed this myth about themselves, and all agreed that they did. They were convinced that their judgments and conclusions were not at all influenced by affect or mood. Bower continues:

> I was not prepared for the dramatic impact that these emotions have had upon our subjects' behaviour. We find that people simply cannot override their emotions: their emotions appear to leak out in nearly everything they do. Moreover, this occurs despite their attempts to do otherwise. Cognition is suffused with emotion.[15]

Think about this when church members, staff, and board members criticize your ministry. Cognition is suffused with emotion. Begin to pray and wonder whether the criticism is born out of a coping mechanism of

---

14. Bower, "Affect and Cognition," 400.
15. Bower, "Affect and Cognition," 400

projection; that is, the member is placing his or her disaffected emotion of the self onto you. Also, think about the myriad of emotions that are inextricably tied to the perceptions of the people bringing harsh judgments. Pray that God would perform a deep inner and emotional healing upon those suffering from disaffections. Pray that their eyes would be opened to acknowledge their own deep woundedness and to cease in their wounding of others. Wounded people wound people. This is the story of human suffering. This is the story of people suffering from disaffections, distorted pathos, and the poisoning of the mind by unbelief and distorted assumptions about one's neighbor.

If we want a community to arrive at orthopraxy, we must cultivate an environment of orthodoxy and orthopathy. Right doctrine alone will lead to a cerebral Christianity devoid of compassion and love. Right affections alone will lead to a compromising Christianity without necessary boundaries. However, a commingling of orthodoxy and orthopathy guides the flock into the right practices. And when we think of right affections, it is not only of right affections for and about God, but also for and about our neighbor.

Look deeper as a pastor to see the emotions that may be influencing perceptions, judgments, cognitions, and assertions. Perhaps if Pastor Jordan could have returned to the place of his wounding, he would have stopped the tedious arguments over the direction of the church and asked the board members to simply share the emotions they were feeling at the moment. He would have asked if there was a grief about their current losses that had not yet been expressed in a worship-integrating lamentation. Perhaps his empathizing with their grief would have created an atmosphere for healthy expression of these emotions rather than their remaining on the surface of stuck and distorted cognitions. Perhaps an existential study of Lamentations with the church board, with opportunities to share genuine and pathos-laden testimony, would have assisted them in navigating the obvious grief that they all shared. This would then have conveyed a legacy of empathy and rightly directed grief rather than slander and disaffection.

Transforming affections is the work of the Holy Spirit—affections to feel purely, truly, and virtuously toward God, self, and the world. However, when the affections are poisoned, much damage can be the result. A history of credibility is sponged away with the turning of affections. Perhaps empathy creates the potential for disaffections to be ameliorated; but if not, it remains a good legacy to leave when one may shake the dust from one's feet and transition, for a poisoned mind is not easily swayed.

Hubris

The city of Iconium would eventually become divided, some aligning with the Jews and others with the apostles. This created such a tumult that an assault was contrived to stone Paul and Barnabas. Now, this is yet another sign that it may be time to shake the dust from one's feet, when a pastor is "used despitefully" (Acts 14:5) or when harm is being plotted against the pastor. And the harm may not be in the form of a physical assault, but will usually come in a narrative assault, a disparaging of character, and a plotting with other influential leaders to have the pastor removed or reviled.

The Greek construction is interesting here; "despitefully" comes from the Greek ὑβρίζω (*hubrizo*), which connotes one exercising violence, abusing, or misusing one to spite him or her. It is to reproach or treat shamefully. The word is etymologically derived from *hubris*, which conjures up a sentiment of insolence, overbearing behavior, injurious intent, and maltreatment.[16] This word has come to us in our English language as well to signify shameful reproach from the context of posturing oneself as superior to another.

Hubris is what comes before a fall (see Prov 16:18). It is the positioning of oneself through self-promotion to act or declare oneself as superior with maleficence in mind. If one can obtain a certain threshold of influence, then one can carry out shameful plans to reproach another. In this case, it was Paul and Barnabas who were the recipients of the Jews' hubris. In our context, a pastor often becomes the object of a church, staff, or board member's hubris if this pastor does not necessarily align with the vision or direction of this member's imagined course for the church.

However, it is also important for the pastor to guard against his or her own hubris. In our own pain, we are not to treat others shamefully or reproach them as a means of promoting our own influence among the body. The greatest temptation is vis-à-vis the creation of a bully pulpit to promote oneself as superior when preaching. Much abuse has

---

16. Zodhiates, *Key Word Study Bible*, 73.

come when pastors veer from the sacred sphere of preaching God's Word to promulgate hubris.

Pastors, let the Word convict. Stand at these pulpits in the spirit of John the Baptist, that we should decrease and Jesus increase (see John 3:30). The Holy Spirit can convict under the preaching of the Word. The Word will accomplish in due time what is needed for the body. As shepherds, we are to expose sin and provide public discipline, if need be, but not with an agenda of garnering influence, but rather with a pure motive of seeking the restoration of the soul affected.

Hubris is pride that seeks the destruction of another. It is the abhorrent distaste of another to the extent that one's desire is to see him or her irreparably damaged. Hubris has been destroying the church from its inception. Hubris is derived from the fallen and sinful nature, with its antithesis and antidote in the principle of humility. Jesus informs us of such humility in the Sermon on the Mount. Jesus would become the lens by which the law could be rightly interpreted.[17] And He states something of a heavenly principle: "Blessed are the poor in spirit, for theirs is the kingdom of heaven" (Matt 5:3).

The "blessed" state is so much more than the colloquial happiness that we think of in terms of situations that generate contentment. Rather, this is a state of satisfaction.[18] When we are poor in spirit, humble, and seeking others' best above our own, we find a sense of satisfaction unparalleled by the buffet of this world's offerings. *Kenōsis*,[19] emptiness, volitional

---

17. Please see Hebrews 3:1–6, where Jesus is envisaged as a second Moses, more superior in the scope of the work accomplished. Indeed, many see Jesus' ascension to the mount to deliver a sermon that reinterpreted the law of Moses as a recapitulation of Moses' Sinai experience of obtaining and giving the law to the people.

18. See Zodhiates, *Key Word Study Bible*, 1735, where he defines the Greek word for blessed (μακάριος) to mean "fully satisfied." And further, he defines this state as one who has the kingdom of God within one's heart because of Christ, appealing to the use of the word in Matthew 5:2, 11. Having God's kingdom within one's heart is the means to true satisfaction or blessedness (see Luke 17:21).

19. *Kenosis* (κενόω) is a Greek construction found most prominently in Philippians 2:7. This is the great hymn of Christ's subjugation to incarnation and thus voluntary surrender of his status in heaven to become a high priest intimately acquainted with human suffering. *Kenosis* is thus to empty and refers to Christ when He laid aside equality with or being in the form of God. It can also mean "to make void," "deprive of force," "render vain," "consider useless and of no effect." It is sometimes utilized to convey the cause of emptiness and a king who exchanges his kingly robe for sackcloth. Please see Rogers Jr. and Rogers III, *New Linguistic and Exegetical Key*, 452, and http://www.greekbible.com/l.php?keno/w_v-3aai-s—_.

surrender of pride, power, and affluence for the sake of Christ, is to find true satisfaction and to leave a kingdom ethos as a legacy!

Pastor Jordan had lamented that the congregation was being divided and that he had become the center of such division. For example, there were those who advocated for him to remain and others who insisted he must go. Relationships that had developed over many years were being eroded and dismantled because of the differences of opinion on the matter.

Pastors, you are not responsible for the division that may ensue because of you being you. You can be no other than who you are and who God called you to be. When one camp opposes your ministry because of dissatisfaction for some reason or another, you need not apologize for prayerful preaching, sound teaching, and passion for the kingdom. This is often misunderstood and outright rejected when some choose to believe lies and use the lies to convince the people of their "just" cause.

What I will say next is grievous and I challenge us all to reflect on the matter. Perhaps pastors who become the object of controversy will know that there is a greater work occurring in the division, grievous as it may be. What if division is inevitable for any minister that seeks to preach Christ?

John Peter Lange posits such a question in the following manner,

> Such a division is by no means wholly unacceptable to a faithful teacher; the Lord Jesus, indeed says that he came into the world to produce such a division (Luke 12:51). The Lord fulfills that saying, whenever he convulses the kingdom of darkness through the agency of his servants, creates a salutary disturbance, and teaches men to depart from iniquity. He will hereafter, on the day of judgment, exercise his awful authority, and make that division complete.[20]

Indeed, your relentless calls to repentance will cause some to delve further into darkness and animosity. The convulsing of the kingdom of darkness will create context, revealing the differences between the sheep and goats. As the kingdom of darkness convulses, a greater outcry will result in calls for your removal. Accusations will be the arsenal of your opponents and the whole body will take greater note of those instruments of God's kingdom and those instruments of carnality.

---

20. Lange, *Commentary on the Holy Scriptures: Acts*, 263.

However, some congregations will not take the great pains to remove the dross when revealed. Some instruments of persecution will remain with great influence and God will send yet another prophet to convulse the congregation until his bride is without spot or wrinkle. The unrepentant will eventually face the final judgment, which will be the last sieve at work to illuminate his true children from the religious, his sons and daughters from those feigned, the humble from the proud.

Pastors, if you have created controversy not from a platform of malfeasance, but from an obedience to preach and pray, then shake the dust from your feet without doubt or guilt. God has used you to convulse the kingdom of darkness in that place. Then Lange asks a question that we all ask when resigning a post, "why is it so painful to endure?" And herein is his reply: "Because it completely crushes man's own will. The apostles would possibly have preferred to die rather than to flee."[21]

Martyrdom is often perceived as more glorious than departure. That is, we as a culture will affirm a pastor for enduring a church split, standing in the face of absolute persecution, maintaining a post where one is rejected. And I do want to be careful here; it is often God calling those individuals to remain and so they must. But what if God calls you to resign as pastor? Is there shame in that? The church culture may answer with a resolute yes. And yet the Lord may applaud your departure with an affirmation that you are being obedient.

A few months after Pastor Jordan had resigned from the church, he was attending another church in the town to which his family had moved. He knew no one. He had a distant acquaintance with the pastor of the church. While worshipping, a man approached him and simply stated, "I do not know what you may have faced. But I feel the Lord is delighted in your decision to do what is best for your family." He then departed as gently as he had come. Of course, tears emerged as a grateful posture of the Lord's prophetic affirmation, which consoled the pain of his rejection.

God comforts those who mourn. He comforted Pastor Jordan. He comforts His children and releases them from assignments after the kingdom of darkness has been convulsed and the agent of such convulsion is rejected. Lange observes the blessing associated with resignation when he both asks and answers the question,

---

21. Lange, *Commentary on the Holy Scriptures: Acts*, 263.

> Wherein does the blessing which attends it consist? Through its means the will of God, and not that of man, is done. Hence, it produces the richest of fruits of every kind; thus, the preaching of the apostles produces faith, the Lord gives testimony to them; their flight is a source of blessing—they carry the word to a wider field of labor.[22]

Pastors, your resignation opens the door for you to carry the kingdom-convulsing message to another town, to another people, to another region. You will bless another community because you are faithful to preach repentance and the remission of sins in Christ. Your rejection is your flight for the gospel, not your flight away from the gospel. Know that God's will is being accomplished even in the wholesale rejection of your ministry.

Lange continues to comment on the blessing of division when he states what we have heretofore explored, the blessing of exposure:

> Their results, the church undergoes a sifting process; the real sentiments of the heart are manifested; it is during the struggle that truth demonstrates its value, that faith reveals it power, that love exhibits new energy, and the church is edified.[23]

In paradoxical fashion, the church is edified through admonition, sifting, and exposure. Division exposes the true hearts of people who had been able to shield their true nature under the cover of feigned peace. Struggle in a church can be the result of the preached Word, of ruffled feathers, of pride surfacing, of authority being undermined, of slander exposed. Any time a heart is exposed, there is an opportunity for admonition and repentance. The church may lose some of its members, but it is likely the members of dishonorable purpose. The church is sifted and sanctified through the means of division. The servant who has been faithful to convulse the kingdom of darkness at any church can leave with this legacy in mind. He or she has waged war on the kingdom of darkness.

Now, on one point, I do differ in opinion with Lange. He proposes that a servant does depart from a work "in order to enter a new battlefield, but not to seek a place of rest."[24] I differ, for the Apocalypse illustrates otherwise. When the woman who had given birth to the male child had endured much persecution from the dragon, she was given two wings.

---

22. Lange, *Commentary on the Holy Scriptures: Acts*, 263.
23. Lange, *Commentary on the Holy Scriptures: Acts*, 263.
24. Lange, *Commentary on the Holy Scriptures: Acts*, 263.

And as a great eagle that might swiftly depart from one place to another, the woman departed to a wilderness where she was nourished for a time, away from the serpent (see Rev 12:13–17).

Even as she finds her place of rest, the serpent does not rest to agitate her further by spewing water from his mouth to drown her and extinguish her holy influence. The very place of her rest comes to her rescue. The earth itself opens to swallow the flood of waters meant for her destruction. This implies that for many, if not the whole of the church, there is a place of rest in the wilderness, away from the battles where one may mend one's wounds and prepare for the next assignment, where fighting is sure to take place. Rest is not antithetical to God's work. The wilderness is not to be despised but embraced. The wings come from God, not from shame. The wings are to give you flight and rest is to hone your virtues as a minister of the gospel! As Lange portends, "The righteous cannot be ruined, when oppressed in one place, it finds a refuse elsewhere; even when prostrated, it arises with augmented power."[25]

Physical Threat

Finally, we come to the third city listed by Paul in 2 Timothy 3, that of Lystra. The saying "Trouble can follow you" could aptly describe the situation in Lystra. Paul had exited Iconium and was preaching in Lystra, and a healing had occurred that brought the entire city to the precipice of declaring Paul a god, namely Jupiter. Paul indeed renounces such treatment and the vanities of idol worship.

However, trouble had followed Paul and Barnabas. The Jews of Antioch and Iconium had followed Paul with the express purpose of completing what they had started. Indeed, their "antagonism" was so great that it was "measured by the fact that they travelled more than a hundred miles to oppose the missionaries and were unimpressed by any attempt to turn the pagans of Lystra to the worship of the God of Scripture."[26] Keep in mind, pastors, that some will go to great lengths to destroy the ministry God has given you.

They had convinced the people of Lystra in ironic fashion to stone Paul. The very people who had been ready to deify Paul now demonized Paul and he was left for dead after a stoning. This offers a caveat here. A

---

25. Lange, *Commentary on the Holy Scriptures: Acts*, 264.
26. Peterson, *Acts of the Apostles*, 411.

community or a church can be fickle like any other human institution. "They first bring garlands, then stones!"[27] Do not be surprised, pastor, when the very ones who have welcomed you with celebration are the first to cast stones at you when the opportunity is ripe.

We should note the correlation as well that the more one confronts the kingdom of darkness through the audacity of preaching, the greater the assault from this kingdom to destroy a person. As Lange also notes, "Those who are most courageous in assailing the kingdom of darkness, are surrounded by the most numerous of foes."[28]

A pastor should come to expect stones to be thrown if he or she is to preach the counsel of God. If a pastor's teaching confronts the cultural subtexts that reinforce wickedness within families, souls, and communities, then he or she will be an object of great scorn. The enemy has a way of convincing even those within the circle of the pastor to pick up stones.

Thus, the threat of life is also a sign that one may need to depart from a community. Threats against one's own life or the life of one's family may be the last sign of a needed departure. Now, we should note that such threats do not necessarily equate to an unequivocal departure for God may be planning for one to experience the gift of martyrdom. In discerning this, we as pastors should be aware that this is an immensely personal decision, revealed to the individual by the Holy Spirit. We should not despise a pastor who departs a community under physical threat; nor should we assume that the gift of martyrdom or physical suffering is God's intention for all pastors.

Paul was delivered and departed from three cities, and yet this was not the case in Corinth. Jesus Himself revealed to Paul when he was residing and preaching at Corinth that he was to remain.

> One night the Lord said to Paul in a vision, "Do not be afraid, but speak and do not be silent, for I am with you, and no one will lay a hand on you to harm you, for there are many in this city who are my people." (Acts 18:9–10)

Therefore, I would propose that to remain in a city when there is the threat of physical harm is a highly personal decision incumbent upon personal revelation from Jesus. When the Lord communicates to a pastor or missionary or any other servant to remain, then one is to

---

27. Lange, *Commentary on the Holy Scriptures: Acts*, 270.
28. Lange, *Commentary on the Holy Scriptures: Acts*, 270.

remain. We explored the life of Polycarp, to whom it was revealed that he would receive the gift of martyrdom. Paul also was prepared to die in Jerusalem (see Acts 21:13). However, if this is not personally unveiled as an assignment from heaven, it is appropriate to depart and shake the dust from one's feet and journey to another city.

Paul miraculously survived the stoning, and having arisen, departed from the city to bring the gospel to Derbe. This completes the triad of cities listed by Paul to Timothy in 2 Timothy 3:11, and perhaps has shed light on helping a pastor discern when to depart a work and begin anew in another community. The Lord "delivered" Paul from the envy of Antioch, the disaffections of Iconium, and the physical threat and stoning of Lystra. He was drawn out of calamity and liberated from the violent intentions of the enemy. See figure 5 below.

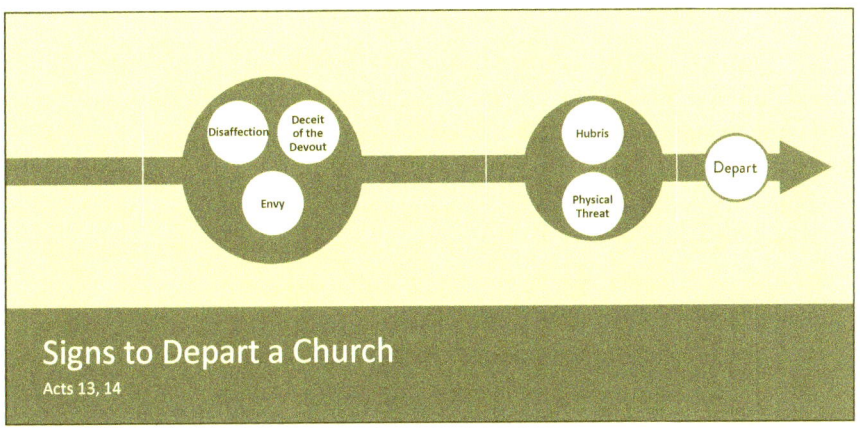

Figure 5: Signs to Depart a Church.

As a tool for helping pastors discern whether to transition, I have developed a fourteen-item screener with a Likert scale and cutoff scores that may help a pastor decide whether to move from a church (see Appendix A). We also know that Paul returned to all three cities to confirm the souls that had been saved and exhorted them to continue in the faith, as tribulation will accompany all who enter the kingdom of God (see Acts 14:22).

Who knows, pastor, if God will have you return to the very place where you were expelled to encourage the saints and exhort them to continue through great tribulation? God's ways are certainly beyond finding out, and in a turn of irony, He may send you back to rejoice in the work that may have beforehand been mired in human envy, disaffections, and physical harm. Legacy has a way of finding you in due time. Your impact was likely larger than you could imagine.

Coercive Terminations

Marcus Tanner has written about coercive pastoral terminations, exploring pastoral survey data and distilling certain factors that adversely affect a pastor's well-being and family life. In citing a study by Lee, he notes,

> When both the frequency and the impact to the minister of each intrusive demand were taken into account by Lee, the frequency and impact of personal criticism, presumptive expectations, and boundary ambiguity were significantly correlated with measures of burnout.[29]

Now, we have identified through survey data salient features that led either to a forced termination of a pastor or ministry burnout. The first is personal criticism. Personal criticism can chip away at a pastor in a way that dampens enthusiasm and strips him or her of personal dignity and worth. If chronic enough, the pastor will grow weary of such criticism and find that he or she can no longer serve a congregation who no longer appreciates this pastor's call or, worse, cuts him or her with words of constant criticism.

The second feature, presumptive expectations, can draw the ire of church members and especially board members, if a pastor was hired with the expectation of growing a church quantitatively, rescuing a church from decline, or bringing back the glory days of a church. These presumptive expectations are neither fair nor helpful. Rather than viewing the pastor as a servant who may direct the church in an altogether different direction with a new vision with a qualitative view in mind, the pastor is expected to grow an empire. If he or she does not, the expectation is not realized, and a forced termination may be looming.

Third, boundary ambiguity is noted as a measure of pastoral burnout. In many cases, no one really knows who is leading the church. Is the pastor leading the church? Does the church board lead the church? Is there a system of elders leading the church? Or is the staff collectively leading the church? Is there a charismatic figure in the church who has

---

29. Lee, "Specifying Intrusive Demands," found in Tanner and Zvonkovic, "Forced to Leave," 714.

garnered a following? These dynamics are far too common in the church, which leads to an ambiguity of leadership. If these leaders do not agree, then one can utilize his or her influence to force the resignation of the pastor. The dynamic of boundary ambiguity can weigh on the pastor who is navigating such dynamics and lead to resignation.

Furthermore, we find that prolonged adversity of such factors takes a toll on the emotional and physical health of a pastor. Duke Divinity School performed a survey of 2,500 church leaders and discovered that 10 percent reported being depressed. However, 40 percent reported being depressed at times or "worn out" some or most of the time. From the responses collected, 76 percent of clergy were either overweight or obese.[30]

With nearly half reporting intermittent and recurring episodes of depression and a staggering three quarters reporting being overweight, it is no wonder that we find a flight of pastors looking for altogether different vocations. Burnout is a real phenomenon and pastors often will decide to transition for their own physical and emotional health, but also for the well-being of their family.

In perusing the literature, Tanner identified the following trend concerning forced resignation of pastors.

> Barfoot et al. (2005) described forced termination as occurring when "a pastor may abdicate his post due to the constant negativity found in personal attacks and criticism from a small faction within the congregation from whom the minister feels psychologically pressured to step down from his or her service of ministry." Greenfield (2001) described forced termination as a process whereby "clergy killers" blame the minister and/or family for the church's problems in highly public attacks.[31]

Indeed, the greater the public attack, the greater the emotional and physiological stress a pastor and his or her family endures. The smearing campaign of prominent church members, although often only a small frac urch, can cause immense damage to the church family and in particular the pastor.

Crowell's 1995 survey of 386 ministers from 48 denominations indicated that approximately 25 percent of pastors have faced forced termination at some point in their ministerial career.[32] Some voluntarily

---

30. Tanner and Zvonkovic, "Forced to Leave," 715.

31. See Barfoot, "Forced Pastoral Exits," 3. See also Greenfield, *Wounded Minister*. Both are cited in Tanner and Zvonkovic, "Forced to Leave," 716.

32. Crowell, "Forced Pastoral Exits," cited in Tanner and Zvonkovic, "Forced to

choose to work in altogether different profession. The self-esteem and confidence of an individual is obviously shaken when experiencing such a disruptive change.

Tanner then proceeds to list a litany of consequential effects from forced termination, citing multiple articles, and worth noting here.

> The body of work of LaRue (1996a, b, c, 1997a, b) is suggestive of many life changes for clergy who have been forcibly terminated and for their families. Many changes occurred: 64% of clergy spouses had to change jobs, and 66% of children were forced to change schools. Change in the clergy members' self-confidence has been found: 58–59% of pastors had a drop in their self-confidence as a leader in LaRue's and Barfoot's work. Family problems have been suggested: in LaRue's work, 54% of pastors reported a heavy emotional toll on their spouse, while Barfoot reported that families experienced a diminished ability to trust people (71% and 67%). Health was a concern: emotional health problems were identified by 59% of Barfoot's sample, and 10% of LaRue's sample reported a major illness within one year of forced termination.[33]

Pastor Forest departed after scrutiny and slander began to inch nearer to his children. He was given wings to rest in the wilderness, where his children would be protected and his wounds mended for a season. While working in an altogether different vocation, he was asked to give a presentation concerning an optimal meeting agenda to include some opportunities for continuing education. As he began the presentation, he experienced physiological stress that he was as yet unfamiliar with. His heart began to pound, his hands began to sweat, he felt altogether nervous and inadequate, and if intently listening, one could detect a slight quiver in his voice.

Pastor Forest had sought pastoral counseling after his resignation and brought this up in one of his sessions. While processing, he realized that the experience at his previous ministry post had affected his confidence in presentations of any sort. He found it difficult to trust himself with any project or leadership endeavor, and wondered if this would eventually improve. His counselor was keen to identify that experiences need not define who we are; God defines who we are. People often misunderstand this.

Leave," 716.

33. Tanner and Zvonkovic, "Forced to Leave," 717.

Pastor Forest would find consolation in his counseling even if belonging remained elusive. Not long after, the COVID-19 crisis would come, and he and his family would shelter in place and all local churches would broadcast their services online. This reinforced a type of isolation but also created an opportunity for greater emotional investment in his children. He taught them lessons, explored the questions of their hearts, embraced them in the rocking chair, read them stories of redemption, found a place of prayer on his front porch, and shed tears concerning the state of the church. His platform for preaching may have been taken, but his platform for intercession remained. In what had been a disruptive transition, God was now transforming him into a legacy of deliverance for his children using small but grand moments of love, affection, and tender exchanges.

Chapter 9

Legacy of Irrelevance

> All scripture is inspired by God and is useful for teaching, for reproof, for correction, and for training in righteousness, so that the person of God may be proficient, equipped for every good work. (2 Tim 3:16–17)

THERE IS A HERESY that has infiltrated the postmodern church in the West, that of "relevance." We see it written on church signs and websites; we see it popping up here and there. "Relevance" is a code word deciphered as applications that seem to relate to modern social life, often with an emphasis on current media, music, and art, over and above *sola Scriptura*.

That is, we find that we live in an age of "grace," a kind of grace that has been redefined to justify our modern habits and justify our sinful acts. The preacher that focuses on an Old Testament passage runs the risk of being dubbed a "legalist" or judged as out of touch with relevant Christianity. An inevitable consequence is the doctrine that the Old Testament is irrelevant to the believer because it contains anecdotes of people who were under the law and we are people not under the law. Thus, the extrapolation is made that if we are not under the law, then the whole of the Old Testament is irrelevant or inapplicable to us today.

Pastor Wyatt was accused of not preaching from relevant New Testament passages during his pastoral tenure. This was baffling, as he made attempts to complement both the Old and New Testaments during the delivery of his sermons. However, Paul is clear to Timothy regarding his view of Scripture: Paul has the whole of Scripture in mind when encouraging Timothy to perform the tasks of a pastor. For this chapter, we will focus on a hermeneutic of Scripture as irrelevant love and the following quadrilateral function of the whole of Scripture for the pastor: doctrine, reproof, correction, and instruction. Indeed, the four *pros-* statements (doctrine, reproof, correction, and instruction) relate to the one *hina-* statement, "that the man of God may be thoroughly equipped," providing a correlation where orthodoxy (doctrine and reproof) and orthopraxy (correction and instruction) are precipitating factors to the equipping of God's servants.[1]

Legacy of Irrelevant Love

Let us begin with an introduction on the notion that all Scripture is inspired. To assert the claim that certain Scriptures are irrelevant to the Christian is absurd. As sacrificial and ceremonial rites have been fulfilled in Christ, many Christians have extrapolated this to mean that the narrative and doctrinal statements of the Old Testament must also be discarded from practice. Paul, however, creates a polemic against this argument in the one phrase "all scripture is inspired by God." Peter would confirm this when he writes, "Because no prophecy ever came by human will, but men and women moved by the Holy Spirit spoke from God" (2 Pet 1:21).

So that the men who prophesied in the Old Testament were moved by the same Holy Spirit who inspired the prophets of the New Testament. Why would the Spirit make Himself irrelevant to a later generation when the Word is for the human heart of all ages? The same exhortation, reproof, and admonition that was required then is needed now, as the human heart continues to entertain sin, veer off track, and surrender to the course of the flesh.

It is by the bold preaching of repentance that the human heart is pricked once more and called back to God. To claim that some portions of Scripture are irrelevant is to denigrate the Word and to introduce a notion that can lead one into heresy as one may be tempted to jettison entire portions of the Scriptures.

Second, to assert that the Old Testament prophets were somehow inferior because they were under the law also does not portend to the narrative of Scripture. As stated above, the Holy Spirit worked upon the

---

1. Nullens, "*Theologia Caritatis*," 46.

prophets of the Old Testament just as He did with the prophets of the New Testament. The work is by the same author (the Holy Spirit) and thus has the same results. The past is not inferior to the present in terms of the Holy Spirit's work. This would imply that the Holy Spirit Himself had somehow matured in His work on willing vessels because of the passing of time or because of the work of Christ. Indeed, the work of Christ forever changes human history, but this does not translate into making the work of the Holy Spirit inferior in the past juxtaposed with the present. I would suggest that to offer a juxtaposition whatsoever is to discredit the work of the Holy Spirit throughout all epochs of human history.

We must avoid the erroneous move of making the Old Testament obsolete as an extension of affirming what Christ did to fulfill the law of sacrifice. Though the Christian need not sacrifice lambs for atonement, he or she reads the ceremonial laws and is both exhorted and admonished when reading the rites of purity. The heart henceforth longs for inner purity when reading is given permission to enter the soul. The ceremonial law continues to point to Christ and thus remains relevant to every believer of every time. Sermons from the Old Testament are as necessary today as they were in the presence of those hearing it for the first time. The human condition has not changed, and thus the Word of God to this human condition has likewise remained unchanged. If we are truly honest with one another, though we are "freed" from the law, there remains the temptation to sin in our liberty—to slander, to covet, to undermine authority, and so on.

The Reformation movement brought Christendom back to an ethic of Scripture as moral authority with the now-familiar tenet *sola Scriptura*. The reformers would often refer to the Scriptures as a manuscript that is both the *regula fidei* (rule of faith) and *regula morum* (rule of meaning). These two leading principles in the understanding of Scripture would create a lens where purpose, epistemology, and trust are all inherent in the whole of Scripture. The Scriptures are trustworthy because of *autopistis*, meriting credibility as self-attesting in a way that describes a mediation of sorts. That is, the Scriptures both testify to and can create context for divine encounter. It is this divine encounter as witnessed by the Scriptures that portends heavenly authority be ascribed to the text.[2] Therefore, it is divine encounter that remains a leading principle in the inspiration of the Scriptures as authoritative text from God

---

2. For a discussion on evangelical views of authority of Scripture, see Nullens, "*Theologia Caritatis*," 39.

Himself. The divine encounter ensues when one reads the Scriptures, for God interprets the heart of the reader for the reader.

To ponder that Scripture is "God-breathed" is to realize that words come from encounter. Speech is the fruit of Presence. That is, revelation becomes much more than grammar and punctuation marks. It is much more than codifying principles, delineating algorithms, reifying protocols, or even a mere behavioral code. It may include these existential items, but also transcends them as revelation is also encounter. It is fellowship with God; it is God breathing on us. Scripture is God-breathed for it is a medium, among others, that God uses to whisper upon our souls. As Webster asserts while channeling Karl Barth,

> Revelation is thus not simply bridging a noetic divide (though it includes that), but it is reconciliation, salvation and therefore fellowship. The idiom of revelation is as much moral and relational as it is cognitional.[3]

Nullens, and by virtue of his citation, Vanhoozer, give emphasis to this view of Scripture and authority by elucidating the need to view Scripture through a covenantal lens of love and relationship. If Scripture is God-breathed, it is therefore dynamic. If Scripture is a metanarrative of love, fellowship, and redemption, then it calls us to the same. Indeed, Nullens would argue that Scripture only becomes formative when it is encountered, not codified. This encounter is a changing of the heart from stone to flesh, from cold to hot, from dispassionate to passionate. The cynic becomes believer, the atheist becomes engulfed in the flames of kingdom passion, the religious lose their scales, and the codes become divine encounters. This is summarized by Vanhoozer's statement, "Scripture is a divine covenant document before it is an ecclesial constitution."[4]

Love then becomes irrelevant to a world of power, codes, and sterile principles. Love becomes irrelevant to systems of oppression. Love is irrelevant to self-promotion. Love says for us to bow low and draw near. Love considers others better than ourselves. Love turns the other cheek, goes another mile, and brings a clearer ethic drawn from the wisdom of Scripture. Love is relational where principle is static. The dos and don'ts of any morality can never be realized by written code but only by flaming hearts engulfed with the purity of love. A pastor is to bring love to

---

3. Webster, *Holy Scripture*, 16, cited in Nullens, "*Theologia Caritatis*," 41.

4. See Nullens, "*Theologia Caritatis*," 45, where he cites Vanhoozer, *Drama of Doctrine*.

bear upon the congregation in such radical fashion that it decries the current systems of self-promotion and oppression of others to create a world of self-kenosis and elevation of others.

The whole of Scripture is God-breathed to move us to love of God and neighbor. This is to be irrelevant and to move away from the relevance heresy that has so infiltrated the church. The heresy of relevance is encapsulated in "trendy church." It is being enamored with buildings, attendance, and money to the extent that relationships are lost. It is emphasis on leadership over covenant, fads over faith, amusement park children's church over discipleship, and staff over community. It is a pastor who is CEO more than shepherd, church board that is more stockholder than elder. It is emphasis on church growth through attendance of events more than life growth through discipleship and covenantal love.

If a *theologica caritatis* (theology of love) is the remedy for a heart-sick church or for suffering in silence vis-à-vis loneliness, then we must take intentional efforts to shed the idolatry that plagues our conversations. Pastors must relate to one another with personal inquiries—"How are you really doing? How are your wife and children? How is your heart? How can we love each other in this moment?" Mullens explicates this further with the following: "It is only through love that we can come to the truth: *caritas quaerens intellectum* (love seeking understanding)."[5] And Goethe adds his amen with the following contribution: "one can know nothing except what one loves; and the deeper and more complete one desires the knowledge to be, the more powerful and dynamic must the love, indeed the passion be."[6]

We use language like "the right bus" and "the right seat on the bus" to describe our staff, but what if we did away with the culture of staff? What if we were able to dismantle the CEO-organization-corporation infrastructure of a church and create a covenantal model of elders and deacons revealed by the Holy Spirit's work upon an individual to serve? The right person with the right skill set with the right "fit" has become so normalized in our conversations that we do not think twice to engender such conversations and sometimes obsess over such configurations. We long to obtain that "rock star" staff member from another church and sometimes court these staff members, thinking that this added person will provide explosive momentum to grow our church. But what if we

---

5. Nullens, "*Theologia Caritatis*," 43.
6. Deeken, *Process and Permanence in Ethics*, 32.

were to have a missional lens within the church—that God will bring people with prophetic burdens, that love will reveal the servant, that the Holy Spirit will comfort the church, that "positions" may not need immediate filling, that servants serve and are not rock stars at all, but little known, with a spirit of condescension, and live a kenotic life? What would the church look like within this epistemological rubric?

Paul reveals a *theologica caritatis* when he defines the purpose of the command he gives Timothy: "But the aim of such instruction is love that comes from a pure heart, a good conscience, and sincere faith" (1 Tim 1:5). So that the virtues of purity, conscience, and faith become the bedrock of a life that thoroughly loves. Indeed, Howard Marshall summarizes this kind of loving lens of authority with the following: "Agape sums up the quality which should result from obeying Paul's command or perhaps from obedience to the gospel message as a whole. It is to some extent a criteria of true preaching."[7]

If one were to use a hermeneutic of covenantal love, then one might also view the false teachers illustrated in both epistles of Paul to Timothy as those with wrong loves, wrong affections, erroneous desires that lead to short-sighted philosophy and teaching for the purpose of elevating the self. Max Scherer helps us here with the following description: "All evil is caused by the intoxicated soul of erroneous loves and the disposition of 'resentment.'"[8]

In a previous chapter, we explored a legacy of opportunity in perilous times through the opportunity to love selflessly. Paul also lists various vices during perilous times that can be envisaged as misplaced loves and affections. Perilous times encompasses being "lovers of themselves," "lovers of money," "unloving," and "lovers of pleasures" (2 Tim 3:2–4). Wrongly placed loves will misconstrue Scripture for personal gain and will contort its use to lobby for one's position. For the one without a pure heart, the principle becomes the god of one's affections so that wounding someone else is an acceptable casualty.

Legacy of Irrelevant Doctrine

After Paul asserts that the entirety of Scripture is "God-breathed," he goes on to describe its functionality. He states that all of Scripture is to

---

7. Marshall, *Critical and Exegetical Commentary on the Pastoral Epistles*, 369.
8. See Nullens, "*Theologia Caritatis*," 46, for the citation of Scherer.

be considered when formulating doctrinal statements. Therefore, our credal statements ought to contain the whole of Scripture. The spirit of every creed should be to encompass the whole of the redemptive metanarrative.

"Doctrine" is derived from the Greek word διδασκαλία (*didaskalia*), which is the instruction belonging to a teacher. It is the curriculum taught and refers to the authority by which the instructor has been entrusted to teach. Thus, how do we derive a curriculum of teaching? What source do we use? Paul is clear here: it is the entire Word, the Old and New, the whole of the redemptive metanarrative, beginning with creation and ending with re-creation. There is a story arc that would be missing if we failed to instruct the body of Christ with the stories of Abraham, Moses, the judges, the prophets, and the kings. Imagine the loss of theological doctrine and instructions on how to pray if we considered the Psalms irrelevant and thus non-applicable. We must guard against the giant leap that many Christians are making that being free from the law means we are free from the claim of the Word. Fulfillment does not lean into eradication. There is much to learn from instructions imbedded in the Old Testament.

As Glover summarizes Paul's view of Scripture, he gives us the following:

> The Jew had indeed from of old the oracles of God and the law of God; and Paul had no question in his mind as to the truth, the validity and the permanence of the Law; he was a thorough Jew here and accepted without criticism. Without criticism, but not without interpretation.[9]

Indeed, Paul would bring a whole new allegory to the story of Israel in the wilderness, who drank from the rock, who was Christ Himself. He would allegorize the seed motif to emphasize the grammatical singular of this word as a reference to Christ as the seed to bless the nations (see 1 Cor 10:2–4 and Gal 3:16). And yet both explications reveal that Paul considered the Old Testament application as "relevant" to his current mission and doctrine. He was not creating new doctrine as much as he was building on prior revelation through the lens of Christ.

All of Scripture is God-breathed and thus all of Scripture is the curriculum for the basis of instructing the body of Christ. Divine speech is divine speech. We ought not to place one as superior over the other, but

---

9. Glover, *Paul of Tarsus*, 33.

to investigate how each divine speech complements and fulfills one another. Yes, we have the book of Hebrews, which introduces us to superior language, and yes, Christ is superior to the sacrificial offerings of the Old Testament, but this superiority does not make the Old Testament irrelevant but rather gives us a new lens by which we can interpret the Old Testament. Therefore, in this way, the task of the pastor is to introduce a legacy of irrelevance as an antagonistic virtue to the heresy of relevance—that heresy of relevance being a wholesale jettison of the Old Testament in favor of motivational speeches over theological exegesis.

Doctrine is credible not necessarily because of its origin but because of its persistent transformation of the human soul. When I say "origin," I mean to intimate that we are not to overrealize the credibility of a text because it is Johannine or the writings of Peter, or from any other authors of Scripture. Rather, "The Scripture makes the test of its own validity to be in what it can do"[10]—the entire transformation of a human soul, the regeneration of a depraved spirit, the restoration of a life lost in mire, and the redemption of a lineage of scandal as that soul encounters God in sincere reading of Scripture.

Indeed, I would argue that the texts of Scripture that make us the most uncomfortable are the ones that are likely to benefit our soul. We ought not ignore previous truth in the name of dispensationalism. Neither should we deny previous truth from our sense of curriculum and doctrine. Previous truth is certainly interpreted with greater revelation and disclosure in mind, but not apart from it.

Henry Ward Beecher does not necessarily mention doctrine in his polemic and sermon on Scripture, but does give us a thought as to the whole of Scripture in what it teaches us, including law when he says,

> It was not necessary to teach us that men were creatures of sorrow and trouble. It was not necessary to teach us that human passions were rampant and rioting. It was not necessary to teach us that the world groaned and travailed in pain. All history and all experience taught us that. But it was necessary to teach us that we had some relation to wickedness in man.[11]

The metanarrative is a constant refrain of human depravity illustrating, and doing so even doctrinally, that we need rescue. The whole of

---

10. A quotation from Henry Ward Beecher's sermon on "The Holy Scriptures," reprinted in Beecher, *Forty-Eight Sermons*, 327–42. Found also in Fant and Pinson, eds., *20 Centuries of Great Preaching*, 4:343.

11. Beecher quoted in Fant and Pinson, eds., *20 Centuries of Great Preaching*, 4:348.

humanity is sinful, born into wickedness, with a preponderance to sin. We are hopeless without a Savior, without Christ, without the love of God to pardon through His Son Jesus Christ. The curriculum, then, unveils our heart of sin and the redemptive plan of God to define the very nature of love, a definition that stands elusive without the irrelevance of Scripture—irrelevant for it is dissonant with normative human inclination and kingdoms, for it juxtaposes our nature with divine nature, our kingdoms with the heavenly kingdom.

Doctrine is irrelevant to human nature for it opposes human nature. Doctrine provides such an altogether counter current to human inclination as to propose an epistemology that unravels carnality at its core.

> The doctrines of humility; of meekness; of gentleness, of non-resistance under injuries, the whole schedule of Christian dispositions which were marked out by the Saviour, shine as though they were so many gems and jewels brought down from the bosom of God."[12]

And all the while, the doctrine, although a jewel itself, is only meant to compliment the true jewels in the bosom of God, you and I. Listen once more to the prophet: "They shall be mine, says the LORD of hosts, my special possession on the day when I act, and I will spare them as parents spare their children who serve them" (Mal 3:17).

Doctrine is dissonance. It is unapproving of our instinctive ego, dismantles our systems of oppression, runs contrary to our pride, pushes against our cravings for power, and prophetically decries our towers of Babel. Doctrine is irrelevant to the heresy of relevance, for it speaks contrary to the human nature to build autonomous empires, to shun genuine authority, to sacrifice holiness on the altar of church growth. A pastor who leaves a legacy of orthodoxy in teaching that unveils the human heart has left a good legacy, even if rejected by the builders who build on a different foundation.

Legacy of Irrelevant Conviction

All of Scripture is used for "reproof" (2 Tim 3:16), from the Greek ἐλεγμόν (*elegnon*), which is rendered "conviction." This is used only twice in the New Testament, here in 2 Timothy and in Hebrews 11:1. It

---

12. Beecher quoted in Fant and Pinson, eds., *20 Centuries of Great Preaching*, 4:349.

connotes not only the charge on the basis of which one is convicted, but also the unveiling of the truth of that charge.[13]

Thus, although our English "conviction" may be the closest term defining this Greek construction, it falls short in describing the two functions of the nature of reproof. One function is to render a charge. Perhaps this is a charge of wrongdoing or a charge of warning. But the charge is not yet enough to fulfill the scope of reproof. The truth of the charge must also be fully realized for the culmination of this action. The whole of God's Word provides the charge that we are indeed sinful but moves beyond this to the display of the truth behind this charge. The whole of God's Word thus reads the human heart more precisely than one's own intuition. Indeed, to take God's Word seriously, we must first admit that we do not read it—rather He reads us!

This is the intimation of the Greek ἐλεγμόν, the reading of the human heart to convict, reprove, admonish, and reveal the truth of such a charge. If the heart is willing, the fruit of repentance can be the result. For the revelation of truth is for the cause of repentance, and the fruit of repentance is none other than restoration of the child of God.

Perhaps we can bring greater clarity to this Greek construction by exploring its only use elsewhere in the New Testament, in the epistle to the Hebrews: "Now faith is the assurance of things hoped for, the conviction of things not seen" (Heb 11:1).

The word translated "conviction" is ἐλεγμόν. Some translations may use the word "evidence," but "conviction" is likely a better translation. Used in this context, we find that ἐλεγμόν is an inner work not seen by the aid of human vision but seen rather with the existential confidence of the qualities that are less corporeal and more spiritual in nature. That is, faith and hope are correlated with ἐλεγμόν to give us more nuance into the intent of the meaning, so that ἐλεγμόν is a work in the human heart that is often perceived rather than seen, felt rather than touched, qualitative rather than quantitative. It is the revealing of truth in the human heart and deep transformation birthed out of a charge made possible by the Word reading the human heart.

Karl Barth has written that it is both impossible and necessary for ministers to take on the task of speaking of and for God. He works through his own sentences to illustrate the seeming paradox of this task and yet exhorts that it be done nonetheless. He can find the strengths and

---

13. Zodhiates, *Key Word Study Bible*, 1712.

weaknesses of both the dogmatics and the mystics in attempting to speak for and of God. He suggests that the dialectician is likely positioned most ideally for such communication but in the end comes to terms with the degradation of even its rhetorical palace.

Life is from death; you have from surrendering; you receive when you give; the first is last and the last first. These dialectics, Barth suggests, are the devices the apostle Paul used so widely to communicate the kingdom. In the end, in Christocentric fashion, Barth looks to Christ as the end of the minister's task to speak of and for God. It is all summed up in the person of Jesus. Somehow, and quite mysteriously, we simply speak of Him, exalt Him, magnify Him, as if this is the only task that amounts to anything substantive in the kingdom.

Barth speaks of Jesus as the Word as something of a penetrating work when he says,

> The fact is that a man cannot believe what is simply held before him. He can believe nothing that is not both within him and before him. He cannot believe what does not reveal itself to him, that has not the power to penetrate him.[14]

So that which is both without and within leads one to believe. The witness is one part; the encounter is the next. The witness has the opportunity for encounter for it is only divine encounter that penetrates the soul. The eyes can see the pathos of the one who testifies. The ears can hear with what great conviction the preacher speaks. However, it is the Spirit of God who so comingles with divine speech to penetrate the heart like a spear wreaking havoc and slaying the serpent's template for destruction. God revealed as Immanuel is the Word made flesh and must be encountered as we would encounter one another. Jesus reveals the intent of the heart as He did with the woman at the well. He penetrates, He pierces, He impales the old creation hanging to pride with the clench of death.

Barth rightly suggests there is a strength in the mystics, and it is imbedded in the following: "We must reckon with the mystic's awareness that God never aids man in his growth but fundamentally aids him only in his decline."[15] Your decline is a paradox but may be the very key that opens the door to greater possibilities with God. The more you decrease, the better able you are to speak for and of God. The greater the condescension, the greater the urgency to speak with fire. Like floating down a

14. Barth, *Word of God*, 202.
15. Barth, *Word of God*, 203.

stream whose destination is humility, let the currents of God's grace move you and let the breakers, though formidable, overtake you.

As a pastor, leave a legacy where the truth of the charge against human depravity is unveiled and the conviction that one is guilty be felt like an earthquake in the human heart. Conviction is a convulsive encounter giving way to repentance and condescension. This is irrelevant to the popular mechanics of Maslow's self-actualization, or motivational speakers providing seven steps to being the best you, or obsessions with leadership methodology to promote one's organizational prowess. Get low, preacher; preach truth that convicts, provide context for persistent repentance, and utter the name of Christ. This is the pastor's legacy when expositing the Scriptures to a congregation.

Legacy of Irrelevant Correction

All of Scripture is also used for correction. Where "reproof" is a charge with the truth revealed concerning the basis of the charge, "correction" is the way made plain on how one may amend his or her ways—from the Greek ἐπανόρθωσις (*epanhorthosis*), which means "to set right again."[16] It is used only here in 2 Timothy 3:16. And we have already noted the difference between reproof and correction, both of which are substantiated on the entire Word of God. Correction is irrelevant for it is contrary to natural inclination. If we are honest, we do not necessarily crave correction. A pastor will create a context where the people of God crave correction, for in it is the development of righteous character. We live in a church culture where correction is anathema. There are those who can do no wrong. If correction is applied, the one corrected pounces on the one correcting with accusations to evade such correction.

Henri Nouwen provides a corrective course for the minister tempted with relevance in his *In the Name of Jesus*. He reflects on his time living with the intellectually disabled and becomes aware that all the relevant and practical aids that enabled him to interact with others failed him. His books, lectures, and academic accolades were not enough to offer genuine friendship to his neighbors.

> Not being able to use any of the skills that had proved so practical in the past was a real source of anxiety. I was suddenly faced with my naked self, open for affirmations and rejections, hugs

---

16. Zodhiates, *Key Word Study Bible*, 1715.

and punches, smiles and tears, all dependent simply on how I was perceived at the moment.[17]

And isn't anxiety that which mitigates a step into irrelevance? We are anxious in this setting and thus labor to be relevant, to offer a contribution that matters, to be noticed and affirmed for our words, work, and worth. Our naked self, our vulnerable frailty, and our just being present are inferior if there is no agenda, talent, or worth to offer. Pastors succumb to this anxiety by running the rat race of relevance and finding new ways to adapt to the cultural shifts of their day. But what if in doing this we lose ourselves? What if we lose our humanity? What if we lose our way of relating to others? What if, like Nouwen, God would like to strip us of the trappings of our books, titles, lectures, and reputation so that we can start anew on relating to God and others? A pastor will leave a good legacy of irrelevance if the corrective course is given to a congregation accustomed to basing one's identity on title and influence rather than love and relationship.

For Nouwen, he was

> Forced to rediscover my true identity. These broken, wounded, and completely unpretentious people forced me to let go of my relevant self—the self that can do things, show things, prove things, build things—and forced me to reclaim that unadorned self in which I am completely vulnerable, open to receive and give love regardless of any accomplishments.[18]

The pastor can only leave a legacy of irrelevance as he or she becomes irrelevant to accomplishing grace rather than receiving grace. Love is received genuinely when one is vulnerable, when one is open to being frail, when one is not afraid to be humble, to face shame head on, to reckon with failure and allow love to overcome the fear that binds us in the need to produce.

Nouwen is "convinced that the Christian leader of the future is called to be completely irrelevant and to stand in this world with nothing to offer but his or her own vulnerable self."[19] And we must become convinced ourselves. When a plan crumbles, a project falls apart, your vision unravels, and your friends flee as you are being stoned—perhaps

---

17. Nouwen, *In the Name of Jesus*, 28.
18. Nouwen, *In the Name of Jesus*, 28.
19. Nouwen, *In the Name of Jesus*, 30.

then we come to the end of ourselves as defined by titles and become a self redefined as loved and loving.

The great irony of accomplishment is despair. For there is no amount of accolade, reputation, or competence that can remove our loneliness. Indeed, accomplishment reinforces our loneliness as we decorate our walls with rewards and titles but sit in that room alone. Nouwen is right to observe,

> While efficiency and control are the great aspirations of our society, the loneliness, isolation, lack of friendship, and intimacy, broken relationships, boredom, feelings of emptiness and depression, and a deep sense of uselessness fill the hearts of millions of people in our success-oriented world.[20]

The greater the success, perhaps the greater the despair and separation. Success has become an idol in the Western church and has come to be illustrated by large crowds, big buildings, and an abundance of cash. But what if God is correcting us through means of the Word? Paul was clear to emphasize that the corrective rod of Scripture provides for a heart that is open to be read. What if COVID-19, having shut the doors of our churches, has become an obvious censure of what we have defined as success—that is, big buildings and big crowds? What if God is using the horrific nature of a deadly virus to redeem His people with intimacy? The church that is wealthy is poor. What if Christ is revealing the Laodicean dilemma in our hearts today?—"For you say, 'I am rich, I have prospered, and I need nothing.' You do not realize that you are wretched, pitiable, poor, blind, and naked" (Rev 3:17).

As Nouwen asserts,

> The leaders of the future will be those who dare to claim their irrelevance in the contemporary world as a divine vocation that allows them to enter into deep solidarity with the anguish underlying all the glitter of success, and to bring the light of Jesus there.[21]

Irrelevance rejects success for solidarity with human anguish. Irrelevance is weeping with others, confessing one's frailties, joining the fellowship of suffering, and being present without the need to anxiously undo the pain. Irrelevance asks the hard question that Jesus places before

---

20. Nouwen, *In the Name of Jesus*, 33.
21. Nouwen, *In the Name of Jesus*, 35.

Peter: "Do you love me?" (see John 21:15-19). The question is also the answer, a polemic opposing relevance. This question to begin all other questions penetrates the ache of the human heart.

> Often it seems that beneath the pleasantries of daily life there are many gaping wounds that carry such names as abandonment, betrayal, rejection, rupture, and loss. These are all the shadow side of the second love and reveal the darkness that never completely leaves the human heart.[22]

Where the second love will always fail us, it is useful for pointing us to the first love, which never fails. We must feel the sting of the second love for it will compel us to pursue the first love. And it is in this world, where few ever really come to feel a limitless love, where we are to declare that one is loved regardless of the shadows that penetrate the human heart.

The first love is always present, but is one reciprocating the first love? This is the question Jesus asks of Peter. The question restores his confession of love as the question is raised no less than the number of times Peter rejected Christ. Jesus responds to Peter's yes with a charge: "Feed my lambs" (John 21:15). Yes, pastor, feed the lambs that leave you, that bite at you, that go every which way that seems right to them. Feed the lambs in a society where autonomy is an idol and where many cannot see that their own wealth and power is a snare to their first love. Feed the lambs with an irrelevant message of human depravity and the need for a Rescuer. Feed the lambs with a corrective message born from a heart of prayer. Be the vulnerable example and crush the idols of prestige, false confidence, and feigned control.

I was discussing with my wife, not too long ago, the ache I feel from a lack of a community that is covenantal in how we love one another. I dare say, I may not know what this truly feels like. In part, this is because we have moved often, nearly every four years, and I do wonder if time is a necessary ingredient in forming these kinds of relationships. When pastoring, I was under the impression that these relationships were forming, but I was mistaken. I am convinced that the Western church does not know how to operate in covenantal love with one another. It appears that the church comes together more as a professional relationship with a common objective. It is the mission or project that unites the church members together rather than a profound love for one another. Listen to the narratives that comprise your church; is it possible

---

22. Nouwen, *In the Name of Jesus*, 40.

that those shared narratives reflect a mission trip, project, purpose, or labor that becomes the thread that unites their stories?

We are driven by mission and have forgotten how to love. As one moves from one job to another if the compensation is right, people move from church to another if the setting or project is right. We placate our loneliness by telling ourselves that we are working for the kingdom. But we are left wanting at the end of this work, back where we started, lonely. We do not know love for we do not know vulnerability and the capacity to be with someone without a common project to work on. In our purpose-driven culture, we have forgotten covenantal love. Take away the common mission, and people do not know how to relate to one another.

I am convinced that I do not know how to love in this manner, for the loneliness comes as a poignant reminder that I too was a professional acquaintance to the community I pastored. I ache to know this love, and perhaps the Lord is redefining this love within me through the medium of my current loneliness and wilderness. Perhaps this is my own reckoning—I who remain aloof and estranged. God reveals the ache, to deepen our pursuit of love.

Nouwen ends his chapter on relevance with an appeal to contemplative prayer as a renewal of our love for God and our commitment to be loved by Him vis-à-vis immersion in His presence. It is a reminder that theology is "Union with God in prayer."[23] Theology as a discipline fails us if it is strictly moral and principled without the relational intimacy to ground our motives. If we are solely motivated to be right rather than relational, we often find ourselves embroiled in conflict.

> But when we are securely rooted in personal intimacy with the source of life, it will be possible to remain flexible without being relativistic, convinced without being rigid, willing to confront without being offensive, gentle and forgiving without being soft, and true witnesses without being manipulative.[24]

Legacy of Irrelevant Instruction

The entire Word of God is to be used for "training in righteousness," from the Greek παιδεία (*paideia*), meaning the whole training and education of children (which relates to the cultivation of mind and morals,

---

23. Nouwen, *In the Name of Jesus*, 44.
24. Nouwen, *In the Name of Jesus*, 45–46.

and employs for this purpose commands and admonitions, as well as reproof and punishment).²⁵ παιδεία is thus a wholistic concept of education. It conveys not only a sense of knowledge but an enculturation of righteousness vis-à-vis the instilling of virtues. παιδεία utilizes a broad spectrum of commands, admonitions, reproofs, and punishment as revealed by the entire Word to instruct the child, the disciple, the church member, and the student.

Indeed, as I write now, my children attend a classical Christian school with this title, Paideia Academy, whose intent it is to educate the child with this Greek construction in mind. The mission of Paideia Academy is helpful here as it brings a nuance to the definition of the Greek construct.

> Paideia Academy is an instrument to assist parents in carrying out the biblical mandate to bring up their children in the paideia (training and admonition) of the Lord. We employ the Western classical tradition of learning, rooted in a distinctly Christian worldview, that cultivate godly affections and wisdom in our students in order to graduate virtuous men and women, who in Christ advances the Kingdom of God.²⁶

παιδεία instructs not only the mind but also the body. Thus, the curriculum includes the training of and ultimately care for the body. Moreover, παιδεία cultivates an environment of soul care, curbing sinful passions and encouraging orthopathy. παιδεία is concerned with the enhancement of virtue in the human soul. παιδεία uses as a tool the concept of chastening, knowing that God chastens those He loves (see Heb 12:6). God continues to use παιδεία through the medium of His Word to remove the Egypt out of us through the chastening of wilderness experiences.

So, the Word can now and should always chasten our current notion of the church. Mark Sayers has offered such an instruction in his book *Disappearing Church*, where he chronicles the rise of relevance in the contemporary church. He observes that there was a fundamental belief that fueled the emergence of the relevance obsession in the church.

> The assumed belief was that people were uninterested in Christianity because they found church traditions alien and

---

25. See Rogers Jr. and Rogers III, *New Linguistic and Exegetical Key*, 506, and http://www.greekbible.com/l.php?paidei/a_n——-asf-_.

26. See Paideia Academy's mission statement at "Paideia at a Glance," https://paideiaknoxville.org/at-a-glance/#1529770230953-d8278915-2f8b.

> unwelcoming. If the church could be made relevant—with culturally relevant forms instead of traditions and ritualized trappings—then Christianity would flourish in the Western world again.[27]

So, liturgy became obsolete, casual was the new normal, mystical union with God was replaced with coffee and motivational speeches, sacred space was replaced with a concert arena, and discipleship became enamored with entertainment and Disney-like experiences to keep people coming back. The truth of the matter is that traditions have not been eradicated but new ones have emerged that embrace a cultural relevance that lamentably has diminished the countercultural message of the gospel and the distinction the church has always illustrated in society. We define flourishing when the culture accepts us, juxtaposed to the gospel, which defines flourishing as being persecuted for the name of Christ.

Sayers asserts that the inevitable end of the relevance heresy and the longing pursuit of the church to stay relevant in culture is the emergence of the religion of self. It is a resurrection of ancient Gnosticism with "an attempt to retain the fruits of Christianity and the solace of faith while maximizing the individual's authority."[28] The only authority that remains in the ash heap of relevance is the authority of self.

The myth of me tells a story that the future is brighter and more intelligent when the self is elevated and autonomous. The dangerous heresy here that has infiltrated much of the church is the central tenet of Gnosticism, that truth is found within the individual. One must peer inside one's own soul to find truth rather than finding truth in the disclosure and revelation of God.

We must surrender to the microscope of God and His Word to find the depravity of our own soul. Because of this, church is becoming more about personal preference than covenantal community, individual prophetic insight than pastoral authority, and catering to public opinion than expositing God's Word. Relevance picks and chooses certain Scriptures over others to fit a worldview of the self. Relevance seeks comfort over holiness, image over transformation, and corporation over community. The myth is, as such, that for the institution to survive, we must adopt the sleek protocols of secular organizations, take polls, create an electric atmosphere, cater to the senses, upend traditional authority. If

---

27. Sayers, *Disappearing Church*, 34.
28. Sayers, *Disappearing Church*, 57.

there was ever a time that we needed to capture the παιδεία of God vis-à-vis the whole of Scripture, it is today.

Pastor Cesar found himself at the end of an accusation that his sermons were not relevant enough. One of his board members provided stinging feedback that he ought to steer away from Old Testament texts and provide greater practical application if he wanted the church to grow. This board member also provided a book on communication written by communication industry gurus as an exemplar model that he should follow. His board member was also uncomfortable with certain "types" of people who were waiting in the church lobby who were seeking counseling at the church. She lamented that she felt uncomfortable with these kinds of people present and suggested that the church was not the proper venue for this kind of counseling.

Pastor Cesar also implemented a church-wide survey to perhaps discover why the church was shrinking, which became a perpetual thorn in his side. For staff and board members would confront Pastor Cesar if he did not make every change suggested by the survey. One board member continually asked, "Why have the services not been shortened? Why do we not have a separate hospitality room? Why this or why that?" In essence, the central question was, "Why are we not bending to every suggestion of popular opinion?" The temptation is to create a culture of accommodation rather than accountability, comfort rather than transformation, and happiness rather than holiness.

Sayers asserts that the revitalization of Gnosticism in our culture has also infiltrated the church, where "the public sphere (of church) ultimately was subservient to the wishes, wants, and desires of the individual. In such an environment, people had grown ghostly because they were only half there; the script of culture had taught them to view public spheres as spaces in which to self-create."[29] Certainly we do not call it Gnosticism in the church; we have spiritualized self-creation and personal fulfillment with prophetic terms such as "personal revelation" or a "personal word." Indeed, church has become more about personal revelation than about communal love. We jump from one prophetic conference to another looking for a personal word to fulfill the meaninglessness we feel because of cultural pursuits.

In the end, the personal word cannot save us, and we come to the same conclusion of Solomon, that everything is vanity (see Eccl 12:8).

---

29. Sayers, *Disappearing Church*, 97.

In this culture, the pastor is suspect if he or she does not have the same personal revelation of a person of influence within the congregation. The pastor is then perceived as lacking in spiritual intuition, insight, or revelation and needs to be instructed in a gnostic way. This is where spiritual authority is blurred and where the individual is king or, at worse, a god unto him- or herself. There is no real authority outside of the autonomous will. Sayers asserts bluntly that "the church was never called to help individuals self-create."[30] Indeed, the church is called to undo our self-created selves and become sons and daughters of God beholden to the will of God.

Sayers proceeds to offer a critique of my own tradition that was personally insightful. He states that relevance has led many traditions to focus on the immanent to such a degree that there becomes an obsession with "the professional presentation panache of Pentecostal churches." Now, he does not single out Pentecostal churches as he sees relevance taking hold in all churches, but with differing manifestations. However, I do take to heart this critique as I look upon the landscape of my own tradition and must confess that there are many who spin their wheels attempting to accomplish a stage presence, or a star-studded service, or an online precision where community can be lost in our attempt to execute a service in excellence.

Indeed, "excellence" has become a keyword in many Pentecostal services and implies a smoothly rehearsed band and praise team, an online package, and a preacher who connects with charisma. Again, none of these attributes should be considered caustic or unworthy of pursuing, but relevance pushes the pursuit at the expense of genuine community with our flaws and vulnerable weaknesses. C. S. Lewis sums it up aptly when he says,

> Christians have largely ceased to think of the other world that they have become so ineffective in this one. Aim at Heaven and you will get earth thrown in: aim at earth and you will get neither.[31]

In other words, the people of God are not in hot pursuit of the culture of this kingdom, but a wholly different culture—a kingdom culture. We bring a countercultural message and existence that should look distinct and different from the culture of this world. Ah, but the rub may be that

30. Sayers, *Disappearing Church*, 97.
31. Lewis, *Mere Christianity*, 134.

our attendance shrinks, our revenue dries up, and our buildings are not a sleek modern fanfare. Our community loses pretense and image, and we find what we have known all along; we are broken and prone to weakness. We come to know that we are in desperate need of true community to heal; we need God's love to love our neighbor. Rather than a mere common mission to rally around, we find that there is a common love to live around. It is by living in the kingdom of God in an already–not yet epistemology that we discover Jesus again, that we discover the gospel again, that we learn that presentation is not king, our autonomous wills are not gods, and our fancy Hollywood-style presentations on social media are not the telos of our ministry. Love is the end, the telos, the place of rediscovery, the gospel that convicts, and the calling from our Savior.

Legacy of Irrelevance—Kingdom In-Breaking

And so, what is the result of good doctrine, reproof, correction, and instruction? The fruit is the teleological completion of the human heart and behavior for good works (see 2 Tim 3:17). Without the entire Word, we have an incomplete thesis by which to utilize the tools for telos. This is why the heresy of relevance is just that; it is a redefining of Christian community to be devoid of discipline, admonition, reproof, and thorough instruction. Relevance appears to be a cultural code word appealing to our postmodern sentiment and justifying our current way of life. However, the Scriptures do just the opposite. The Word calls us out of our current cultural context to transform us so that we penetrate the sleeping culture with the jolt of God's countercultural kingdom message and to awaken the soul from the slumber of idolatry and so-called relevance.

So, how do we emerge from this heresy of relevance and at the same time navigate Barth's dilemma? Where there are strengths of dogmatism, there are also imbedded weaknesses; where there are insights with mysticism, there are also pitfalls; where there are safe places for the dialectic, there are also philosophical circles. To be sure, every rhetorical style of speaking for and of God will have its inherent weaknesses, because of human frailty, but praise God that He decides to place his treasures behind the frailty, coarseness, and weakness of human jars of clay (see 2 Cor 4:7).

There is another way for the ministers to speak of and for God that needs to be added to Barth's litany of necessary impossibilities.

It is the way of story. A pastor who is facing the heresy of relevance must help the flock inextricably weave his or her own story with the Christian metanarrative of Scripture. We must see ourselves in Abraham's dilemma of deciding whether to slaughter his own son. We must see our own courage in taking up the sling and stone to slay Goliath. We must see our own fear when escaping the death threats of Jezebel, running to hear the whisper of God. We must preach narrative even when taking up a text of principle. Minsters must speak of and for God by speaking parables, as Jesus did. We must somehow, with the Spirit's enablement, create stories of purpose, morality, virtue, and fruit. We must, like Bunyan before us, communicate the truths of God's Word through the perilous journey of Christian and Hopeful. We must, with divine guidance, create worlds such as Narnia where there are witches and creatures both nefarious and righteous. We must get at the inner soul who desperately longs to touch the mane of Aslan and ride along His sprint to bring liberty to the captives.

And when the story cannot find words in the expression, I would also add to Barth's ways of speaking for God the medium of song. We must learn to sing again. We must write the hymns that celebrate the narratives of God's immanence. We must sing of God's power to throw both the chariot and the rider into the sea. We must call upon God in song to vindicate His children. We must appeal to heaven with songs for comfort, for strength, and for resilience in the journey.

Steve Land has written about Pentecostal spirituality in this manner, explicating that for Pentecostals there is an appropriation of redemptive narrative to be one's own in Pentecostal liturgy. "Everybody became a witness to Calvary and his or her own crucifixion with Christ, the biblical Pentecost and a personal Pentecost, the healing of the disciples and his or her own healing and so on."[32]

Therefore, we do not merely read words on a page, but we become immersed in the story of God, His immanence in creation, and become witnesses to the same event that the disciples witnessed. We witness the cross of Christ when a sinner becomes saved. We witness the day of Pentecost when a believer becomes baptized in the Holy Spirit. We witness the healing of the atonement when efficacious prayer penetrates the body with the virtue of Christ. We witness the power of the kingdom of heaven over the kingdom of darkness when demons are exorcised. We are called

---

32. Land, *Pentecostal Spirituality*, 73.

thereafter to tell these stories, the narratives, our part in the story of God. Pastors, preach God's breaking into your world from His world to a people who desperately long for their own beholding of Jesus as Savior, Healer, Holy Spirit Baptizer, Sanctifier, and Soon-and-Coming King!

We must continue to sing songs of our hope, of our passion, of our love, and of the kingdom to be consummated,

> I love to tell the story, for those who know it best
> Seem hungering and thirsting to hear it like the rest;
> And when in scenes of glory I sing the new, new song,
> 'Twill be the old, old story that I have loved so long.

> I love to tell the story,
> 'Twill be my theme in glory,
> To tell the old, old story
> Of Jesus and His love.[33]

It is the telling of story and the motif of song that conjures up the existential longing for Jesus, the revisioning of one's own being translated within a new kingdom. Pastors, we must integrate all the rhetorical styles of preaching, including dogmatics, mysticism, dialectics, story, and song, and do so from the whole of Scripture. We must reclaim the narratives that are being propagated within our society, and to do this we must preach; we must speak for and of God. No matter how insufficient we may be, no matter how incomplete the rhetorical style, no matter how impossible it might be, it is necessary. Tell the story to all; tell them of His glory, the old story that is also the new story for it is ever appropriating the new of community, family, birth, and vision. Tell of the cross, the atonement, the resurrection, the birth of the church vis-à-vis Pentecost, the miracles, the healings, the restorations; and tell the story of the Soon-and-Coming King!

Finally, one should note that this may be a lonely journey as it will become increasingly unpopular, and many may be terminated because they are a voice crying out in the wilderness.

Pastor Cesar was asked to resign when he did not follow the script of the popular survey. The narrative in this context is that if we have a new pastor with relevance, then the church will grow again. Pastor Cesar's irrelevance became a snare for the ones he was leading. However, he need

---

33. Hankey and Fischer, *African American Hymnal*, 821.

not be ashamed of what he deposited, for he leaves a legacy of irrelevance that perchance helped some to have eyes to see that the kingdom of heaven is so unlike the kingdoms of this world. And if this occurred even to one soul, then perhaps this seed will grow to help others see that the last thing we need in the church is yet another relevant church—accommodating the preferences of our culture and autonomy.

Rather, the need for today is an altogether different church where people know each other, where the kingdom of heaven breaks in, and where Christ reigns in the hearts kindled with fire from on high. When accused of preaching Old Testament passages, resound with the affirmation, "I am guilty of this." For the Old Testament story is also my story. The New Testament story is also my story. The whole of Scripture is our story, and the *Logos*, the Word become flesh, is the one who is the beginning and ending of our story. Preach the entire Word, pastors, and God will be with you to leave a legacy of irrelevance.

Chapter 10

Legacy of Apologetic Evangelism

> As for you, be sober in everything, endure suffering, do the work of an evangelist, carry out your ministry fully. (2 Tim 4:5)

PAUL PROVIDES AN EXTENSIVE charge to Timothy in chapter 4 of 2 Timothy. In this charge, he states that Timothy is to preach the Word in whatever season he is in. He is to rebuke, exhort, and utilize sound doctrine as the medium by which he is to perform both functions of the pastor (that is, rebuking and exhorting).

Of note, pastors are usually more comfortable with the exhorting function of pastoral ministry; the rebuking function can become increasingly uncomfortable throughout the course of one's ministry. As an anecdote, Pastor Xavier was able to proclaim messages of rebuke in a corporate setting when preaching but retreated when personal rebuke became necessary in the context of council or staff meetings. Whenever he did meet with members or staff in private to confront certain behaviors, a seed of resentment grew to the extent that some staff members consorted with the church board in an effort to undermine his authority and ultimately call for his resignation. Pastors must lean into conflict, not retreat away. Pastors must exercise both exhortation and rebuke as God-given tools of the office; this is an imperative aspect of the pastoral office.

Paul provides the rationale for this ongoing ministry of pastors, for the time will come when congregations, churches, and communities of faith will not endure sound doctrine. The word "endure" is an interesting one to posit in relation to sound doctrine, for it implies that sound doctrine requires a semblance of patience with a connotation that this is a rigorous exercise. The word comes from the Greek ἀνέχομα (anechomai), which is "to bear up," "to endure," "to put up."[1] The use of this construction implies a barrage of antagonism to sound doctrine so that the one hearing must endure *in* sound doctrine as the *teachers* of the age will make every attempt to convince the hearer *out* of sound doctrine.

Indeed, this is the travesty of Paul's prediction. A time will come, and is likely already present, when the church takes upon themselves the authority to hire certain individuals who will teach to their itching ears. And what are these ears itching for? The word κνηθόμενοι, illustrates a tickle or scratch. It is a people who are intentional to look for interesting and spicy catchphrases or information. The itching is only relieved by a self-justifying message of these new teachers.[2] Paul is clear: the ears are itching for sinful desires of all sorts. It is the same *teachers* Paul had warned of a mere chapter earlier when he described them as "Holding to the outward form of godliness but denying its power. Avoid them!" (2 Tim 3:5).

The *teachers* envisage a form of godliness, but with no real power, their real agenda is to cater to the human passion in defiance of the Holy Spirit and sound doctrine. And when we have church boards that are a result of popular election, these board members then become voices for a faction so that, as in politics, the board members are advocating what the people who elected them desire for the direction of the church. This is why popular elections in church governance have become such a travesty, for it portends to the snare of satisfying the populace or in some cases a cohort that is most vocal in opposition. And yet, Paul predicted this when he asserted that churches will ἐπιθυμία (ep-ee-thoo-mee'-ah), literally "heap" or "pile upon" for themselves teachers who pander to human preference. Like a politician who seeks to pique curiosity and acquiesce popularity, the pastor now is beholden to the same board who hired him. If the people are unhappy, the pastor is in a position where he or she must muster up teaching or vision that placates the board and by proxy members of influence. Pastors can easily become the ponds of church boards.

---

1. Rogers Jr and Rogers III, *The New Linguistic and Exegetical Key to the Greek New Testament*, 506.

2. Rogers Jr and Rogers III, *The New Linguistic and Exegetical Key to the Greek New Testament*, 506.

I was speaking with a director of an orphanage during my time as a pastor and he informed me quite frankly that he had learned that he must do whatever the church board asks if he wanted to keep his job. In all his years of ministry, he had learned that his administrative role was simply to accommodate the board; any disagreement could be misconstrued and jeopardize his vocation.

When Paul uses ἐπιθυμία to describe the state of churches, he uses the future indicative active tense of the word. This denotes a prophetic envisioning of many churches who, rather than being the passive victim of false teachers, will intentionally look for these kinds of teachers by extending an invitation for them to be their pastors. The word image is like a pile or heap of carcasses—catering to the dying flesh while ignoring a living soul.

To defend holiness, God's entire Word, and kingdom principles is to create context in our modern church ecclesiology of politics for the pastor to be terminated or asked to resign. The church is not the victim but the medium by which these false teachers flourish. Thus, we need courageous pastors who are apologetic in orientation—defending the truth at the expense of their popularity. It appears that we have lost a generation of pastors. Who carries the legacy of Leonard Ravenhill, David Wilkerson, and Steve Hill?

An Apologetic Legacy

Pastor Xavier can recall the painful business meeting where a board member, newly voted in, claimed to have accepted the nomination for one purpose only, and that was to force Pastor Xavier to resign. His basis for this singular intention was a claim that he was following the agenda of the people who elected him. Sure, Pastor Xavier was ignorant to the size of influence of this cohort, but certainly had to face the fallout of such a splintering assertion.

This member undermined the current meeting agenda, inserted his motion that Pastor Xavier ought to resign, and proceeded to moderate the meeting by inquiring into the other board members' thoughts on the matter. Pastors, you must know your polity. In this instance, the pastor is the chair of a council meeting and moderates the meeting and sets the agenda. If this is the case, pastors must put a stop to board members who attempt to run a meeting, undermine pastoral authority, and introduce agenda items from the whim of the moment or from a personal cause.

Pastor Xavier processed the dynamics of this meeting with a mentor, and what this mentor said seemed to hang in his mind in the ensuing months: "They have essentially stripped away any influence you have to lead, and without influence, you cannot lead." Pastor Xavier began to see the realization of this statement in the months to follow. Resistance escalated against his efforts to lead, not only from board members but also from staff members.

The time, therefore, is coming and has come when people will want teachers that appeal to their own preference, style, and thoughts of how liturgy and direction should proceed. We are living in times where church councils or boards will feel the need to cater to those who "elected" them out of a perceived need that he or she is there to exercise his or her influence to direct the church.

In another instance, Pastor Xavier was faced with a board member who asserted that international people were leaving the church because of his preaching. She stated that pastor Xavier's preaching must change and must become more relevant for international people to remain. Pastors, when hearing these kinds of statements, it will be important to perform some sort of investigative inquiry.

For example, how many international people communicated this to the board member as a reason for leaving the church? Is the board member actively inserting his or her own opinion when talking to these individuals? When the church board deems it more important to cater to the will of the people rather than the will of God, the board has essentially turned inward rather than outward, and it will require much courage of the pastor to redirect the church to seek the will of God. Call for prayer and fasting; call the church to humble itself before the Lord so that seeking direction is from a posture of looking up and out rather than down and in.

The time will come when form Christianity will become increasingly prevalent. Form Christianity emphasizes appearance over the inner life, corporation over community, optics over ontology, structure over spiritual reform, popular opinion over theophany, human elections over divine appointment, filled seats over filled hearts, revenue over relationship, institutional fame over kingdom fame, human "lordship" over divine love. Form Christianity will continue to build its own kingdom until the Lord Himself humbles this community. Pastors, be on guard, for many would rejoice to see you go if you spent your days preaching as a voice in the wilderness.

The fruit of assorting such teachers in any community is the turning away from truth and the embracing of fables. Again, Paul employs the use of the word μῦθος (*muthos*). We should note the source of turning to the myths that can become so prevalent. The source begins with the inability to endure sound doctrine. This proceeds to accumulating teachers who will justify the human need to wink at sinful nature and lustful desires. This is like Israel's kings asking the prophets to prophesy something positive concerning the fate of Israel rather than the truth, which was a harbinger of calamity.

Paul provides several examples that are antithetical to sound doctrine and that deserve corrective discipline through the pastor. For example, we find a litany in Paul's first letter to Timothy when he describes some examples of the "lawless and disobedient":

> this means understanding that the law is laid down not for the righteous but for the lawless and disobedient, for the godless and sinful, for the unholy and profane, for those who kill their father or mother, for murderers, the sexually immoral, men who engage in illicit sex, slave traders, liars, perjurers, and whatever else is contrary to the sound teaching. (1 Tim 1:9–10)

A pastor leaving an apologetic legacy will have confronted the profane speech that can splinter a congregation. A pastor leaving an apologetic legacy will have spoken out against violence and murder of all sorts. A pastor leaving an apologetic legacy will have admonished those who refuse to submit to proper ecclesial authority. A pastor leaving an apologetic legacy will have defended purity and confronted sexual immorality of all sorts, whether it be heterosexual or homosexual immorality. The pastor leaving an apologetic legacy will have preached the word with great conviction confronting lies, false accusations, and gnostic influences attempting to contaminate the simplicity of the gospel.

Paul addresses those who are contrary to sound doctrine once more in his second letter to Timothy when he writes,

> For people will be lovers of themselves, lovers of money, boasters, arrogant, abusive, disobedient to their parents, ungrateful, unholy, unfeeling, implacable, slanderers, profligates, brutes, haters of good, treacherous, reckless, swollen with conceit, lovers of pleasure rather than lovers of God, holding to the

outward form of godliness but denying its power. Avoid them! (2 Tim 3:2–5)

The apologetic pastor confronts the love of wealth—the avarice that can easily become a god in our society, which equates happiness with luxury. The apologetic pastor introduces and defends the virtue of suffering in an age where the prosperity gospel has obscured suffering, at best, or rejected it as a lack of faith, at worse. The apologetic pastor will confront the love of self that is the result of a society ever bent on autonomy as human actualization, where this has become a golden calf. The Facebook likes, the obsession with seeing oneself on a screen, the comments on social media and the retweets that stroke a person's ego—the apologetic pastor will call for the destruction of these idols in the human heart.

In the same way, the apologetic pastor is less concerned with institutional preservation and more concerned with the legacy of the gospel. Thus, the buildings, programs, preservation of the status quo, and cultural structures that insist on keeping the pistons moving are given less or even no importance to a community who is transformed by the Spirit. As Craig Loscalzo asserts, "The pulpit must learn to proclaim Christ while being a loyal critic of institutionalized religion." Loscalzo cites Buttress, who further asserts, "We are witnesses to grace, not to institutional success stories."[3]

The apologetic pastor will ignore and perhaps refute the temptation of a marketplace church where attractive fads and techniques are utilized to gain members, thinking that somehow this will translate to personal discipleship. Newbigin is keen here in his critique of such missional missteps when he states that the church must "Exclude ideas which have been too prevalent in 'evangelical' circles, ideas which portray the Church in the style of a commercial firm using modern techniques of promotion to attract members."[4]

The apologetic pastor will honor the family system, obedience to parents, the authority of the home, and the order of creation, the lines of authority that God has ordained. The apologetic pastor will help a congregation envision obedience as surrender and submission as kenosis, and create a disciplined community where one is indeed working his or her salvation in fear and trembling. "Where there is no [disciplined] vision, the people cast off restraint" (see Prov 29:18).

---

3. Loscalzo, *Apologetic Preaching*, 24.
4. Newbigin, *Gospel in a Pluralist Society*, 226.

However, we should also note, the apologetic pastor is not merely concerned with the gospel's influence on domestic or private concerns. As Lesslie Newbigin asserts, "To be faithful to a message which concerns the kingdom of God, his rule over all things and all peoples, the Church has to claim the high ground of public truth."[5] If the kingdom will come to reign all, then we must promote a gospel that influences all of life. The kingdom ethos is to guide, influence, and interpret all spheres of society. An apologetic pastor is not merely interested in helping people manage their checkbooks, parent their children, or enhance their marriages. These are important facets of life, to be sure, but are not the only parts of living that the gospel and the kingdom ought to inform. The apologetic pastor helps the congregation to be a living epistle that interprets all of society. The kingdom is to reign over our work, our politics, our charity, our education, our entertainment, our music, our healthcare, our business, etc. The apologetic pastor will advocate a kingdom perspective on all spheres of living as there is no crevice to be hidden from the light of God.

The apologetic pastor will hold in esteem various expressions of gratitude. The Eucharist will be the very embodiment of gratitude as this sacrament is regularly practiced. This sentiment will become existential as the apologetic pastor instills a culture of gratitude. Grumbling and complaining is often stymied in a congregation where a culture of gratitude is esteemed. We are thankful for our brothers and sisters regardless and because of their flaws. We thank God that He houses treasures in vessels of clay. Joy is the fruit of gratitude. The apologetic pastor will defend a polemic of gratitude and will be intentional to create structures in liturgy where gratitude can be expressed. For example, the liturgical practice of testimony is one component that assists pastors in creating such an environment. Testimony is a wonderful segue into the Eucharist. We are thankful for the body and blood of Jesus, who heals us from our sins and diseases! It is His blood that also binds us together as community, a family, and a corporate body in His body.

Newbigin is helpful here as well when he characterizes the local church as a hermeneutic of the gospel. That is, the gospel is not merely written words, but a community living out the gospel in the kingdom of God in the ordinary work of life and the not so ordinary mystery of the Holy Spirit at work in the community. He states that a community that

---

5. Newbigin, *Gospel in a Pluralist Society*, 222.

is a hermeneutic of the gospel is first a community of praise. He qualifies this by saying that the church "Is a place where people find their true freedom, their true dignity, and their true equality in reverence to One who is worthy of all praise that we can offer."[6]

Newbigin goes on to argue that thanksgiving is part and parcel to being a community of praise and contrasts this with a society that leans into the demand for human rights. He states that the church offers a message of human rights only as an advocate for someone else, not the self. A congregation that is a hermeneutic of the gospel and apologetic for God embodies a kind of gratitude "That can spill over into care for the neighbor," and is not necessarily therefore "The expression of commitment to a moral crusade."[7]

Radical gratitude is not a cause but an existence. It is not a means; it is a way of life. It is not an obligation, but an expression of a heart who worships from a genuine posture of utter thanksgiving for a gift undeserved. The church must recapture an epistemology of gratitude, not as a mere form, but as a corporate expression of regard for God and for neighbor. Jesus has given us the Eucharist, which we can regularly practice, and testimony, which we can regularly profess, not as trite liturgical components of community, but as life-giving rehearsals of our story with Christ.

The apologetic pastor will raise a standard of holiness where we are continually seeking God's holiness to be our holiness through acts of regeneration and sanctification. Water baptism is this initial sacrament that begins a lifelong journey of holiness. Foot-washing is the sacrament that bears repeating as it creates context of sanctifying the body of Christ. Regular opportunities for repentance are calls the apologetic pastor utters for the body to create the potential for the spot and wrinkle to become undone in the bride Christ is perfecting (see Eph 5:27).

The apologetic pastor will preach, live, and display the extremity of a kingdom love that condescends, becomes incarnational, and surrenders one's agenda. Such a love disarms the critics, silences the demonic opposition, and better yet, inculcates a kingdom ethos. We love through embrace, and embrace also includes correction. We love with the consideration that others are always better than ourselves. The other is worth our time, our condolences, our comfort, our listening ear, our smile, our prayers, our dreams. Our ambitions for a healthy congregation

---

6. Newbigin, *Gospel in a Pluralist Society*, 228.
7. Newbigin, *Gospel in a Pluralist Society*, 228.

must begin and end with love. Revive the *agape* feasts pastors—become an ardent defender of radical hospitality. We are currently in a moment where violence runs the streets in many cities in the context of a plague that has unearthed undercurrents of violence. When lawlessness rises, the love of many grows cold (see Matt 24:12). This should not be in the body of Christ. The apologetic pastor will charge the flock to love with greater veracity in a society that escalates with animosity.

The apologetic pastor will confront the perjuring of truth, the twisting of doctrine, and the breaking of covenant. The apologetic pastor is unafraid to create accountability and discipline within the church. The apologetic pastor will have to disfellowship members from time to time in hope that the buffeting of the flesh will restore the soul through repentance of sin. The apologetic pastor will confront those who accuse without merit, who flaunt influence by diminishing another. The apologetic pastor will mediate exhortation, consolation, and encouragement and confront those who despise others from jealousy, covetousness, or difference.

Newbigin extrapolates further that a congregation as hermeneutic will be a community of truth. But we must be on guard, as the means of disseminating truth does not become "Modern propaganda, but must have the modesty, the sobriety, and the realism which are proper to a disciple of Jesus."[8]

An apologetic pastor does not make mere attempts to market truth in catchphrases or slogans to place on a T-shirt or bumper sticker. We are not a people who make truth claims but rather live out truth claims in covenant with God and neighbor. We do not galvanize social media for attempts to "get out the message," as a pep rally would to celebrate a brand. Rather, an apologetic pastor and congregation live every day in our private and public spheres in a way that declares the truth through love, service, holiness, and becoming that which is lovely in Christ. If a congregation is to defend God, it must give hope where there is despair, and it can only do so when it "Renounce[s] an introverted concern for their own life, and recognize that they exist for the sake of those who are not members, as sign, instrument, and foretaste of God's redeeming grace for the whole of life of society."[9]

Betrayal will be a harbinger of birth pains as the Parousia of Christ nears, but the apologetic pastor will confront those that betray the faith

---

8. Newbigin, *Gospel in a Pluralist Society*, 229
9. Newbigin, *Gospel in a Pluralist Society*, 233.

and will be unafraid to implement loving discipline. He or she will confront the proud, the haughty, those seeking power and influence as a means of elevating their own ego, and those who narcissistically resent those who are thought to be inferior. The apologetic pastor will introduce ascetic practices as means to crucify the flesh. Fasting, confession, prayer, and repentance will be regular disciplines in the church. Hedonism, Epicureanism, Gnosticism, and nihilism are confronted on a regular basis as the apologetic pastor contends for the faith and advocates for a true form of godliness—contentment, care for the orphan, and care for the widow. The marginalized will be a priority and a joy to serve within such a congregation.

Such is the legacy of the apologetic pastor and be not surprised if such a pastor is rejected and asked to resign if the culture of the church would rather invest in fading structures of fads, trends, curb appeal, appearance, and online presence. We have been warned.

Legacy of the Evangelistic Pastor

Concomitant with being a herald, messenger, or preacher of the gospel are the afflictions that necessarily come. This is because the word being spoken offends the lusts of the flesh. Paul affixes afflictions to the gospel earlier when he posits the following to Timothy: "Do not be ashamed, then, of the testimony about our Lord or of me his prisoner, but join with me in suffering for the gospel, in the power of God" (2 Tim 1:8).

It is time that pastors shake off the utopian perspective that a preacher is altogether always loved by the same community he or she preaches to. Certainly, this may occur at times, and when it does, it is a gift. However, the pastor ought not always look for internal miscues when afflictions arise in his or her ministry. Afflictions are inevitable; suffering to some extent will occur; and the exhortation to Timothy is the same for us— endure! Endure the waves of false accusations; endure the flame of the furnace; endure the betrayal, the opposition, the pain, the sieve. Discern, as we have already discussed, when to shake the dust from your feet, but rejoice when God takes you to another city for the sake of proclamation. One of the most difficult tasks for my wife and I was to discern whether to endure or move on. This is a most personal decision, and a pastor needs to be encouraged when making either decision.

Next, Paul charges that Timothy perform "the work of an evangelist." I would like to spend some time meditating on this charge. For it appears to be a charge that one perform the work regardless of the office of an evangelist. Moreover, there are certainly all kinds of idiosyncratic definitions of this kind of work. Moreover, I find myself wondering if this kind of work aids the pastor in enduring affliction. For it may very well be that when the religious offense has spilled over in vitriol against the pastor, reprieve is found in the sinner who turns to a Savior, a wounded soul who finds a refreshing spring, and a lonely pilgrim who finds a companion who provides a cup of cold water for his journey.

The Greek εὐαγγελιστοῦ (*evangelistou*) is one who declares the good news. It is as simple as the definition confers. It does not prescribe a method or conjure up a paradigm of steps that one must follow. It does not imply that one method is superior to another. It does not describe any other form of declaration than mere proclamation that there is indeed good news. It does not infer the context, location, phraseology, or phenomenon of such declaration. In short, Timothy is being asked by Paul to do the work of speaking the good news.

We might appropriate this kind of work into our own ministry as pastors by meditating on Phillip, who was described as an evangelist, and thus is a prototype of the office. We begin with this description in Acts: "The next day we left and came to Caesarea, and we went into the house of Philip the evangelist, one of the seven, and stayed with him" (Acts 21:8).

The New Testament church was beginning to recognize these offices very early as descriptions were being given to certain individuals within the church. We find that Phillip was one of the first to hold this office and it would behoove us to reflect on his ministry as a way of defining "the work of an evangelist."

We begin in Acts 8. What begins the dissemination of the gospel was imbedded ironically in persecution. As Saul was persecuting the church, the people scattered abroad to avoid imprisonment, and everywhere they went, they spoke of the good news. Another lesson here: persecution is indeed a seed of the church, causing one to reach greater audiences than if persecution were not present.

Phillip sojourned to Samaria and it is recorded that there he preached Christ. The Greek word is κηρύσσω (*kerusso*), which is "to preach, herald, and proclaim," so that preaching Christ is simply proclaiming Christ. Preachers speak of the good news that Christ died, was buried, was resurrected, and is coming again.

We further learn that miracles accompanied Phillip's preaching, and many would come to give audience to his preaching because of these signs (see Acts 8:6). It is unclear whether doing the work of an evangelist necessarily includes miracles, but indeed this was the case with Philip. For with Philip, exorcisms and healings occurred because of preaching the gospel of Christ in Samaria. In short, the signs accompany those who believe and substantiate the veracity of preaching Christ. The evangelist proclaims Christ and the signs follow the proclamation as the Lord may direct. As David Peterson notes, "In Acts, signs and wonders establish the credentials of a prophet before all the people and all authenticate or verify the prophet's message by actually conveying a partial realization of the salvation proclaimed."[10]

The evangelist is a herald where kingdom in-breaking occurs in the context of gospel proclamation. He or she becomes a tangible expression of the already–not yet tension of the kingdom upon the earth. Perhaps this is why we hear of miracles when someone enters the places of Samaria, a people rejected by Israel but embraced by the Lord, who reveals His glory to the marginalized and ostracized. Phillip continues the ministry that Christ began when evangelizing a scandalous woman of Samaria.

Second, Philip is taken to an Ethiopian eunuch as a next episode in his work as an evangelist. He explains the prophet Isaiah to the God-fearing gentile. Thus, the work of an evangelist is also to exposit and instruct the meaning of the Scriptures.

I would like to take a brief excursus on this work of an evangelist—that of hermeneutics. And I would like to converse with Eugene Peterson on the topic in his book *Working the Angles*. Peterson also peers into the exchange between the Ethiopian Eunuch and Phillip, the evangelist. He does this by distinguishing between one who is a guide and one who explains. The Eunuch returns Phillip's questions with a question: "How can I [know], unless someone guides me?" (Acts 8:31). Peterson goes on to assert, "But the explainer, the exegete, leads the meaning out of the text; the guide, the hodogete, leads you in the way of the text."[11]

The evangelist is incarnational in this sense. He journeys with, which is more than merely explaining the way. Exegesis is necessary but

---

10. Peterson, *Acts of the Apostles*, 281
11. Peterson, *Working the Angles*, 128

may not complete the instructional component of an evangelist. One may need to jump into the chariot and go along for the ride until a pool of water emerges to provide a divine opportunity for immersion with the holy. What may set apart the evangelist from the teacher is the journey itself. A pastor who is also an evangelist risks the differences to embody the journey. The Ethiopian eunuch and Phillip, as Peterson notes, were quite different men entirely, but found a place of convergence from an ancient prophecy in Isaiah![12] Indeed, perhaps differences become the common dictum of the evangelist, with inherent examples displayed here by Phillip and the eunuch and also in the Parable of the Good Samaritan. Evangelists perhaps have the uncanny ability to envision the alien as his or her neighbor.

Phillip guides the Ethiopian eunuch to Christ. This is the central tenet and dogma of the evangelist's message. Peterson cites Martin Luther as having asserted that "We always read the Scriptures with an eye for *was Christum triebit*, 'what impels to Christ.'"[13] Christ is imbedded in the tapestry of every Scripture. God has been revealing His Son for millennia. Perhaps the evangelist's legacy is one that can also see Christ in the story of Scripture and in the ordinary lives of the sheep. Perhaps the evangelist pastor moves the flock to see Christ as all in all in the very fabric of human existence (see Col 3:11).

The evangelist is also the baptist, immersing new believers in water as one lays claim to the Christian faith. Phillip preached Christ, exposited the Scriptures, was an instrument of various miracles, and baptized new converts in the faith (see all of Acts 8). This is the work of an evangelist and performing this work is tantamount to making full proof of your ministry.

Pastors have the same reasons that we all have for omitting the proclamation of the good news in what is now a postmodern and perhaps post-Christian society, where Christ is fine if accompanied by a sundry of idols among our relative palate. We offer the following: "They will not listen to what we say," or "I do not have the relationship to tell them of the good news," or "I fear rejection," and so on.

I was able to recently run an inquiry through church metrics tracking the number of baptisms from 2015 through 2018 at the church I pastored.[14] The church baptized sixty-four candidates, the majority of which

---

12. Peterson, *Working the Angles*, 127.
13. Peterson, *Working the Angles*, 128–29.
14. Please see https://www.churchmetrics.com. This is a free software tool that

were children. There were only two individuals baptized in all of 2016. Thus, on average, sixteen people were baptized per year, most of which were children who were growing up in the faith and part of the families who attended the church. I find myself wondering if this represents most of our churches in the US, so I began looking for research done by Pew Research Center's Religion and Public Life Team to investigate further.

Although Christians remain by far the largest religious group in the United States, this percentage of the population has declined significantly. Over the course of 2007–2014, the percentage of adults who describe themselves as Christians has dropped from 78.4 to 70.6.[15]

Once an overwhelmingly Protestant nation, the US no longer has a Protestant majority. In 2007, when the Pew Research Center conducted its first Religious Landscape Study, more than half of adults (51.3 percent) identified as Protestants. Today, by comparison, 46.5 percent of adults describe themselves as Protestants.

While there have been declines across a variety of Protestant denominations, the most pronounced changes have occurred in churches in the mainline Protestant tradition. The share of adults belonging to these churches declined from 18.1 percent in 2007 to 14.7 percent in 2014. This is similar to the decline seen among US Catholics, whose share of the population declined from 23.9 percent to 20.8 percent during the same seven-year period.

In contrast with mainline Protestantism, there has been less change in recent years in the proportion of the population that belongs to churches in the evangelical or historically black Protestant traditions. Why this population has largely remained unchanged is poorly understood. However, the African American church has not declined as the other Protestant churches have, which should precipitate inquiry on the part of the Christian community. Perhaps we should be interviewing African American pastors regarding what it is that sustains the African American congregations. Table 3 below summarizes the data from the 2014 Pew Research study.[16]

---

tracks certain metrics for churches such as attendance, baptisms, small group attendance, and so on.

15. See Pew Research Center, "Chapter 1: The Changing Religious Composition," https://www.pewforum.org/2015/05/12/chapter-1-the-changing-religious-composition-of-the-u-s/.

16. See Pew Research Center, "Chapter 1: The Changing Religious Composition," https://www.pewforum.org/2015/05/12/chapter-1-the-changing-religious-composition-of-the-u-s/.

Table 3: Biggest Declines Seen Among Mainline Protestants

Biggest Declines Seen Among Mainline Protestants

	Among all U.S. adults			Among Protestants		
	2007 %	2014 %	Change	2007 %	2014 %	Change
Evangelical tradition	26.3	25.4	-0.9	51	55	+4
Mainline tradition	18.1	14.7	-3.4	35	32	-3
Historically black Protestant tradition	6.9	6.5	-0.4	13	14	+1
NET Protestants	=51.3%	=46.5%	-4.7	100	100	

2014 Religious Landscape Study, conducted June 4-Sept. 30, 2014. Figures may not add to 100% due to rounding.
PEW RESEARCH CENTER

While the overall Christian share of the population has dropped in recent years, the number of Americans who do not identify with any religion has exponentially increased. Nearly 23 percent of all US adults now say they are religiously unaffiliated, up from about 16 percent in 2007. While most of the unaffiliated describe themselves as having "no particular religion," a growing share say they are atheists or agnostics. This is indeed a harbinger for the church. How do we reach a growing agnostic and atheist population? How do we answer the questions of those who are cradled with doubt? How do we introduce the gospel in the demonstration and power of the Spirit? See table 4, which summarizes the data on the group that has been described as either non-Christians or the "nones."[17]

---

17. See Pew Research Center, "Chapter 1: The Changing Religious Composition," https://www.pewforum.org/2015/05/12/chapter-1-the-changing-religious-composition-of-the-u-s/pr_15-05-12_rls_chapter1-05/.

Table 4: Composition of the Religious "Nones"

Composition of the Religious "Nones"

	Among all U.S. adults			Among the religiously unaffiliated		
	2007 %	2014 %	Change	2007 %	2014 %	Change
Atheist/agnostic	4.0	7.0	+3.0	25	31	+6
Atheist	1.6	3.1	+1.5	10	13	+3
Agnostic	2.4	4.0	+1.6	15	17	+2
Nothing in particular	12.1	15.8	+3.7	75	69	-6
Religion not important	6.3	8.8	+2.5	39	39	0
Religion important	5.8	6.9	+1.1	36	30	-6
NET Unaffiliated	16.1	22.8	+6.7	100	100	

PEW RESEARCH CENTER

One can note that the proportion of atheists in the US population has nearly doubled over a seven-year period. The "nones" have increased by a total of nearly four percentage points. The epidemic of faithlessness continues to grow while the faithful shrink. Indeed, if this trend continues, then we are to see a future where the US population will increasingly be a mission field, ripe for the gospel. Please see figure 6 for the trend data from the Pew Research Center.[18]

---

18. Pew Research Center, "Appendix C: Putting Findings," https://www.pewforum.org/2015/05/12/appendix-c-putting-findings-from-the-religious-landscape-study-into-context/.

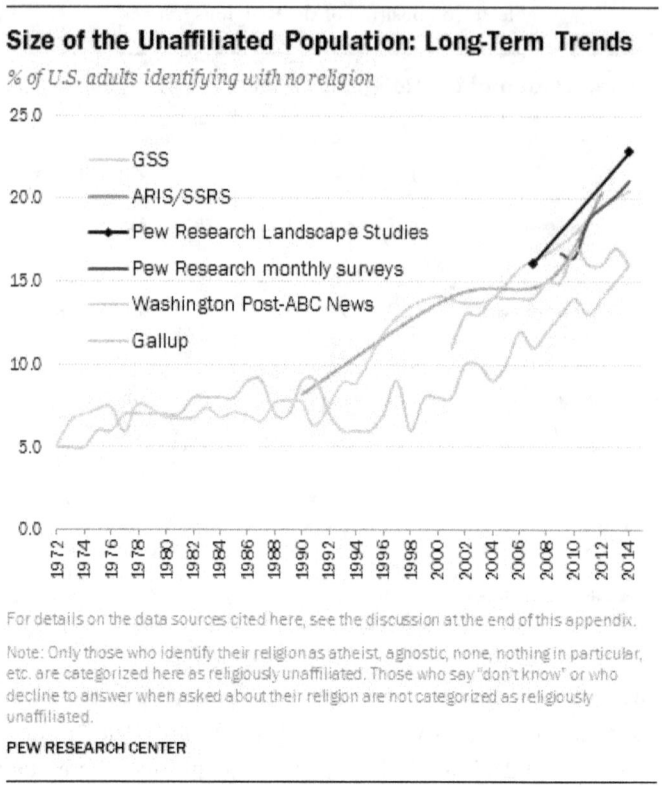

Figure 6: Size of the Unaffiliated Population:
Long-Term Trends

If these trends continue, we are looking at 25 percent of the US population classified as "nones" or atheists/agnostics in a few short years.

We must ask ourselves the honest question as pastors, am I doing the work of an evangelist? If I am truly honest with myself, the answer would be that very little of the work I did would be considered the work of an evangelist. I spent most of my time as a pastor either counseling Christians (an area of discipleship) or administrative work (staff development, budget, council, and planning meetings). Where are the evangelists? Where are the Billy Grahams among us? Where are the Charles Finneys among us? Where are the D. L. Moodys among us? Where are the John Wesleys? How can we capture and infuse the imagination with excitement to antagonize the fear of doing the work of an evangelist? How can we as pastors make full proof of our ministry?

There are some instances where I might consider what I did the work of an evangelist. I spent ten days in the African country of Tanzania preaching the gospel in a crusade where nearly ten thousand people came to hear the gospel each night. Each night of the crusade, nearly one thousand people came to know Jesus. Certainly, there were also signs following, where some were being delivered from demonic spirits and others were testifying to a healing work in their bodies. I returned the next summer to do the same kind of work, and we saw similar numbers coming to know Jesus. I saw more conversions in that ten-day period than I did during the entire five years of pastoring the local church. I consider that work to be the work of an evangelist and was given much less effort, time, and resources than all the other demands that came with pastoral ministry. Indeed, I spent the majority of the last six to eight months of my pastoral tenure mediating conflict, for the church had turned to an inward focus and we as a body lost our missional emphasis.

Paul is exhorting us today as well, "do the work of an evangelist;" fulfill your kingdom assignment, pastor! Model for the sheep the passion for souls that can sometimes be lost in the organizational fervor of maintaining the current church infrastructure or programs. Call prayer meetings to cry out for souls. Amid these prayer meetings, wait on God to impart a vision on how to reach your community. Provide an opportunity for the Holy Spirit to work among the preached gospel with signs following—miracles, healings, and exorcisms. Perhaps your city will also be described as a place where it was shaken, and they were all filled with the Holy Spirit and spoke the word of God boldly (see Acts 4:31). Or perhaps and quite miraculously, the whole city may gather to hear the word of the Lord (see Acts 13:44).

Moreover, as we do the work of an evangelist, we must as pastors anticipate that signs will follow. The commission of Jesus inscribed in the Gospel of Mark plainly informs us that "signs will accompany those who believe" (see Mark 16:17–18). Paul reports to the church at Rome the following: "By the power of signs and wonders, by the power of the Spirit, so that from Jerusalem and as far around as Illyricum I have fully proclaimed the gospel of Christ" (Rom 15:19).

Paul's ministry throughout his missionary journeys included the proclamation of Christ and the forgiveness of sins. Accompanying this message were signs and wonders as propagated by the Holy Spirit. Although many came to hear the good news because of the signs, the Holy Spirit was also wooing and drawing souls to Christ.

Legacy of Proof

Finally, how does one—and in our case, a pastor—fulfill or make full proof of one's ministry? The Greek πληροφορέω (*pleirophoreo*), which is "to fulfill," is a term is found only in biblical or patristic Greek and has the intimation of thoroughly accomplishing something. It is equivalent to the term *pleroo*, which is "to fill up."[19] The ministry of Timothy is to be fully established and brought to an expected end. It is to be completed, reaching the goal that was always intended for Timothy. It is to be fully proved and confirmed with the fullest of evidence.

To gather a yet greater sense of this word, we turn to the other use of this word by Paul, in his letter to the Romans. When writing of Abraham, he employs πληροφορέω and says, "No distrust made him waver concerning the promise of God, but he grew strong in his faith as he gave glory to God, being *fully convinced* that God was able to do what he had promised" (Rom 4:20–21). So πληροφορέω can also connote persuasion or convincing. Abraham did not stagger at the unbelievable remarks from God that he would have a child in his later years, indeed his twilight years. He was advanced in age but still believed; he was beyond his years of bearing children and yet still hoped against all hope. He committed to being strong in the faith and gave glory to God for what would be a fulfilled promise. He was convinced or πληροφορέω that God would discharge his Word accordingly, and thus would perform the miracle where it concerned him and his wife.

Therefore, Paul provides an imperative to Timothy that he complete his ministry. There seems to be a couple of thoughts here describing the intent Paul has for Timothy's ministry. The first and primary intent appears to be teleological. That is, Timothy is to complete the task by which he was called. He is to fill up that which was imparted to him. He is to not leave things unfinished, not contribute his partial passion to the ministry, no matter how formidable. He is to thoroughly accomplish the work of God that began with the gift given to him through the laying on of Paul's hands (see 2 Tim 1:6). In completing his work in a teleological fashion, not only is Timothy completing the work of the Lord allotted to him; he himself is also being completed.

This is the nature of telos. We find that Jesus provides a double entendre for telos when He washes his disciples' feet in John 13. He loves them to their end by coming to His end. He accomplishes them by

---

19. Zodhiates, *Key Word Study Bible*, 1749.

accomplishing the cross. He leads them to everlasting life by ending his own corporeal life, which would soon be translated into a glorious life. The Christian irony is this: we complete Christian ministry by coming to the end of ourselves. Telos is accomplished when we are undone. Love is an unravelling of opulent robes, the taking of a towel, and the expending of our ingratiating lives for the life of a servant.

Second, there is the *proving* aspect of πληροφορέω. That is, Timothy is to walk in a manner where the ministry itself is substantive proof that he indeed is a called servant of the Lord. This seems to be in part connected to the task of doing the work of an evangelist as it is etymologically linked here. This appears to be the secondary intent of Paul in his imperative to Timothy.

Therefore, one may fully discharge one's duties in the form and medium of being an evangelist. One is to proclaim the good news, instruct in the Scriptures, anticipate signs following, and baptize new converts. One is to be whisked away according to the Spirit's purpose and there continue preaching the gospel. A pastor may find him- or herself in Jerusalem one moment, feel a burden for Samaria the next, only to be walking along an Ethiopian eunuch in a chariot on his commute back home. And if this is not the end of the story, a pastor may then be drawn inexplicably to Caesarea to preach the gospel. Who knows if the one convert from Ethiopia did not go with this transformative message to his home country to become an evangelist himself and thus shake the nation of Ethiopia with the gospel?

Souls being added to the kingdom thus appears to be the tangible *proof* of one's ministry. In a partial sense, it is the πληροφορέω of Paul's imperative to Timothy. It completes the quadruple imperative where Timothy is to first watch in all things; that is, he is to employ discernment while serving in Ephesus. Second, he is to endure all afflictions, for they will surely come. Third, he is to do the work of an evangelist. And finally, he is to complete or make full proof of his ministry.

I often look back as a pastor and still wrestle with whether I had fallen short in terms of the enduring imperative. Certainly, I was in the fire of many afflictions over the course of the last year as pastor. Did I retreat when I should have fought? Did I withdrawal when I should have engaged? Did I let the fiery trials chase me away? I do believe I will be asking these same questions for some time as I navigate my own grief and reflection on my season as pastor. The questions may not all be answered in due time, but the asking of such questions is a good exercise for the soul, for it has the potential to lean into prayer, where the answer becomes the presence of God. And as David so aptly prayed, we can appropriate such prayers when we as pastors lean into God's presence: "From you let my vindication come; let your eyes see the right" (Ps 17:2).

Vindication does not come from our lofty arguments, from our witty presentations, from our rhetorical skills at debate. Vindication is not etiologically found in the defense of human friends or advisors. It is not found in the arguments and even loyalty of those most fiercely aligned with you as pastor. No, friend and co-laborer, your vindication comes from a most glorious source, the very presence of the living God. O Lord, let my vindication find its source simply in Your presence. Let this become the appeal of the pastor evangelist. O Lord, look upon our affliction, our wonderings, our woundedness, and answer us simply with Your presence. The need for understanding is no longer a need when we walk and talk with our Beloved. And we can travel this pilgrimage with a song upon our lips:

> I'd stay in the garden with Him
> Tho' the night around me be falling;
> But He bids me go; thro' the voice of woe,
> His voice to me is calling.
>
> And He walks with me, and He talks with me,
> And He tells me I am His own,
> And the joy we share as we tarry there,
> None other has ever known.[20]

Finally, Paul recapitulates this four-tiered imperative with an illustration from his own life. He remarks that his departure is at hand. He has fought the good fight fully and completely. He has kept the faith as Abraham, without staggering or doubting the hand of the Lord. He has finished his course, his marathon, his race, and ran it well. He is anticipating the crown of righteousness awaiting him in glory (see 2 Tim 4:7–8). He loves the Parousia of Christ and waits for Him to come again. Paul is nearing the culmination of telos, completing his ministry as he himself is being complete by Christ.

Pastor Xavier and the leadership felt a burden for a neighboring community. Churches were closing in this community; there was a

---

20. Miles, "In the Garden," 787.

long-standing history of violence, single-parent homes, and drug addiction. The city itself was attempting to revitalize some parts of the community through gentrification of some of the residential areas, but this appeared to displace residents—an unintended consequence.

Thus, he partnered with churches to hold evangelistic crusades. His church also held a day in the park to provide services, counseling, games, and ultimately a gospel crusade. He planted a church in the community with a core group of leaders who remain to this day preaching the gospel in albeit difficult soil.

Indeed, many have argued that to do the work of an evangelist is to plant churches and be a missionary. William Barclay calls evangelists "The rank and file missionaries of the Church."[21] William Combs reminds us that the New Testament evangelist founded multiple churches in various locations.[22] Thus, Pastor Xavier was doing the work of an evangelist by planting a life-giving church in a neighboring community. There the church is bearing witness to the good news that Christ has come to save us from our sins. Some plant, some water, and some receive the increase (see 1 Cor 3:6–8).

The evangelist pastor and his or her church congregation must bear in mind that there are various seasons to evangelism. We should not always reflect on the "glory" days of a "fruitful" work as being an indefinite season. Evangelism may prove to be a long season of sowing and plowing. This kind of work can be the most frustrating, for one may cry out to God in despair as to why the great effort with so little results. Or one may be in a season of watering, constantly nourishing the seed but not yet seeing the buds, the flowers, the green shoots breaking through the soil. One does not always enjoy the season of reaping a great harvest. Indeed, the harvest may be yet for another servant who reaps the work that you labored for. I say all of this to remind the evangelist pastor, do not kick against the goads of the season God has you in. And do not be ashamed to speak of this season, believing as Abraham, hoping against hope, that God will reap a harvest in due season.

---

21. Barclay, *Letters to the Galatians and Ephesians*, 174.

22. Combs, "Biblical Role of an Evangelist," 40. Combs also cites the following works by authors who substantiate the role of an evangelists as primarily the planting of churches: Lincoln, *Ephesians*, 250; Bruce, *Colossians, Philemon, and Ephesians*, 347; MacArthur, *Ephesians*, 143; Lloyd-Jones, *Christian Unity*, 192; Saucy, *Church in God's Program*, 139; McClain, "Evangelism as God Sees It," 21; Baxter, *Gifts of the Spirit*, 174, 179–80.

Pastor Xavier recalls one of the church board members lamenting that she ever took part in a church plant in our neighboring community. The board member stated that they should never have invested in this endeavor, that it was in the end a bad idea. She went as far to say that the new church plant was only interested in the financial contributions that the main campus church could provide for their operations to continue.

Pastor Xavier remembers reacting internally to this remark with a sense of antagonism and rebuttal but he did not altogether make this known verbally. This church-planting team had sacrificed greatly on behalf of the burden to reach souls. They were not remotely interested in financial gain but longed to see support from the entire body of Christ, more so in the form of presence, encouragement, and the serving together in a community with rocky soil. If he had this moment back, he would offer a sharp rebuke of this member and a call for us all to have the mind of Christ in regard for each other. This church-planting team had bravely stepped out into the unknown, were performing the work of an evangelist, and were finding that in their own obedience, Christ was completing them!

Finally, we should not overlook one function of the evangelist pastor and legacy that the church requires—preaching repentance. The evangelist pastor finds him- or herself gravitating to the preaching of repentance, calling for it, admonishing the sheep to draw near to Christ through confession of sin, and weeping between the porch and altar.

Combs, citing Van Gelderen, distinguishes the pastor and evangelist in the following manner: pastors "lead the sheep," where evangelists "shear the sheep."[23] So in this sense, fulfilling the work of an evangelist is also completing the task appointed to you by God to preach against sin and call the flock to repentance. This may be all the Lord has called you to do for a season and then He may catch you up in a whirlwind and drop you somewhere else where you are called to minister truth to one solitary soul for a season.

Great is the mystery of God and His plan for our lives! Therefore, the evangelist pastor should not be discouraged if rejected by his or her own if he or she has faithfully discharged the duty to call the flock to repentance. This is indeed a part of doing the work of an evangelist. Often, the sheep defy the shearing, as it may show the leanness of the sheep underneath

---

23. See Combs, "Biblical Role of an Evangelist," 42.

the fullness of their wool. It is this leanness that the Lord is attempting to expose through the work of the evangelist.

In summary, we have explored the work of an evangelist being a dualistic role. That is, the pastor is both evangelist and apologist. As apologist, our congregations are living hermeneutics to defend the gospel and interpret praxis from pathos. As evangelists, we bear the good news wherever we are able. In essence, this is a part of completing the ministry, but in a much more existential way, it is the completing of ourselves in Christ. Imagine leaving a legacy where one comes to the end of self only to be completed by Christ! This is a legacy worth leaving. Pastors, preach the good news, contend for the faith, and watch as God brings telos to life in your own heart. You leave a legacy to spiritual sons and daughters for they behold a man or woman ablaze for God and then become ablaze themselves. He makes us whole, for the preaching of the good news is not only for the ears of the sinner but for ears of the preacher as well.

Chapter 11

Legacy of Invitation

> Do your best to come to me soon. (2 Tim 4:9)

PAUL ENDS HIS SECOND epistle with an inclusio of invitation in the context of being forsaken. He begins in 4:9 with an invitation to Timothy to come shortly and ends with the same invitation in verse 21 for Timothy to come before winter. Ah, the winter season, one that can portend isolation and loneliness. I believe Paul models for every pastor the need to commune with someone not involved in the immediate context of the work. This is a communion of consolation and presence and every pastor or pastor in transition needs this.

Indeed, if we look at the structure of Paul's last remarks, there is a pattern that evolves into the following schema, an A–B pattern that consolidates the juxtaposition of coming and forsaking.

    A—Come shortly (4:9)
        B—Demas has forsaken . . . (4:10)
    A—Luke is with me . . . (4:11)
        B—Tychicus is sent (4:12)
    A—Come and bring . . . (4:13)
        B—Alexander, no man stood with me . . . (4:14–16)
    A—The Lord stood with me . . . (4:17–18)
        B—Erastus in Corinth, Trophimus is left sick . . . (4:19–20)
    A—Come before winter . . . (4:21–22)

The act of forsaking the shepherd has prophetic undertones. Jesus himself would fulfill this prophecy when He went on to say, "Then Jesus said to them, 'You will all fall away because of me this night, for it is written, 'I will strike the shepherd, and the sheep of the flock will be scattered'" (Matt 26:31).

Jesus cites Zechariah 13:7 as the prophetic literature He is fulfilling when the soldier comes to strike His flesh with the pummeling of a whip, the crowning of thorns, and the nailing of the cross. When Jesus is arrested, those closest to Him flee, scattering in the night, which is the prophetic result of being struck. The prophet is hopeful, however, for he reveals that it is in the striking wherein the sheep are refined and purified (see Zech 13:7–9)

Therefore, the striking has redemptive qualities, for the hand of the Lord will turn upon the sheep in chastisement, refining them as gold is tried in the fire or silver is purified with the flame. This refinement will lead to greater ownership by God of His people. Meditate on this, pastor; the sheep who persecute you invite the correction of the Lord, who refines His sheep for greater possession over their lives. The sheep, in turn, learn to call on the name of the Lord with greater veracity and impunity, laying claim to a divine heritage because of complete surrender.

Demas appears to be one of these sheep who left Paul to pursue the present world. In essence, Paul was deserted by Demas. We know Demas had accompanied Paul on some of his missionary journeys for he is mentioned as being present with Paul as he wrote to the Colossians and to Philemon (see Col 4:14 and Phlm 24). Paul considers him a fellow laborer in these instances when sending his greetings, but this is juxtaposed by his now lamenting Demas's departure. And the intimation here is that Demas has departed from the faith. Demas loves this present world and, as the apostle John has wherewith stated, those who love this present world do not have the love of the Father in them (see 1 John 2:15).

O, the travesty of being a servant of Christ in one breath only to traverse as a servant of the world in the next. Paul laments this departure but appears to record the departures of Crescens and Titus in a different light, as missionary departures. Although we do not know any specifics of the probable missionary journeys, Paul does not add the specifier of them having departed from the faith or having done wickedly, as he is prone to do when describing the abandoning of the faith and church discipline. We also know that Paul devotes an entire epistle to Titus, who is pastoring at

Crete. Luke alone was with Paul—Luke, a beloved companion of Paul's, having been faithful in friendship, in recordings, and in ministry.

Thus, the invitation to Timothy weighs heavy on Paul, for the isolation grows thick with the pending winter. Tychicus has left for Ephesus, likely another missionary journey. It is unclear if Tychicus is coming to give Timothy reprieve at Ephesus so that Timothy could join Paul, but this is implied, and Paul implores the church at Ephesus to accept Tychicus (see Eph 6:21–22). It appears Paul is making ministerial provision for Timothy to have somewhat of a sabbatical and to commune with him, imprisoned and in isolation.

We come, however, to the most nefarious of characters in this story to end Timothy—Alexander the coppersmith. We first learn of Alexander in Acts 19, where he was put forward to offer a defense of the goddess and temple to Diana (see Acts 19:33). As the riot commenced into the theater and the entire town, as it seems, entered an assembly, Alexander was drawn as a man of influence among the community that crafted metals. Paul had preached that the stone idols were not gods at all, thus threatening their trade and commerce. However, before Alexander could convene with an address, the town clerk disbanded the assembly, stating that it was an unlawful gathering and that proper legal protocol must be followed.

Second, we come to know Alexander from Paul's first epistle to Timothy, where he describes having given Alexander "over to Satan that [he] may learn not to blaspheme" (1 Tim 1:20). Thus, we find that Paul, who was no doubt personally disparaged and injured by Alexander, also had to exercise church discipline because of blasphemy. He disfellowshipped Alexander to provide a space whereby he may repent. We know of a personal injury because Paul exercises the use of the personal pronoun. What kind of evil this was is largely undetermined as Paul does not provide specific examples. However, he does not shy away from an imprecatory prayer in appealing for divine retribution. Imprecatory prayers can often be uncomfortable and church culture is prone to pray for retribution against the spiritual forces compelling an individual rather than the individual him- or herself. Paul is, however, clear here and elsewhere: may the Lord also provide to the individual the fruit of correction from seeds of dissension that were sowed.

Therefore, we do know that Alexander formulated a resistance to Paul's words or doctrine. And it is implied that he influenced many people within Ephesus, for Paul laments that none had stood with him when he gave his first defense. Moreover, Paul would treat those forsaking him differently than he did Alexander, who stirred up dissension. For Alexander, church discipline was the correct intervention. For those who were drawn away by his words, great mercy and forgiveness was the correct intervention.

Paul prayerfully appeals to the Lord in two ways: first, that the Lord "reward" Alexander according to his works, and second, that those who were dissuaded would not have this blemish posted to their account. Indeed, the word λογίζομαι (*logizomai*) figures large in Paul's theology on justification as he writes to the Romans: "He received the sign of circumcision as a seal of the righteousness that he had by faith while he was still uncircumcised. The purpose was to make him the ancestor of all who believe without being circumcised and who thus have righteousness reckoned to them" (Rom 4:11). So that in Paul's meditation on justification, every human soul has an account in relation to their soul and regarding eternity. This account has the imputed righteousness of Christ when one comes to believe in Him. This is the premise that Paul is asserting when using Abraham as an example that what justifies a believer is his or her faith. It is faith that credits the imputed righteousness of Christ to one's account, so that when Paul is imploring the Lord not to hold the people's abandonment to their account, he longs for their eternal or soul account to remain free from blemish.

Paul, like Moses before him, interceded for the flock, even for those who opposed him. What love, mercy, and tender forgiveness must have gripped Paul! And yet, how does one discern when to enact discipline vs. mercy? For Alexander, Paul appealed to the Lord to perform justice; for the rest who were influenced, he appealed for mercy.

Pastor Trevor would find himself in a similar situation when some of his church board members opposed him, not only in the direction for the church, but concerning his character; there were none who stood with him. During the public meetings with the state director, there were none who vocalized their support without prompting. And yet, Pastor Trevor feels a sense of sympathy for them, longing for the tender mercies to fall upon them. For many, they had never been to a board meeting where such insults flew out of the mouths of those elected. Certainly, the utter shock must have paralyzed any unction to speak on his behalf.

Some months after resigning from the church, Trevor caught himself lamenting with a friend that none stood up in public to come to his defense. After finishing this conversation, he realized that such tender mercies for those who remained silent were still in need of full maturation in his own heart. Perhaps the mere utterance is not enough. From the deep recesses of the heart, he must feel the statement emerge with great force, "Lord, do not hold this to their account." Perhaps it is in making this appeal on behalf of others that he can find the source of his own healing. Perhaps, like Steven before him, Pastor Trevor may glimpse the glory of our Savior if he can simply and genuinely utter. "Lord, do not hold this sin against them" (Acts 7:60).

And so, as pastors, we must rely on the Lord standing with us when all forsake us. Pastors, you must preach the Word of God amid the most vehement of opposition. It is the Word of God that manifests His glory, which displays the evidence that God is with you.

During persecution, preaching is the antidote. It is the instrument of warfare entrusted to the pastor, to be wielded in great veracity for the congregation. The pastor being opposed is not to preach less, but more. Do not take sabbaticals during opposition; defer this for another season of harmony. Call for special services of prayer and preaching. Call the church to assemble and disclose that there is much warfare in the community and proceed to walk the sheep through the valley of warfare with the rod of God. When all have forsaken you—your supposed friends, the staff, and the leadership—preach! Preach to the lost, to the sheep, to all who will give an audience. Let the Lord vindicate you through the anointing that accompanies the preached Word. Begin preaching during the midweek service. Pastors, you have been called to preach, and so perform this duty with the heavy hand of the Lord compelling you to speak with a fire caught up in your very bones (see Jer 20:9)!

Pastor Trevor can recall, a few weeks after his resignation was called for, that the very person who had begun to call for his resignation came to him after service. He made a statement that at once surprised him. He stated that God was with him. He did not sense that this statement was disingenuous in the moment, but likely forgotten soon after as he continued to call for Pastor Trevor's resignation.

Nonetheless, let the majesty of God take possession of your tongue and magnify our Christ. Lift up the name of Jesus with such a great throng of celebration, love, and fervency that the people of God join in the praise of our God. God has a way of either melting the dissent away in the flame of love or expelling it with the might of His judgment. Perhaps God, through preaching, will close the mouth of the lion, deliver the pastor from the evil work lurking within the congregation, and preserve His servant for the heavenly kingdom.

Timothy, O Timothy, come before winter. Come and hear my honest wound, my honest insecurity, my loneliness and solitude. Timothy, come before the roads are impassable, before my heart is trodden down with my own thoughts, which need the temperance that you bring. Timothy, do not delay; do not hasten another day. Come with the friendship that I hold so dear, with the safety of a faithful ear. Come and share in my burden to love a people who despise me, to pray for a people who despitefully use me, to continually lay down who I am for who the Lord is.

Where are you, Timothy? Where are the ones who visit, who offer their presence without pomp or circumstance, without pretense, without an agenda, without the need for me to be anyone else but myself?

> Do thy diligence to come before winter. Travelling would be difficult then, if not impossible, and perhaps the white snow would be the shroud of the apostle. Anyway, he has been delivered once for a brief space out of the mouth of that lion—Nero. But it is not easy to believe that this ferocious lion, satiated for the time with blood, should seek to devour him no more. But a Roman prison in winter is a very desolate place, and he who has been hurried from place to place by his keepers has left even his warm cloak behind him, and hopes to cover himself with that black goat's-hair skin when winter comes. Bring the cloak, Timothy, and the papyrus books—old vellum manuscripts, perhaps the roll of Isaiah and the prophets; let not Timothy forget them, for there are songs of prisoners in those inspired prophetic rolls. And let Timothy remember that St. Paul wants to see his face again.[1]

It seems to me that Nero is not the only lion whose mouth is shut in the moment. God has shut the mouth of Alexander on behalf of Paul so that the gospel is preached, and the enemies scattered. And yet Paul is not at Ephesus; rather, he is imprisoned at Rome, awaiting his destiny before a Roman emperor. Surely, he asks for the small comforts of a theologian and Christian; the cloak for warmth, the scrolls for comfort, but more importantly, the presence of Timothy.

Of all requests, this is one is particularly noteworthy. When in the prison of our call, the winter of isolation, the dungeon that can so easily bemoan despair, Paul asks for Timothy. Pastors, we must turn to the prophets; we surely need the cloak to shelter us from the storm. But

---

1. Homily by W. M. Statham, "2 Timothy 4:21."

more than this, we need Timothy to hear of our great adventure and our great woundedness. We need an audience who will nod without a word in acknowledgment that the wound is worth feeling in another soul. A wound is worth the travel, for a companion awaits whose soul is dear. Pastors, there is a Timothy for you! There is a companion who will bring you the prophetic scroll and the comfort that accompanies this word. His presence will aid you as you wrap yourself once again in the cloak of God's Word and the fellowship of His servants. But you must invite him into your world!

The Invitation

The question remains, therefore, are you leaving a legacy of invitation? That is, are you inviting someone into your cell? It is the legacy of invitation to one's home, to one's prison, into one's life that can be a most potent balm for a healing moment. For a description of the power of invitation, we turn to one whose life was changed by a simple invitation, Rosario Butterfield.

Butterfield was both an open lesbian and Syracuse professor with tenure. She advocated for the LGBT community and lived with a lesbian partner. She had written an editorial that sparked great interest from both the secular progressive and Christian communities. However, one letter stood out, for it provoked her to question her own presuppositions. It was a letter from Pastor Ken Smith, from the Reformed Presbyterian Church in Syracuse. The letter included an invitation for more dialogue. It was not an invitation to church, not an invitation to a gospel crusade, not an invitation to immediately convert, but simply a letter for discussion in the setting of a dinner.

I do not want to demure the invitations to churches, crusades, or immediate conversion, but would like for us all to reflect on the power of a simple invitation to a dinner table, where the context of genuine love can be on display in a way that gives an unbeliever a glimpse into the heart of God by opening the heart of the vessel where God dwells. Here is how simply Butterfield describes the invitation: "We had a nice chat on the phone, and Pastor Ken invited me to dinner at his house to explore some of these questions."[2]

---

2. Butterfield, *Secret Thoughts of an Unlikely Convert*, 9.

The questions Pastor Ken invited her to explore around his dinner table were the ones he expressed in his letter, which were questions regarding the suppositions that supported Butterfield's claim in the op-ed article in the local newspaper. These were questions on hermeneutics, faith, and claims on morality. This intellectual challenge is what provoked Butterfield to initially accept his invitation.

Butterfield reflects on her initial meeting with Pastor Ken and his wife, Floy. She strikes a chord that it is invitations like this that may be a central tenet lost in what is now the commercial enterprise of the church. "Ken and Floy invited the stranger in—not to scapegoat me, but to listen and to learn and to dialogue."[3]

The notion of the stranger and alien coming into our homes seems quite frightening in the world of hyper-privacy and autonomy in which we traverse. I would argue that we fear people knowing the real me, the story that may be full of brokenness, struggle, and the misbehavior of our kids. We fear that our fellow Christian will judge us for not being perfect. We fear that our Christian brothers and sisters will have little to no grace for a bad day, a misspoken word, or a moment of anger. We fear the unbeliever will misunderstand or somehow cause us to stumble. So, we go on living private lives and then wonder why we feel so lonely.

What began as an invitation culminated in transformation. This is the power of invitation—a simple gesture at first glance, but an altogether loving and sacrificial act. Butterfield had spent much time with Pastor Ken, his son, the Bible, and even in prayer before the moment of her conversion. She had even begun to attend church, wrestling with existential questions and tenets of her own childhood. Her gay and lesbian friends were also noting a change and she could not hide the kind of change occurring in her affections that seemed to be changing her grounds of morality and way of thinking. Listen to the beauty of her conversion experience and reflect on the fact that this experience began with an invitation to dinner:

> That night, I prayed, and asked God if the gospel message was for someone like me, too. I viscerally felt the living presence of God as I prayed. Jesus seemed present and alive. I knew that I wasn't alone in my room. I prayed that if Jesus was truly a real and risen God, that he would change my heart. And if he was real, and I was his, I prayed that he would give me the strength of mind to follow him and the character to become a godly

3. Butterfield, *Secret Thoughts of an Unlikely Convert*, 11.

woman. I prayed for the strength of character to repent for a sin that at that time didn't feel like sin at all—it felt like life, plain and simple. I prayed that if my life was actually his life, that he would take it back and make it what he wanted it to be. I asked him to take it all—my sexuality, my profession, my community, my tastes, my books, and my tomorrow.[4]

This is the crisis-dialectic moment for Butterfield. She comes to the end of herself and there finds a new self. She surrenders all her presuppositions and the sturdy *moral* ground that had up to this moment felt so secure and sure. She *repents* even though it feels incongruent existentially. She is in the presence of God with a sacred moment that would radically transform her life. She has found God, or rather discovered that He has always been knocking on the door of her heart. What began as a seed of invitation has flowered into an encounter with God.

Paul's invitation is to a fellow laborer, Timothy. Pastor Ken's invitation was to an unbeliever. Invitation is the key here. Are we inviting people into our lives both to hear our pain and to provide solace to another? Do we break bread with others? Do we open our doors to our neighbors? Even as I write this, I am challenged with the paucity of my own invitations. I am always waiting for someone to invite me into relationship and then wonder why I receive so few invitations. Perhaps it is because we are all waiting for someone else to make the first move. We should take note that it was the travelers to Emmaus who invited Jesus to stay with them for dinner, quite before they recognized Him as Jesus. Indeed, perhaps God will disclose Himself to you at the dinner table with those you have invited to dinner (see Luke 24:29–32)! Moreover, loneliness may be a season divinely orchestrated to teach us that we in truth, are not alone. Rather, there are some companions near that we simply do not see or hear. This is the lesson that Hannah Hunard must teach us.

Invisible Companions

In Hannah Hurnard's allegory *Hind's Feet on High Places*, Much-Afraid finds herself on the shores of loneliness. Although she continues to have her companions, Sorrow and Suffering, the Shepherd must depart for a season. This is a time for Much-Afraid when she feels quite alone, walking

---

4. Butterfield, *Secret Thoughts of an Unlikely Convert*, 21

the shores in a sense of solitude and wandering across landscapes with a mere word from her Guide, that He will come when she calls.

As she walked, "an icy wind came shrilling across the billows, stabbing sharp as a knife."[5] The winter had come for Much-Afraid, and it was the winter of loneliness, the space where she must believe a mere Word. It was a time when the landscape did not change with each step and where the horizon congealed into a mirage of a sorts, where change was hoped for but not apprehended.

But it was here where her walk changed; there was a confidence, a strength, and a resolve that had never been present. A mark had come to her soul, an indelible imprint that could not be sponged away. Something, or rather Someone, had produced an inner resilience to persevere.

She recalls her past, the Valley of Humiliation, the timidity, the fear, and the silence that took hold of her tongue whenever there was a cause to cry out for justice and admonish the wickedness that had erupted around her. She says, "I was that woman, but am not that woman now."[6]

And O how the winter has this proving effect on the soul! There is refining of the silver and the removal of dross when winter comes. There is a kind of loneliness that stands on the Rock of Ages only to fall upon in it in our own brokenness (see Matt. 21:44). There is a changing of the guard, peering into the wells of salvation, and a crafting of a soul for the imminent war of the ages. What had happened to Much-Afraid was her coming to the end of her grief and thus the end of herself. She was at the last stage in Kubler-Ross's model of grief, where "we start the process of reintegration, trying to put back the pieces that have been ripped away."[7] This is acceptance, and it had come upon Much-Afraid as it does for all who go through the loneliness of loss, grief, pain, and death.

And yet the description here is uncanny. Acceptance is a flower that grows out of the furnace of Egypt. It is a desert rose that withstands the elements of the heat that bears down ever so oppressively on the seed of faith. Acceptance that solitude, loneliness, and winter has come has the potential to bear "the stamp of royalty," as an entourage may herald the

---

5. Hurnard, *Hinds Feet on High Places*, 40.

6. Hurnard, *Hinds Feet on High Places*, 40.

7. Kubler-Ross, *On Grief and Grieving*, 25. Kubler-Ross goes into intricate detail explicating the five stages of grief, a theoretical framework of grief apprehended by her own observations in psychotherapeutic work. She states that one will experience the following stages when navigating grief: (1) Denial, (2) Anger, (3) Bargaining, (4) Depression, and (5) Acceptance. Acceptance is the final stage, marking the end of grief and beginning of a reintegrated life.

coming of a king's son or daughter.[8] Think of it, Beloved; your winter and current or future loneliness may be the very limp required to mold you for the robe, the ring, and the imprint of divine DNA.

When acceptance comes as it may, and an inner life is reordered, a vision emerges. The beauty that was once obscured by a myopic lens of degeneration is remade. But this time, the lens can see the beauty in the furnace. The loneliness becomes joy when acceptance is the substrate of one's living. That is, the flower that is now growing in the winter is as colorful, breathtaking, and wonderful even as it stands alone. Acceptance of one's lot, one's suffering, one's assignment to walk a little on the sands alone is a divine filter to lay again a memorial stone that invokes the name Ebenezer (see 1 Sam 7:12).

However, there are, to be sure, enemies of acceptance, adversaries of freedom, and an antagonist that would love nothing more for one to remain in a stage of anger or despair to the extent that a metamorphosis would occur in a sinister way. We find in our allegory that these enemies are thus named, and their names are Resentment, Bitterness, and Self-Pity. O how tempting it is to give in to our adversaries! Or rather, to extend the wrong invitation to these enemies of our soul.

As pastors or people of faith, it is critical that we extend invitations and that we leave a legacy of invitation for our parishes. However, we must leave a legacy of wise invitation, for there are those who would like you to stoke the flames of resentment. Resist this kind of invitation.

There is an ironic comfort, albeit transient, when we make our lodging with these enemies. They promise shelter away from loneliness, only to deceive us in the end. Their comfort is no comfort at all, but a trap that ensures that our loneliness would become faithlessness, that our loneliness would become cynicism, that our loneliness would have us resent all who come with genuine love. In turning aside to such companions, we would never trust again as long as these companions have our hand. We would traverse life with a sarcastic jadedness that beauty is not to be found in the dance upon this earth. The winter will never cease, and I might as well remain on these shores of desperation or, worse yet, return to Egypt and become enslaved.

These enemies were the same that caused all of Israel to crave for Egypt when in their own wilderness. The pity was so great, the resentment of Moses so grand, and the bitterness of hope deferred engendered

---

8. Harnard, *Hinds Feet on High Places*, 40.

such a giant that idolatry was at their door. When all we know are the pods that come to the pigs, we lament when the pods are taken away in preparation for a feast. And yet the prodigal can still remember. He can remember the royalty from whence he came. He can remember what great love was lavished upon him. He can come to his senses once more even in the most heinous of circumstances.

We should not assume that winter is a consequential winter in all providential dealing with humanity. Those who come to its realms are not always prodigal. The winter can be an instrument in the hand of God to perfect His servant. And so it is with Much-Afraid; she meets an evil triumvirate who has come for her testing. And every wounded warrior may perceive a certain vulnerability to each of these adversaries. For me, a pastor who deeply resonates with Much-Afraid, Self-Pity is a giant that stands across the valley mocking me along the way, catering to my need for vindication and laying a snare that I would require others to understand me.

Yes, you have been misunderstood, your intentions scandalized, your deep desires misconstrued. And so, Self-Pity nourishes this wound, and yet it also provides a kernel of a mistake, a mistake enough to reorient you to the wounds of a Savior. For Much-Afraid, his strategy was surely intended for her harm when he remarks, "It really seems as though the one you follow takes delight in making you suffer and leaving you to be misunderstood, for every time you yield to him he thinks up some new way of wounding and bruising you."[9] Take note, pastors. The adversaries who mock and despise you will inevitably make a mistake in their case of words against you, for a word will invoke a promise made from the Shepherd to you and thus will invoke something of an other-worldly courage to resist once again. And having done all, stand. For when one submits to God and resists the devil, the devil can do nothing other than flee (see Jas 4:7).

O how the enemy can misspeak! But this is the ray of light that can break into your winter, O wounded warrior! When you are bruised, look to the bruising of Your Savior. When tempted to pity your circumstance, your journey, your pilgrimage, look to the one who was despised and rejected of men. Look to a man disfigured, misunderstood, hated, and despised. Look on Him, Beloved; look on Him and be healed. Look at the Shepherd and find the flower of acceptance. Look at Him and withstand

---

9. Hunard, *Hinds Feet on High Places*, 43.

the stones of resentment. Let bitterness morph into a heart that gives birth to a glorious sonnet, "Father, forgive them, for they know not what they do" (see Luke 23:34). Come outside the camp to meet with Him in the garden. Know that the pressing of the olives in that garden is for the nourishment of others. Do not make the desire that you be understood into an idol. For this desire can often lead to self-pity and when pity comes to fruition, it can become an idol. Grief also can be worshipped like any other carved image, for grief is in the image of the wounded that refuses healing through the flower of acceptance.

In conclusion, we come to the prophet Isaiah, where we will spend some time in reflection. Who knows if Paul may have been reading this very passage from the prophet whenever Timothy brought him the scrolls. Moreover, Much-Afraid is reminded of a conversation with the Shepherd, words that all pastors must embrace when in the fortress of loneliness. In the allegory, the Shepherd cites the prophet Isaiah when standing at the threshing floor of the Pyramid.[10]

Acceptance

> For dill is not threshed with a threshing sledge,
> nor is a cart wheel rolled over cumin,
> but dill is beaten out with a stick
> and cumin with a rod.
> Grain is crushed for bread,
> but one does not thresh it forever;
> one drives the cart wheel and horses over it
> but does not pulverize it.
> This also comes from the Lord of hosts;
> he is wonderful in counsel
> and excellent in wisdom.
> (Isa 28:27–29)

We begin with the instruments of threshing, the rod and staff. These are the instruments of a shepherd, for David himself sings to us in the Twenty-Third Psalm that it is the rod and staff of God that comforts him when in the valley of the shadow of death. The beating of the seed

---

10. Hurnard, *Hinds Feet on High Places*, 43.

is for the nourishment of others, and it is the rod and staff that perform the beating.

The staff, or *matteh*, was a branch, twig, scepter, spear, or tribe. The staff signified correction in the form of chastisement. A scepter is the very symbol of authority and rule. One of the curious figurative meanings of *matteh* is one that is quite pertinent to the role of a pastor. In this case, the reason for seasons of loneliness and/or correction is found in the etymological link where *matteh* is also bread,[11] so that the staff itself becomes bread for it beats out the grain to become bread for others. Your beating, when it is the staff of God, is not a mere punitive tool of the Lord, but a redemptive one. You become bread, a grain useful to the Master in service as a wounded healer.

Matteh can also refer to the shaft of an arrow (see Hab 3:9, 14). Thus, the treading of the pastor is to become an arrow in the hand of the Lord, piercing the soul with the Word of God for the purpose of repentance, salvation, holiness, and revival. The greater the beating, the sharper the point. How wonderful it is for one to come under the threshing of God's staff. The sorrow of threshing has the destination of fragrance. The staff lashes the caraway seed and what is the result?

Caraway is used in a variety of ways. It is included in essential oils, carvone, limone, and anethole.[12] It is most commonly used as a spice in rye bread, which was likely the use in Israel. Caraway is an ingredient in desserts and casseroles. It is a primary ingredient in the European goulash dish. The leaves can be consumed as herbs, dried or cooked. In the Middle East, caraway pudding, called *meghli*, is a distinct wintertime dish and is the celebratory cuisine when a new baby is born into a family.[13] So think on it, Beloved. When threshed upon, you are the caraway seed. The medium of the threshing is the staff of God for the purpose of producing grain in you. Winter is a necessary season, for it is the foreshadow of a new birth. The aroma of threshing is like a fragrance of something new that has been formed. You become the *meghli*, a dish that signifies life, birth, redemption, and a new beginning. From the depths of your wounds, you become the fragrance of Christ. The threshing has a purpose that one may not readily understand amid the treading. Do not succumb to resentment when under the staff; this is the temptation of loneliness. This temptation mitigates the fragrance of caraway and

11. Zodhiates, *Key Word Study Bible*, 1627.
12. López et al., "Toxic Compounds in Essential Oils."
13. Holmin, *From the Tables of Lebanon*, 164.

entices one to depart from the beauty of threshing. Winter is not without its blessing, pastors. Indeed, serve the very dish of your persecution as a reminder. Create an entire dinner ceremony where *meghli* is the dish and the prayers those of rejoicing that God would deem you worthy of suffering for the Name and that new birth is coming.[14]

The *matteh* eventually became associated with the tribes of Israel as each tribal leader would carry the *mattteh* as a sign of rule or authority (see Num 17:2–10). Identity in Israel was therefore correlated with the *matteh*, and so it is today. We identify with the Suffering Servant as one who both carries the *matteh* and also came under the threshing of the *matteh*. We identify thus with the tribe of Christ as wounded caraway seed fit for the Master!

Second, the rod or the *shevet* is the second term in Isaiah's prophecy (28:27). Indeed, two terms are employed by the prophet not only to bring emphasis to God's corrective action, but also to signify the tremendous fruit that is accompanied by such reintegration of the pastor under such a rod.

The *shevet* was a branch or stick that was most commonly used for fighting, punishing, ruling, or walking.[15] It is used as its counterpart, *matteh*, to signify a spear, arrow, or tribe, but without the connotation of scepter. In a prophetic sense, the word closely resembles the authoritative word of the Messiah (see Ps 2:9 and Isa 11:4). And it is the *shevet* that promulgates the threshing of cumin in Isaiah's pronouncement. And perhaps this is the case so that the one being threshed becomes most closely aligned with the authority of the Messiah. Indeed, what if the threshing is so that a greater authority would be the fruit, an authority that originates in one's greater submission to the authority of Jesus?

The rod grinds the cumin seed into a powder used for spice in traditional Middle Eastern stews. The spice has an earthy aroma and brings a hotter tone when applied to food. But without the grinding, there is not the powder that we call the spice, nor is it good for seasoning a dish. In like manner, we become the seasoning of God under the grinding rod for the purpose of flavoring the world (see Matth 5:13). And if we lose our flavor, what will become of the world? Without flavor, we are unfruitful. Without the grinding, we are but seeds without flavor. We must come under the rod of God and submit to the persecution of this

---

14. See Appendix B for a liturgy of acceptance with *meghli* as a component of this liturgy.

15. Zodhiates, *Key Word Study Bible*, 1664.

world for the aroma to ascend and percolate through the atmosphere and thus beautify God's work among the earth.

It is curious, but not altogether ironic, that Christ would speak of persecution as something worth celebrating in Matthew 5, for it is paradoxically woven into the flavor and fragrance of every believer becoming seasoned. Our maturation is mediated by our persecution and woundedness, with the caveat that this is only true if we do not surrender to the enemies of our resulting loneliness, the lurking devils of pride, self-pity, bitterness, and resentment. O how these enemies mitigate our own grinding, our own surrender into contrition, and our resolution to come under the rod and staff of God.

In conclusion, we have the comfort of the prophet that the threshing is not indeterminate. It is not a phenomenon that perpetuates without cessation. There will be a time where the bruising of the grain has produced the flour necessary for bread to be made. Take comfort, pastors. Your threshing will not always be, but it must happen for a season, for it is the threshing that enables one to become bread for others. Jesus is the bread that came down from heaven, and it was His own threshing that made Him sweet. For Christ is like "white coriander seed, and the taste of it *was* like wafers *made* with honey" (Exod 16:31). And the bruising is so that you also may become bread for others, to nourish their soul with the comfort wherewith you were comforted from your own wounds. But you are not just any bread, but bread of flavor—caraway spice, cumin, coriander—bread not only fit for nourishment, but also sweet to the taste. Thus, loneliness is a time of threshing, pastors. Loneliness will evoke compassion at a time when all others may resent or forget you. Loneliness is your exile moment to see Christ in His glory,

> And among the lampstands was someone like a son of man, dressed in a robe reaching down to his feet and with a golden sash around his chest. The hair on his head was white like wool, as white as snow, and his eyes were like blazing fire. His feet were like bronze glowing in a furnace, and his voice was like the sound of rushing waters. In his right hand he held seven stars, and coming out of his mouth was a sharp, double-edged sword. His face was like the sun shining in all its brilliance. (Rev 1:13–16)

I confess even as I write this, I am lonely upon the shores that resound with the lapping of the waves—a perpetual reminder that I no longer pastor. A part of me misses the phone calls, the emails, the opportunity to be a companion when one is in distress. A part of me misses the fellowship on Sundays and Wednesdays, the community that I once called brothers and sisters. I am in the dessert, with sorrow as my trusted partner. But Faithful indeed is with me in this sorrow to help me know the sorrow of Christ. And yet, loneliness is a human condition that transcends office or role.

I remember calling a friend and staff member of the church I once pastored. I reflected with him that I was feeling lonely, and he made a comment that surprised me. He felt lonely as well. This is a man who had spent over twenty years at the same church, and one would think that he would have deep-rooted friendships there. However, he lamented that this was not the case. In the sea of community, he felt alone. In the crowd where relationships are implied, he felt that none traversed the intimate places of his heart.

Another anecdote comes to mind. I remember that not long before resigning from the church I was sitting with an altogether different staff member at a restaurant. We would from time to time meet to discuss our lives and ministry goals. He had a typical refrain that was a sort of prognostication and metaphor for something deeper. He would with a sort of jest but with brutal honesty say, "I do not know what he likes on his hot dog." By stating this unknown, he was lamenting that he did not know his fellow staff members to the extent that the simple, mundane, and small comforts of life remained yet elusive to his grasp. In other words, he was saying, "I don't really know them." And when we do not really know them, we are tempted to be suspicious of their character and intent. When we do not really know them, we are but members of a corporation in parallel motion without the commingling of the lanes to take the hand of another. When we really do not know one another, we become lonely. For to know and to be known is the beginning of true community. We all long for this; we all desire this; we all seek for communities to be known and to know.

Pastors are particularly vulnerable to the existential state of loneliness. Lifeway Research has recently conducted an epidemiological study polling pastors across denominations and found that more than one in three agree that they feel isolated as a pastor.[16] Loneliness is no discriminator of persons. It invades at any moment, whether at the pinnacle of ministry or at the valley of shadows. It is becoming an epidemic

---

16. Lifeway Research, "Reasons for Attrition among Pastors," found at http://lifewayresearch.com/wp-content/uploads/2015/08/Reasons-for-Attrition-Among-Pastors-Quantitative-Report-Final1.pdf.

in society as our relatedness is diminishing in an ongoing movement into a sense of insulation and distance to prevent the next wound or to shut ourselves out from the criticism of others. Real relationship risks the potential for criticism. The beautiful risk of an open heart is the possibility that this same heart will be trampled. The trampling, however, has the fruit of greater relatedness.

Finally, we must know what becomes of Much-Afraid on the shores of loneliness. Certainly, there is a climactic confrontation on the rocky crags of a cliff by the enemy Pride. Upon seeing her enemy approach, she cries out for deliverance and at once the Shepherd comes to her aid, vanquishing her enemy to the sea. Pride would not, however, be so easily defeated. This battle had been won, and yet there were certainly others to follow. What follows is a tender exchange between Much-Afraid and the Shepherd as she attempts to understand the source of her near captivity by Pride and the relentlessness of Self-Pity, Resentment, and Bitterness. The Shepherd provides an answer we must all contemplate in our loneliness.

> You forgot for a while that you were my little handmaiden Acceptance-with-Joy and were beginning to tell yourself it really was time that I led you back to the mountains and up to the High Places. When you wear the weed of impatience in your heart instead of the flower of Acceptance-with-Joy, you will always find your enemies get an advantage over you.[17]

The weed of impatience chokes the bloom of acceptance. Acceptance is the antidote to loneliness. It is the tool to aid the pilgrim in defeating resentment, bitterness, and self-pity. "Acceptance" is a synonym, if you will, of "surrender." Surrender to your now, despite the loneliness. The loneliness is certainly a threshing, but it is not forever. It is not a destination where you will end, but a mediation to the life ahead. Surrendering to the desert, the winter, the difference, and the discomfort is to see a strange beauty emerging from the horizon of the dune. It is a dessert flower coming out of a seemingly dead cactus. It is the caraway or cumin seed becoming the powder to flavor your next assignment. Loneliness drives one to empathy. For was it not the Spirit of God that drove our Savior into the wilderness (see Mark 1:12)? And are there not redemptive qualities in becoming the scapegoat who is cast into the

---

17. Hurnard, *Hinds Feet on High Places*, 44.

wilderness (see Lev 16:10)? Perhaps you just might meet the One who is outside the camp (see Heb 13:13).

So here is my act of surrender, frail and yet sincere: I surrender to my loneliness. I surrender to the sound of the solitary waves lapping the shore. I hold tightly to my companions, Sorrow and Suffering. I surrender the need to be vindicated by my peers or my authorities. I relinquish the idol of self-pity. I no longer require that justice come to restore my reputation, tarnished by gossip and accusation. I will not bow to the vindication idol. I will accept my lot and become the spice the Lord would have me be. I refuse to resent my current situation. I will not give in to the bitterness that so readily provokes my loneliness. I will hope beyond hope that even now redemption is at play in the unseen, in the small comforts, in the vision of a mountain ahead—a place where God will provide hinds feet for the leaping of canyons and running with the clouds. O how sweet surrender can be and how refreshing the water that comes from the rock struck by the rod in the wilderness, for the refreshing of our souls (see Num 20:11)! Sorrow and suffering may be odd companions—but they are companions with great empathy. So, pastor and believer, leave a legacy of invitation and find that it requires a surrender of sorts, which can create context for God's disclosure. And know that loneliness is not true loneliness if we can truly see. Leave a legacy of invitation; it is the guests we bring into our world who help us navigate sorrow and suffering.

Afterword

This manuscript was on the shelf for about two years. After a counseling session, it was suggested that I dust off the manuscript and submit it for publication. I gave it a try. I rather surprisingly heard back from Wipf and Stock, who agreed to publish the manuscript based on its merit. I was at once surprised and humbled. I did not expect the invitation to publish. Wipf and Stock asked that I tag the manuscript, a process of inserting subtitles, captions, and citations, before the editing process. This request has enabled me to look at the manuscript with a set of new eyes, some four years removed from my own transition.

To be quite vulnerable, I have made several attempts to move away from the desire for conventional pastoring. However, I also find that a flicker of desire remains. I also have attempted to envision pastoring as a *who* rather than a *what*. This has been both cognitively and emotionally challenging for me, as it appears that my identity was enmeshed in the *what* of pastoring.

I still look at job postings for pastors but have not applied. I work as a physician and intellectually attempt to incorporate my work with patients in a way that would be pastoral in nature. Would I respond to a pastoral call? If the Lord was in the call. Have I accepted the past? I confess this is still a blossoming work in my heart. Will I continue to write? I pray and hope so.

In these pages I have attempted to elucidate a notion of legacy that is nuanced and wholly scriptural. My hope for you, reader, is that you have contemplated your own legacy, received healing for your wounds, prayed with tears, allowed your soul to be pricked, and even smiled under the loving gaze of Christ. You have a legacy; now give it away!

Appendix A

Pastoral Transition Screen

A tool[1] designed to help pastors know when to transition from their current pastoring role.

Please answer all questions which seems most intuitively and prayerfully honest to your experience. Please note, that this tool is not to replace direction received in prayer.

Do you perceive that those with influence have come to envy your authority or gifting?

☐ 1 ☐ 2 ☐ 3 ☐ 4 ☐ 5
None Some Several Most All

Have those with influence slandered your reputation?

☐ 1 ☐ 2 ☐ 3 ☐ 4 ☐ 5
None Some Several Most All

Have those with influence opposed your direction and vision for the church?

☐ 1 ☐ 2 ☐ 3 ☐ 4 ☐ 5
None Some Several Most All

Have those with influence convinced honorable men and women to dissent?

☐ 1 ☐ 2 ☐ 3 ☐ 4 ☐ 5
None Some Several Most All

Have those with influence asked you to resign?

☐ 1 ☐ 2 ☐ 3 ☐ 4 ☐ 5
None Some Several Most All

Have any with influence come to your defense in a public setting?

☐ 1 ☐ 2 ☐ 3 ☐ 4 ☐ 5
All Most Several Some None

Have you been wounded by the leadership of the church?

☐ 1 ☐ 2 ☐ 3 ☐ 4 ☐ 5
None Some Several Most All

Have you perceived the leadership is disaffected with you?

☐ 1 ☐ 2 ☐ 3 ☐ 4 ☐ 5
None Some Several Most All

---

1. This tool is derived from principles of "shaking the dust" from one's feet found in Acts 13-14.

Appendix A: Pastoral Transition Screen

Have staff and board meetings become more emotional driven than mission driven?

☐ 1 ☐ 2 ☐ 3 ☐ 4 ☐ 5
None Some Several Most All

Does those in leadership truly love you?

☐ 1 ☐ 2 ☐ 3 ☐ 4 ☐ 5
All Most Several Some None

Have those in leadership mistreated you?

☐ 1 ☐ 2 ☐ 3 ☐ 4 ☐ 5
None Some Several Most All

Have those with influence vocalized their own credentials, experience, or authority in opposing you?

☐ 1 ☐ 2 ☐ 3 ☐ 4 ☐ 5
None Some Several Most All

Have you used the pulpit to shame or reproach others?

☐ 1 ☐ 2 ☐ 3 ☐ 4 ☐ 5
None Some Several Most All

Have you been threatened with either emotional, familial, legal, or physical harm?

☐ 1 ☐ 2 ☐ 3 ☐ 4 ☐ 5
None Some Several Most All

A score of 41 or lower places a pastor at a low risk to resign and transition. A score of 42 or higher places a pastor at moderate risk to resign and transition. A score of 56 or higher places a pastor at high risk to resign and transition.

Appendix B

Liturgy of Acceptance

Lebanese Meghli

Prep Time	Cook Time	Total Time
10 mins	20 mins	30 mins

Author: Margarita @ Tasty Mediterraneo

Cuisine: Mediterranean

Serves: 8

Ingredients

- 125g (1 cup) Organic rice flour
- 150g (1¼ cups) Organic unrefined sugar, milled into powder
- 1 tablespoon caraway powder
- 1 tablespoon cinnamon powder
- 1 tablespoon grounded anise seeds
- 2l (8 cups) cold water
- 8 Teaspoons organic shredded coconut unsweetened
- 100g (1/2 cup) Walnuts (peeled and soaked in cold water)
- 100g (1/2 cup) Almonds (peeled and soaked in cold water)

- 100g (1/2 cup) Pistachios (peeled and soaked in cold water)
- 50g (1/4 cup) Pine nuts (peeled and soaked in cold water)

Instructions

1. Have all the ingredients prepared as indicated in the ingredient's description.
2. In a large cooking pot add the rice flour, the sugar, the caraway, the cinnamon, and the anise and mix them well before adding the water. Add the cold water and mix well. Once it is well mixed, put the cooking pot on the stove at low heat and stir well.
3. Let the mixture cook at low heat, stirring constantly, for about 20 minutes.
4. Remove from the heat, pour directly into small individual cups or in a large serving dish, and let it cool.
5. Once it is cold, add on top of each cup a teaspoon of coconut, and a few walnuts, almonds, pistachios and pine nuts.

Notes

The *meghli* should not have a runny texture but rather hold itself if you try to tilt it.

Recipe by Tasty Mediterraneo at https://www.tastymediterraneo.com/lebanese-meghli/

Liturgy for the following (transition, grief, acceptance, and birth):

Responsive Reading: Isaiah 28:27–29

Call: *Caraway is not threshed with a sledge, nor is the wheel of a cart rolled over cumin;*

Response: *caraway is beaten out with a rod, and cumin with a stick.*

Call: *Grain must be ground to make bread;*

Response: *So one does not go on threshing it forever.*

Call: *The wheels of a threshing cart may be rolled over it,*

Response: *But one does not use horses to grind grain.*

Call: *All this also comes from the Lord Almighty,*

Response: *Whose plan is wonderful, whose wisdom is magnificent.*

Hymn: "All Hail the Power of Jesus Name" (Edward Peronnet and James Ellor)

Prayer

Father God, we come this day to accept the lot You have given us. We know that it is the rod and staff that comes from Your hand. We accept that it is for the purpose of grinding us into the flavor of God for the world to taste of Your goodness. We accept Your rod and staff both as a comfort and as a tool of refinement. We come with humble submission under Your rod for the threshing of our character. We acknowledge that the caraway seed requires the threshing and the grinding to become the spice that can beautify Your creation. We thank You for this dish, the *meghli*, which represents the fruit of threshing for the purpose of new birth. As we partake of this dish, we are reminded that caraway is ground to a powder to provide a season that we taste this day. We thus become the caraway under Your grinding, knowing that this will not be forever, but accept it now today. We know Your plan is wonderful and wisdom magnificent.

The Dish and Discussion

As you partake of the dish, reflect as a family or group on the season of loss and loneliness. Allow the reflections to also navigate the space of gratitude for what one did have prior to the loss. Let the sweetness of the dish move you to reflect on your own threshing and the fruit that comes of it. Discuss how each one has come to accept the current situation. Is anyone in the family or group having difficulty coming to acceptance?

Call and Response: Psalm 22

Call: My God, my God, why have you forsaken me? Why are you so far from saving me, so far from my cries of anguish? My God, I cry out by day, but you do not answer, by night, but I find no rest.

Response: Yet you are enthroned as the Holy One; you are the one Israel praises. In you our ancestors put their trust; they trusted and you delivered them. To you they cried out and were saved; in you they trusted and were not put to shame.

Call: But I am a worm and not a man, scorned by everyone, despised by the people. All who see me mock me; they hurl insults, shaking their heads, "He trusts in the Lord," they say, "let the Lord rescue him. Let him deliver him, since he delights in him."

Response: Yet you brought me out of the womb; you made me trust in you, even at my mother's breast. From birth I was cast on you; from my mother's womb you have been my God.

Call: Do not be far from me, for trouble is near and there is no one to help.

Response: Many bulls surround me; strong bulls of Bashan encircle me. Roaring lions that tear their prey open their mouths wide against me. I am poured out like water, and all my bones are out of joint. My heart has turned to wax; it has melted within me. My mouth is dried up like a potsherd, and my tongue sticks to the roof of my mouth; you lay me in the dust of death.

Call: Dogs surround me, a pack of villains encircles me; they pierce my hands and my feet. All my bones are on display; people stare and gloat over me. They divide my clothes among them and cast lots for my garment.

Response: But you, Lord, do not be far from me. You are my strength; come quickly to help me. Deliver me from the sword, my precious life from the power of the dogs. Rescue me from the mouth of the lions; save me from the horns of the wild oxen.

Call: I will declare your name to my people; in the assembly I will praise you. You who fear the LORD, praise him! All you descendants of Jacob, honor him! Revere him, all you descendants of Israel! For he has not despised or scorned the suffering of the afflicted one; he has not hidden his face from him but has listened to his cry for help.

Response: From you comes the theme of my praise in the great assembly; before those who fear you I will fulfill my vows. The poor will eat and be satisfied; those who seek the LORD will praise him—may your hearts live forever!

Call: All the ends of the earth will remember and turn to the LORD, and all the families of the nations will bow down before him, for dominion belongs to the LORD and he rules over the nations.

Response: All the rich of the earth will feast and worship; all who go down to the dust will kneel before him—those who cannot keep themselves alive. Posterity will serve him; future generations will be told about the LORD. They will proclaim his righteousness, declaring to a people yet unborn: He has done it!

Hymn: "When I Survey the Wonderous Cross" (Isaac Watts)

Prayer

Oh Father, shall we not accept both blessing and difficulty from Your hand? Isn't it the bitter that produces the sweet? We must see in the picture of our Savior, the God who became forsaken so that we all would have communion with You. As the shepherd is struck, the sheep are scattered. Is this also not the pattern that comes to us today? All who respond to the call will follow the way of being struck. All who respond to the call must carry their cross. All who respond to the prophetic burden must carry the weight of God's Word. O how great a Savior we have! Give us strength to suffer with You that we may rise with You!

Discussion

Now discuss the new possibilities of the future. Reflect on the *meghli* dish and ask why one thinks this is the dish to celebrate the birth of a child. Discuss the birth of Christ. Discuss under what circumstances He was incarnated. What did this represent for Israel, for the world? Reflect on the birth of a child in your own family. What did that mean for the family? Discuss each child's birth and reflect on the emotions, circumstances, and prophetic meaning of each birth. Now begin to cast a vision for your future. What new possibilities now exist because of this loss and transition?

Responsive Reading: Luke 2:46–55

Call: And Mary said: "My soul magnifies the Lord, And my spirit has rejoiced in God my Savior.

Response: For he has regarded the lowly state of his maidservant; for behold, henceforth all generations will call me blessed. For he who is mighty has done great things for me, and holy *is* his name.

Call: And his mercy *is* on those who fear him From generation to generation. He has shown strength with his arm; he has scattered *the* proud in the imagination of their hearts. He has put down the mighty from *their* thrones, and exalted *the* lowly.

Response: He has filled *the* hungry with good things, And *the* rich he has sent away empty. He has helped his servant Israel, in remembrance of *His* mercy, As he spoke to our fathers, to Abraham and to his seed forever."

Hymn: "O Come, Immanuel": Veni Immanuel Chant

Benediction

We have now come to the precipice of surrender and acceptance. I surrender to my loneliness. I surrender to the sound of the solitary waves lapping the shore. I hold tightly to my companions, Sorrow and Suffering. I surrender the need to be vindicated by my peers or my authorities. I relinquish the idol of self-pity. I no longer require that justice come to restore my reputation tarnished by gossip and accusation. I will not bow to the vindication idol. I will accept my lot and become the spice the Lord would have me be. I refuse to resent my current situation. I will not give in to bitterness that so readily provokes my loneliness. I will hope beyond hope that even now redemption is at play in the unseen, in the small comforts, in the vision of a mountain ahead; a place where God will provide hind feet for the leaping of canyons and running with the clouds. O how sweet surrender can be and how refreshing the water that comes from the rock struck by the rod, in the wilderness, for the refreshing of our souls (see Num 20:11)! We await the new birth coming from Your hand, O Lord, great and mighty and full of wisdom.

Appendix C

Legacy Interview

THE FOLLOWING IS AN interview with Bob Thompson, pastor of Corinth Reformed Church, who is retiring after thirty years of pastoral ministry. I thought it fortuitous that we can have a glimpse of a pastor who is now at the phase of development where he is to leave a legacy. Thank you, Pastor Bob. I am so grateful for your time and enjoy chasing those sunsets!

> *1. Paul addresses Timothy as son when writing his second epistle to Timothy. As Paul anticipated his imminent death, it appears that he had an urgent message for his son in the faith, prompted to write under the inspiration of the Holy Spirit. In your estimation, what is the urgent message you would like to give to your sons and daughters of the faith? And how does one be intentional to leave a legacy to sons and daughters in the faith?*

I have not been as intentional about engaging in father-son relationships as I could have been. I have some regrets about my own children but especially in ministry I have not been, by nature, someone who enters deep relationships.

In a recent Sunday school class, I reviewed my satisfaction and regrets as I close my time at Corinth. My satisfaction derives from the New Testament metaphor of the church as a building, with Christ as the cornerstone. Corinth has been a place of Christ-centered stability and strength for those wounded and broken by life or by churches.

My regrets connect to the body metaphor given to us by Paul to the Corinthians. As a pastor, I have not modeled or enabled the kind of interdependence I had hoped for the church. My spiritual relationships have been wide but not many have been deep. Some staff and church leaders at Corinth may say I'm too hard on my legacy. With the help of the Holy Spirit, I watched and helped one associate pastor in particular grow and flourish. Early on it felt risky for me to trust him—and for him to trust me, honestly—but it has been beautiful to watch him mature through grace and patience. In the context of this love, he grew as a wise leader himself. All four of our associate pastors are a gift to my successor as lead pastor.

In evangelicalism we tend to hide or excuse our faults and mistakes. I have tried to model transparency and have not shied away from underscoring or admitting my weaknesses, which are many.

2. The apostle Paul was quite concerned about sound doctrine when writing to Timothy. How would you describe the state of sound doctrine today? Is it under attack? What is the role of fathers, pastors, and churches in the preservation of sound doctrine?

It's easier to talk about essentials and non-essentials than to distinguish between what is essential and non-essential. Sound doctrine is under attack with every generation, but not every alteration in our teaching is compromising the gospel or the Bible. As a pastor I had to unlearn some things. I do have fewer essentials on my list than I did in my youth. For example, I learned along the way that ordaining women as pastors or appointing them as leaders is an area where Christians who fall on either side can disagree and still love Jesus!

I have always loved the passage in 2 Timothy 2 where Paul calls ministers to be kind and gracious when correcting even if someone has been taken captive to the devil's work. Keep in mind that I am wired as a peacemaker and look to help people to get along. I typically do not confront by nature, but God does call and use those who confront. It is simply not my gifting. I do not want to affirm false doctrine, but we need the humility and grace of Romans 14–15 when we argue about disputable issues. "In all things charity."

3. Paul writes about honorable vs. dishonorable vessels in the body of Christ when counseling Timothy. What message would you give to pastors who are attempting to faithfully navigate the discerning process of contrasting vessels of honor from dishonor? Is there a place to confront vessels of dishonor? If so, in what way?

I have a chapter in my little book about our transition, *The Unity of Grace*, in which I discuss homosexuality. Obviously in the UCC this has been a large issue of discussion. In terms of church discipline, there is not a New Testament manual on how to address this. Paul addresses these matters on a case-by-case basis. In my view, the matter of honor and dishonor must consider the cultural context.

One clue to Paul's thinking is that he confronts the church at Corinth concerning incest that even the pagans would not tolerate. There is a sense in which cultural mores can and should frame church discipline. My moral values may be absolute, but the application of them requires pastoral sensitivity and attention to individuals. For example, was polygamy automatically disciplined on Paul's day? No, but we would immediately discipline a member who married two or more partners. Some of our spiritual ancestors in the antebellum German Reformed church of the South, including elders and pastors, owned slaves. Today we would quickly dismiss any member who advocated or practiced human trafficking.

We need to consider how church discipline will affect our evangelism, our sharing of the good news. For example, even if we are prolife, if we publicly reprimand or excommunicate a member who has had an abortion, in our current culture how will this impact our ability to invite and include those who need Jesus and his church? On the other hand, if we tolerate overt racism, hate speech, or sexual abuse—well, isn't that one reason younger generations are turning away from faith?

We do not have a formalized procedure for discipline at Corinth. I have tended to take each example of sin or discipline on a case-by-case basis. I am often asked to marry cohabiting couples and believe that is generally the right next step for them. But when I was asked to officiate a wedding for an older cohabiting couple who were well known in the church, I met with them privately and declined. They ended up leaving the church. Honor and dishonor require pastoral discernment in the context of a plurality of leaders in the church.

4. Paul refers to his missionary journeys when writing to Timothy. He refers to God's deliverance whenever he departed places like Antioch and Iconium. What message do you have for pastors who are navigating the wounds of church hurt, rejection from their own, and when to stay vs. when to depart a work of ministry?

I think the default choice in calling is to stay where you are. In 1 Timothy 1, Paul tells Timothy to stay in Ephesus to confront false doctrine. In 1 Corinthians 7, Paul also provides guidance to singles and marriages and even slaves to remain in their status and serve the Lord—although in the case of slavery Paul said one should seek freedom if it is an option. This is part of my argument for staying in the United Church of Christ. However, forty-five years ago, if you asked my wife and me where we wanted to serve the Lord, it would have never been in the UCC. But the Lord put us here, and at times it has been difficult. God rarely places his people in easy places, but where He can use them.

As a first instinct, I would advise ministers to stay where they are, but this is not an absolute rule. We left another church to come to Corinth, and now we're retiring. There are times to move on! Sometimes God is providing a door for freedom from a difficult situation. This is a very personal decision, so look to the Lord and get counsel. We stayed here thirty years, but not because it was easy. We asked the church to stay in the UCC, and the vote was split almost 50/50. It's a long story, but we lost no active members a year before or after that vote, because we tried hard to handle it with sensitivity and respect to all. Such difficult moments can be times when God is refining and using pastors, leaders, and every member.

5. There seems to be a cultural paradigm shift in the church concerning relevance. This culture has defined gender and sexuality in a way that is often incongruent with Scripture. This cultural shift has in many ways penetrated ecclesial bodies, where much debate has ensued. In terms of gender and sexuality, what message do you wish to leave the UCC, ECOT, and your local church? In this prophetic moment, what should be the message of the church?

When I asked my Sunday school class what topics they wanted to discuss before I retire, being transgender came to the top of the list. What I would say here is to establish your moral values but also make a genuine attempt to provide compassion and empathy. There are many reasons and layers to the transgender person and homosexuality debates. The sin nature is certainly a major part, but it is not the whole story. People are deeply affected by the blind spots of their culture and their generation. We must care enough to listen to their story—anyone's story. People need to know they are heard and loved before they are willing to hear and love in return. One of my pastoral principles is that as far as it's up to me, I don't want any conversation to be the last one.

Twenty years ago, a man named Randy said to me, "I am gay but I know Jesus as Savior. I do not have a partner now, but I can't promise you I won't. May I join your church?" I said to him, "All I ask is that you be open to the Holy Spirit." He joined the church and years later came to my office. He said, "I've decided to be celibate, and I wanted you to know. A big reason is you. No man has ever loved me the way you have loved me."

The prophetic message of the church in a generation where sexual confusion is rampant cannot be one that sequesters those we consider pure and stiff-arms everyone else until they repent and behave. We can hold to and even proclaim our values, but we must meet people where they are. In any instance where there is sin or any other action we find inconsistent with our values, we need to change the approach from "Why are you acting this way?" to "What happened to you?" Let's hear their story and love them as they tell us about their journey. Then we open the door to Jesus.

Bibliography

Amos, Mark. *God for Now: Theology through Evangelic and Charismatic Experience.* Eugene, OR: Wipf & Stock, 2020.
Augustine. "On the Holy Trinity." In *Nicene and Post-Nicene Fathers*, 1st series, vol. 3, edited by Phillip Schaff, translated Arthur West Haddon. Grand Rapids: Christian Classics Ethereal Library, 1956.
Barbalet, Jack. "Weeping and Transformations of Self." *Journal for the Theory of Social Behaviour* 35:2 (June 2005) 125–41.
Barclay, William. *The Letters to the Galatians and Ephesians*, 2nd ed. Daily Bible Study Series. Philadelphia: Westminster, 1958.
Barfoot, D. S., Bruce E. Winston, and Charles Wickman. "Forced Pastoral Exits: An Exploratory Study." Working paper, School of Leadership Studies, Regent University, June 2005. http://www.scottbarfoot.com/wp-content/uploads/2011/07/forced_pastoral_exits.pdf.
Barrett, C. K. *A Commentary on the Epistle to the Romans.* New York: Harper, 1957.
Barth, Karl. *Church Dogmatics in Outline.* New York: Harper and Row, 1959.
———. *A Shorter Commentary on Romans.* Edited by Maico. Routledge, NY: Michielin, 2016.
———. *The Word of God and The Word of Man.* Gloucester, MA: Peter Smith, 1978.
Becker, Jurgen. *Paul, Apostle to the Gentiles.* Louisville: Westminster/John Knox, 1993.
Beecher, Henry Ward. *Forty-Eight Sermons.* Vol. 2. London: R. D. Dickinson, 1871.
Bonnke, Reinhard. "Evang Reinhard Bonnke Transferred Leadership to Evang. Daniel Kolenda." https://www.youtube.com/watch?v=NK0Y80YM560.
———. *Living a Life of Fire.*, Longwood, FL: Harvester, 2010.
———. *Raised from the Dead: The Miracle That Brings Promise to America.* Kensington, PA: Whitaker House, 2014.
Bower, G. H., et al. "Affect and Cognition." *Philosophical Transactions of the Royal Society of London, Series B, Biological Sciences* 302:1110, Functional Aspects of Human Memory (August 11, 1983) 387–402.

Brueggman, Walter. *David's Truth in Israel's Imagination and Memory*. 2nd ed. Minneapolis: Fortress, 2002.

———. *The Prophetic Imagination*. Minneapolis: Fortress, 2001.

———. *Sabbath as Resistance: Saying No to the Culture of Now*. Louisville: Westminster John Knox, 2014.

Butterfield, Rosario. *The Secret Thoughts of an Unlikely Convert*. Pittsburgh: Brown & Covenant, 2012.

Chrysostom, John. *The Homilies of John Chrysostom on the Epistles of St. Paul, the Apostle to Timothy, Titus, and Philemon*. London: Oxford, 1843.

Combs, William. "The Biblical Role of an Evangelist." *Detroit Baptist Seminary Journal* 7 (Fall 2002) 23–48.

Crowell, R. "Forced Pastoral Exits: An Empirical Study." PhD diss., Dallas Theological Seminary, 1995.

Dalrymple, Rob. *Understanding the New Testament and the End Times*. 2nd ed. Eugene, OR: Wipf & Stock, 2018.

Deeken, A. *Process and Permanence in Ethics: Max Scheler's Moral Philosophy*. New York: Paulist, 1974.

DeVaux, Roland. *Ancient Israel: Its Life and Institutions*. Grand Rapids: Eerdmans, 1997.

Dickens, Charles. *A Tale of Two Cities*. New York: Popular, 2001.

Duewell, Wesley. *Mighty Prevailing Prayer*. Grand Rapids: Zondervan, 1990.

Dwight, Timothy. *The Conquest of Canaan*. 1785. Ann Arbor: Evans Early American Imprint Collection online Text Creation Partnership, 2011. https://quod.lib.umich.edu/e/evans/N14973.0001.001/1:24?rgn=div1;view=fulltext.

Edwards, Jonathan. "Christian Love." In *20 Centuries of Great Preaching*, edited by Clyde Fant and William Pinson, vol. 3, *Wesley to Finney (1703–1875)*. Waco, TX: Word, 1971.

Erikson, Erik. *The Life Cycle Completed*. New York: Norton, 1982.

Fant, Clyde, and William Pinson, eds. *20 Centuries of Great Preaching*, vol. 4, *Newman to Robertson (1801–1901)*. Waco, TX: Word, 1971.

Fee, Gordon. *1 & 2 Timothy, Titus*. Understanding the Bible Commentary Series. Grand Rapids: Baker, 2011.

Finney, Charles. "How to Promote a Revival." In *20 Centuries of Great Preaching*, edited by Clyde Fant and William Pinson, vol. 3, *Wesley to Finney (1703–1875)*. Waco TX: Word, 1971.

Free, Joseph. *Archeology and Bible History*. Grand Rapids: Zondervan, 1992.

Glover, T. R. *Paul of Tarsus*. London: SCM, 1925.

Greenfield, Guy. *The Wounded Minister: Healing from and Preventing Personal Attacks*. Grand Rapids: Baker, 2001.

Hankey, A. Kate, and William Fischer. *The African American Hymnal*. Chicago: GIA, 2001.

Heffernon, Thomas. *The Passion of Perpetua and Felicitas*. New York: Oxford University Press, 2012.

Herzog, William, II. *Jesus, Justice, and the Reign of God*. Louisville: Westminster John Knox, 2000.

Holmin, Dalal A. *From the Tables of Lebanon: Traditional Vegetarian Cuisine*. Summertown, TN: Book Publishing, 1997.

Hurnard, Hannah. *Hinds Feet on High Places*. London: Tyndale, 1975.

"Jose Altuve Sends Astros to World Series with 2-Run Homerun." https://www.youtube.com/watch?v=XC34yua88z0.

Katz, Jack. *How Emotions Work*. Chicago: University of Chicago Press, 1999.

Kafer, Peter. "The Making of Timothy Dwight: A Connecticut Morality Tale." *The William and Mary Quarterly* 47:2 (April 1990) 189–209.

Kubler-Ross, Elizabeth. *On Grief and Grieving*. New York: Scribner, 2005.

"Lance Armstrong Biography." Biography.com, April 23, 2021. https://www.biography.com/athletes/lance-armstrong.

Land, Steve. *Pentecostal Spirituality: A Passion for the Kingdom*. New York: Sheffield Academic, 2003.

Landa, Apolos. "Shalom and Eirene: The Full Framework for Healthcare." *Christian Journal of Global Health* 1:1 (June 2014) 57–59.

Lange, John Peter. *Commentary on the Holy Scriptures: The Acts of the Apostles*. Grand Rapids: Zondervan, 1955.

Lee, C. "Specifying Intrusive Demands and Their Outcomes in Congregational Ministry: A Report on the Ministry Demands Inventory." *Journal for the Scientific Study of Religion* 38:4 (1999) 477–89.

Lewis, C. S. *Mere Christianity*. New York: Macmillan, 1952.

Lifeway Research. "Reasons for Attrition among Pastors: Quantitative Report." Pastor Protection Research Study. N.d. https://research.lifeway.com/wp-content/uploads/2015/08/Reasons-for-Attrition-Among-Pastors-Quantitative-Report-Final1.pdf?source=post_page———————————————.

López, Maria María J. Jordán, and María J. Pascual-Villalobo. "Toxic Compounds in Essential Oils of Coriander, Caraway and Basil Active against Stored Rice Pests." *Journal of Stored Products Research* 44:3 (2008) 273–78.

Loscalzo, Craig. *Apologetic Preaching: Proclaiming Christ to a Postmodern World*. Downer's Grove, IL: Intervarsity, 2000.

"Lukewarmness or Fervent in the Spirit." *Church of God Evangel* 17:7 (February 17, 1923) 1.

Marshall, I. Howard. *A Critical and Exegetical Commentary on the Pastoral Epistles*. Edinburgh: T. & T. Clark, 1999.

McNaughtan, Neil. *Biology and Emotion*. Cambridge, MA: Cambridge University Press, 1989.

Miles, Austin. "In the Garden." In *The African American Heritage Hymnal*, 787. Chicago: GIA, 2001.

Murphy, Francesca Aran. *Illuminating Faith: An Invitation to Theology*. New York: Bloomsbury T. & T. Clark, 2015.

Newbigin, Lesslie. *The Gospel in a Pluralist Society*. Grand Rapids: Eerdmans, 1989.

Nouwen, Henri. *In the Name of Jesus: Reflections on Christian Leadership*. New York: Crossroad, 1989.

Nullens, Patrick. "*Theologia Caritatis* and the Moral Authority of Scripture: Approaching 2 Timothy 3:16–17 with a Hermeneutic of Love." *European Journal of Theology* 22:1 (2013) 38–49.

"Paideia at a Glance." Paideia Academy. https://paideiaknoxville.org/at-a-glance/#1529770230953-d8278915-2f8b.

Peterson, David. *The Acts of the Apostles*. Pillar New Testament Commentary. Grand Rapids: Eerdmans, 2009.

Peterson, Eugene. *Working the Angles: The Shape of Pastoral Integrity.* Grand Rapids: Eerdmans, 1987.

Peterson J. Z., et al. "Clinical Characteristics Associated with the discrepancy between Subjective and Objective Cognitive Impairment in Depression." *Journal of Affective Disorders* 246 (March 2019), 763–74. doi:10.1016/j.jad.2018.12.105

Pew Research Center. "Appendix C: Putting Findings from the Religious Landscape Survey into Context," in *America's Changing Religious Landscape.* Pew Research Center, May 12, 2015. https://www.pewresearch.org/religion/2015/05/12/appendix-c-putting-findings-from-the-religious-landscape-study-into-context/.

———. "Chapter 1: The Changing Religious Composition of the US," in *America's Changing Religious Landscape.* Pew Research Center, May 12, 2015. https://www.pewforum.org/2015/05/12/chapter-1-the-changing-religious-composition-of-the-u-s/.

Plessner, Helmuth. *Laughing and Crying: A Study of the Limits of Human Behavior.* Evanston, IL: Northwestern University Press, 1941/1970.

Roberston, A.T. *Word Pictures of the New Testament.* New York: Harper, 1932. Available online at https://www.biblestudytools.com/commentaries/robertsons-word-pictures/.

Rogers, Cleon, Jr., and Cleon Rogers III. *The New Linguistic and Exegetical Key to the Greek New Testament.* Grand Rapids: Zondervan, 1998.

Sayers, Mark. *Disappearing Church: From Cultural Relevance to Gospel Resilience.* Chicago: Moody, 2016.

Seeley, David. *The Noble Death: Graeco-Roman Martyrology and Paul's Concept of Salvation.* Sheffield, UK: Sheffield Academic, 1990.

Statham, W. M. "2 Timothy 4:21—Homilies by W. M. Statham." In *The Complete Pulpit Commentary,* edited by Henry D. Spence, vol. 9. Harrington, DE: Delmarva, 2013. Available online at https://bibleportal.com.

Sumney, Jerry. "'I Fill Up What Is Lacking in the Afflictions of Christ': Paul's Vicarious Suffering in Colossians." *Catholic Biblical Quarterly* 68:4 (October 2006) 664–80.

Tanner, Marcus, and Anisa Zvonkovic. "Forced to Leave: Forced Termination Experiences of Assemblies of God Clergy and Its Connection to Stress and Well-Being Outcomes." *Pastoral Psychology* 60 (2011) 713–26.

Trentham, Charles A. *Studies in Timothy.* Nashville: Convention, 1959.

Tsuji, Manabu. "2 Timothy 1:6: Laying on of Hands by Paul for Ordination?" *Annual of the Japanese Biblical Institute* 39 (2013) 65–76.

Webster, John. *Holy Scripture: A Dogmatic Sketch.* Cambridge: Cambridge University Press, 2003.

Wesley, Charles. *Hymns of Worship and Service.* New York: The Century, 1910.

Wilson, Robert. "The Hardening of Pharaoh's Heart." *Catholic Biblical Quarterly* 41:1 (January 1979) 18–36.

Zodhiates, Spiros. *The Key Word Study Bible.* Chattanooga, TN: AMG, 1991.

Scripture Index

Old Testament

Genesis

2:4	71
3:15	69n16, 70
6:11–12	90
28:10–17	69
28:12	69n16
38:10	97

Exodus

1:8	99
3:8	71
4:10	97
4:21	99
7:11	122
7:13–14	103n21
7:22	103n21
8:15	103n21
8:18	123
8:32	103n21
9:7	103n21
9:11	123
10:20	103n21
10:27	103n21
11:10	103n21
14:10	103n21
16:31	215
17:11	15
25:30	35
30:34	35
33:19	89
34–35	103n21

Leviticus

16:10	218
19:8	37
24:5–9	35
24:9	36

Numbers

12:3	107
17:2–10	214
20:11	218

Deuteronomy

23:1–8	101
23:7–8	101
31:6	97
31:7	97
31:23	97
32:4	89

Judges

7:11	97

1 Samuel

7:12	210
21:1–9	36, 38
27:1	91

Job

6:26	91

Psalms

2:9	214
17:2	196
22	226
27:14	97
46:1	114
56:8	22, 92
57–59	90
75	90
112:9	88

Proverbs

16:18	140
29:18	181

Ecclesiastes

2:20	91
2:21	91
12:8	170

Isaiah

6:9–10	97
11:4	214
28:27	214
28:27–29	212, 224
40:3	118
56:3–6	102
57:9–10	93

Jeremiah

2:25	93
18	90
18:1–17	89
18:4	90, 93
18:7	90
18:9	90
18:11	93
18:12	90, 93
18:17	94
20:9	204
31:16	26

Ezekiel

2:3–4	98
8:8	114
41:22	38

Hosea

6:6	40

Habakkuk

3:9	213
3:14	213

Malachi

3:17	160

Deuterocanonical Books

4 Maccabees

1:1	63
1:4	63
4:1	63
4:3	64
4:25	65
5:6–7	65
5:10	65
5:13	65
5:22–24	65
6:18–19	66
6:27–29	67

SCRIPTURE INDEX

New Testament

Matthew

3:3	118
3:17	10
5	215
5:3	141
5:4	135
5:13	214
7:13	69n16
7:14	69
10:1	5
10:5–6	5
10:7	5
10:8	5
10:14	128, 135
10:22	60
11:12	70
11:29	108
12:3–4	37
12:4	35
12:7	40
12:34	94, 130
13:22	56
13:32	53
13:58	133
16:25	50
18:2–4	xix
18:3	74
21:5	108
21:12–23	31
21:44	209
22:14	4, 35
22:37–40	37
23:37–39	22
24:8–9	63
24:12	184
25:21	71
26:31	201
27:1–10	27
27:27	68

Mark

1:3	118
1:12	217
2:23–28	38
2:27–28	40
8:35	50
16:17–18	194
17:17–18	115

Luke

2:46–55	228
3:4	118
6	4
6:12–16	2
7:45	75
9:24	50
9:35	10
12:51	142
16:19–31	72
17:21	141n18
23:34	212
23:43	72
24:29–32	208

John

1:51	69
3:8	73
3:30	141
6:51	35
10:10	70
10:11	71
11:35	21
11:50	79
12:25	50
13:27	27
17:12	27
17:18	2
21:15–19	166

Acts

2:26	2
4:31	193
5:41	80
7:60	204
8	186
8:6	187
8:31	187
9:15–16	3

Acts (continued)

9:16	59
13:42	130
13:43	134
13:43–45	130
13:44	194
13:46	135
13:50	133, 134
13:50–52	135
13:51	128, 130, 135
14:2	136
14:5	140
14:22	147
18:9–10	146
19:33	202
20	20
20:31	20
21:8	186
21:13	147

Romans

1:1	3
2:16	50
4:11	203
4:18–22	58
4:20–21	194
6:8	33
8:28	35, 36
9	88, 99
9:11	36
9:13	89
9:15	89, 94
9:17	89
9:18	89, 94
9:19	94n10, 95
9:20	94n10
9:21	88, 89
9:22–23	96
10:17	51n12
11	103
12:12	60
13	107
14–15	232
15:19	194
16:20	70

1 Corinthians

1:1	3
3:6–8	197
3:12	53
5:4	33
7	234
9:10	58
9:14	58
9:25–27	57
10:2–4	158
12:1–11	28
13:7	60
13:12	49
13:13	xx
15:8–9	3
15:10	33
16:20	75

2 Corinthians

1:1	3–4
2:15–17	38
4:6	5
4:7	172
4:8	70
5:20	1
8:2	87
9:11	87
11:23–29	9
12:9	108
13:4	121

Galatians

1:1	9
3:1	3
3:16	158
5:22–23	107
5:26	107

Ephesians

1:1	3
1:8–9	35
1:9–11	36
3:1	59
3:6	36

4:2–3	107
5:27	183
6:20	2
6:21–22	202

Colossians

1:1	4
1:24	33, 61–62
1:27	58
3:11	188
4:3	59
4:14	201
4:18	59

1 Thessalonians

1:1	4

2 Thessalonians

1:1	4

1 Timothy

1	234
1:1	4
1:2	xii, 11
1:5	157
1:9–10	45, 180
1:18	56
1:20	202
4:1	113
4:12	5
4:14	28
5:22	29
6:3–4	46

2 Timothy

1:1	4
1:1–2	1
1:3	19–20
1:4	19
1:6	8, n10, 19, 31, 194
1:6–7	51
1:8	xii, 19, 32, 33, 56, 185
1:9	19, 34–35, 36
1:13	xviii
1:13–14	20, 43
1:14–15	19
1:15	xvii, 43
1:16	54
1:16–17	59
2	232
2:3	xvii, 55
2:3–10	60
2:8	50
2:9	xvii, 33, 59
2:10	61
2:11–13	55
2:12	60
2:14–26	83
2:17–18	xvii
2:20	82
2:21	88, 99, 103
2:25–26	106
3	145
3:1	109
3:1–9	110
3:2	111
3:2–4	157
3:2–5	181
3:5	177
3:9	112, 121
3:10	129
3:10–11	128
3:10–17	110
3:11	147
3:12	62
3:14–15	44
3:16	160, 163
3:16–17	152
3:17	172
4:5	56, 176
4:6–8	xvii
4:7	xix
4:7–8	196
4:9–22	200
4:10	xvii
4:12	xvii
4:16–18	xvii
4:18	xx
4:21	xx, 20

Titus

1:1–3	4
1:9	44

Philemon

1:1	4
1:7	59
3:10	9, 80
24	201

Hebrews

3:1–6	141n17
11:1	160–61
12:1	70
12:2	60
12:6	115, 168
13:3	59
13:13	218
13:23	32

James

2:13	37
4:7	211
4:14	xx

1 Peter

3:19	73

2 Peter

1:21	153
3:3–4	113
3:9	114

1 John

2:15	201
4:18	100

Revelation

1:13–16	215
1:14	71
3:15–16	29
3:17	165
5:8	22
6	62
6:10–11	78
7:9	71
12:3	69n16
12:13–17	145
21	22

www.ingramcontent.com/pod-product-compliance
Lightning Source LLC
Chambersburg PA
CBHW050844230426
43667CB00012B/2142